Five Irish Writers

Five Irish Writers

THE ERRAND OF KEEPING ALIVE

JOHN HILDEBIDLE

HARVARD UNIVERSITY PRESS
Cambridge, Massachusetts, and London, England   1989

Publication of this book has been aided by a grant from
the Hyder Edward Rollins Fund of Harvard University.

This book is printed on acid-free paper, and its binding
materials have been chosen for strength and durability.

Library of Congress Cataloging-in-Publication Data

Hildebidle, John, 1946–
   Five Irish writers.

   Bibliography: p.
   Includes index.
   1. English literature—Irish authors—History and criticism.
   2. English literature—20th century—History and criticism.
   3. Ireland—Intellectual life—20th century.
   4. Ireland in literature.   I. Title.
PR8753.H57 1989   820'.9'9415   88-34825
ISBN 0-674-30487-X (alk. paper)

This is Susannah's book:
home for the first time,
for good

Acknowledgments

When I first began to consider undertaking this book, Seamus Heaney, Robert Kiely, and Shaun O'Connell offered advice as to where to begin, and made it seem not utterly absurd for a student of American literature to take up the study of even a particular corner of Irish literature. Later, Paul Ericson and Kelly Wemmers read portions of this manuscript and offered very useful criticism, not all of which I was wise enough to follow.

At MIT, the Old Dominion Fund and the Class of 1922 materially assisted my work. Among my colleagues at MIT I wish to thank especially Monica Kearney, a beacon of calm and good sense; Alvin Kibel, for tolerating my many solecisms; and Theo Theoharis, for reminding me that enthusiastic curiosity can be a part of an academic career.

My wife and son came to share my often naive passion for things both Celtic and pseudo-Celtic; without them I would never have climbed to Queen Maeve's cairn or met the inestimable Oscar. My daughter has yet to learn how much she added to the later stages of my work on this book, but the dedication is at least the beginning of an explanation.

Contents

Because many of the works considered here have gone through various editions, I have identified all citations from novels and other longer works by Bowen, O'Brien, O'Connor, O'Faolain, and O'Flaherty parenthetically, giving chapter numbers or titles rather than page numbers. Unless otherwise identified, the sources of the stories, which are also identified parenthetically by title, are the most ample collections available of a given author's work: *The Collected Stories of Elizabeth Bowen* (1981); Frank O'Connor, *Collected Stories* (1981); *The Collected Stories of Sean O'Faolain* (1983); *The Stories of Liam O'Flaherty* (1956).

Introduction

TAKEN singly, the five writers considered in the following chapters are figures of substance and value, whose ongoing colloquy with the conditions of life in their own time—and ours—produced important fiction, whether the standards of importance be quantitative, qualitative, or (as they should be) both. Taken as a group, they represent the most important voices in a distinct generation of Irish fiction writers, those who began their active careers in the decade after the appearance of *Ulysses*. They are, to put it briefly, what most significantly happens in Irish fiction immediately after Joyce.

LIAM O'Flaherty's usual literary voice is loudly declarative and confessional; but the record of his life is marked by confusions and evasions, by alternating periods of noisy publicity and of prolonged and mysterious invisibility, as yet not fully pierced by any biographer. O'Flaherty was born in 1896 in a village on Inishmore (renamed Inverara or Nara in his fiction), largest of the Aran Islands off the Galway coast. His family was large (O'Flaherty was the ninth child), life on an Aran farm materially meager and difficult, and, under the rule of O'Flaherty's iconoclastic and stubborn father, the household was anything but peaceful. O'Flaherty's early education had an uncompromising Gaelic and nationalist bias. In 1908 Liam left the islands to be schooled for the priesthood—not a surprising path for the bookish second son of an Irish family, but rather an astonishing one for O'Flaherty, given his family's unorthodoxy and his own richly deserved later reputation for rabid anticlericalism and agnosticism. His education took him first to Cashel, then to Blackrock College, County Dublin, and finally to the seminary of the Holy Ghost Fathers at Clonliffe.

In his last months at Clonliffe O'Flaherty joined the Irish Volunteers, one of a number of extra-legal nationalist organizations at work in Ireland at the time. But when he abruptly left the seminary, he did not plunge into political activity, but rather enlisted (as did many thousands of his countrymen) in the British army. His service on the Western Front ended when he was seriously wounded in September 1917 by a shell explosion. Invalided out of the army, and having obtained a degree from University College, Dublin, under special arrangements made for war veterans, O'Flaherty spent several years as a merchant seaman and wanderer in the Near East, the United States, Brazil, and elsewhere.

By 1921 he was back in Ireland. As a distinctly heterodox supporter of the Republican cause in the Civil War, he made, in January 1922, his most public gesture of political action. Along with a handful of unemployed men he seized the Rotunda in Dublin, in support both of antigovernment politics and of more-or-less Communist demands for redistribution of food and wealth. The action, dramatic as it was, received no support from any political faction; and the public outcry against the seizure (which led to the destruction of the historic building) compelled O'Flaherty to flee to England. By 1923 he had turned from politics to writing; in that year his first published story, "The Sniper," appeared in a British socialist weekly, and with the active support of Edward Garnett, his first novel, *Thy Neighbour's Wife*, was published by Jonathan Cape.

For more than ten years, he was a prolific writer. By 1935 he had published over a dozen novels and three volumes of short stories, plus two book-length autobiographical works, an account of his journey to Russia in 1930, an exceedingly bitter *Tourist's Guide to Ireland,* several screenplays, a biography of Tim Healy, and a good deal of journalism as well. He achieved momentary fame by way of the film version of his novel *The Informer;* his part in writing the screenplay took him to Hollywood in the early 1930s.

During this productive period, he was an extremely visible and controversial figure on the Dublin literary scene, known especially for his rebellion against the looming influence of Yeats, which brought him into conflict with that other "socialist," Sean O'Casey, but which did not prevent him from agreeing to be one of the Founder Members of Yeats's beloved Irish Academy of Letters. Like not a few of his characters, O'Flaherty lived with (and then married) another man's wife; the husband, as it happened, was the Irish historian Edmund Curtis, and the wife, Margaret Barrington, was herself a writer of fiction. The O'Flaherty's produced one daughter and their marriage seems to have disintegrated by about 1932.

By the mid-1930s his state of mind was profoundly disturbed. According to his own account in *Shame the Devil,* his relative lack of critical and popular success as a writer and his considerable inner divisions brought him to a near breakdown and another period of wandering. His "recovery"—announced on the final pages of *Shame the Devil*—allowed him to return to writing. A long historical novel, *Famine,* appeared in 1937; two more novels and a volume of short stories were published between 1946 and 1953. After 1953 he was virtually silent, save for a collection of stories in Gaelic and a long-rumored but never completed novel. During the 1940s he apparently lived in America; afterwards he lived mostly in Dublin, but was rarely seen. His death, in 1984, came over thirty years after the effective end of his career as a publishing writer.

KATE O'Brien was born in 1897, in the city of Limerick. Her large family (she had eight siblings) was prosperous, at least until 1916 when her father died and Kate went off to Dublin to university. In *My Ireland* she counts herself among "those who were lucky in the circumstances of their childhood." But those circumstances included as well the tragic early death of her mother, whose married life was, O'Brien admits in *Presentation Parlour,* "short and exacting." Perhaps in part because of that death, O'Brien devoted particular affection to her father, "not an easy or a disciplined man," as she says in *Presentation Parlour,* but "an expressive and affectionate parent" *(My Ireland)*. After her time in a Limerick convent school, Kate went up to University College, Dublin, where the ruins left by the Easter Rebellion, and the political turmoil which that event had both signaled and fueled, were still inescapably visible. But O'Brien, then and later, felt little attraction to politics, nationalist or otherwise—a trait shared by many of her characters, and which she would in time attribute in part to the lasting effects of Catholicism and the belief it engendered in "the absolute dominion of personality over system" *(Mary Lavelle,* "Don Pablo").

After taking her degree, O'Brien worked briefly in England and America as a journalist, a teacher, and a secretary; then, in her mid-twenties but still (she says in *Farewell Spain)* "a considerable ass," like her character Mary Lavelle she went to Spain as a governess/companion or "Miss." On her return she married a Dutch journalist, but the marriage was very brief. Her active writing career began with the appearance of a play, *Distinguished Villas,* which enjoyed a considerable success in London, although its run was cut short by the General Strike of 1926. She soon turned permanently to the writing of novels, although she would later rework several of her novels into plays. Her first novel, *Without My Cloak,* was some years in the writing and, on its publication, won both the James Tait Black Memorial Prize and the Hawthornden Prize. It was followed by eight more novels; the last one, *As Music and Splendour,* appeared in 1958.

Her career, successful if never spectacular, had its moments of controversy. Her remarks about the Franco regime in *Farewell Spain* and her portrayal of Philip II in *That Lady* provoked the Spanish government to deny her entry to Spain for many years. Her novels *Mary Lavelle* and *The Land of Spices* were both banned by the Irish Censorship Board, the second on grounds of obscenity—an action so inexplicable as to rouse the objection of Frank O'Connor, who was in general not an admirer of O'Brien's work. For a considerable portion of her later life she lived at Roundstone, County Galway; but she lived frequently in England as well, both during World War II, when she worked in London in the Ministry of Information, and in the last years of her life, which she spent in a village near Canterbury. She died in Canterbury in 1974.

ELIZABETH Bowen was born into a world that has its geographic heart not far from Aran and Limerick, but sociologically and culturally at a great distance from either. The long-awaited heir to an old Anglo-Irish estate, Elizabeth Bowen was expected to be a boy and was prenatally assigned one of the usual family names, Robert. Her father had broken with family tradition by taking up a career in the law which demanded his residence, for at least part of each year, in Dublin, at some distance from Bowen's Court, which stood in the rolling farmlands northeast of Cork City. Bowen's mother came from a substantial Dublin family. Both father and mother were genuinely, if amiably, eccentric, and the surprise of their child's gender, when she was born in Dublin in 1899, did not disturb them unduly. For nearly seven years Bowen was raised in comfort and security, half the year at Bowen's Court, half the year within the safe confines of the substantial Dublin professional classes. Her early childhood had its oddities— she was, for instance, forbidden to learn to read—but her recollections of it make it seem an almost purely idyllic world of prosperous habits, gentle personal quirks, and substantial, well-furnished houses.

The idyll ended in 1906 with her father's breakdown, diagnosed, in the peculiar terminology of the day, as "anemia of the brain." It was thought he might harm his wife and child, and so Bowen and her mother moved to England, there to live for some five years in an assortment of "villas," mostly on the seacoast of Kent. The family's reunion, once her father had recovered, was brief; within months, Bowen's mother was dead of cancer. Elizabeth and her father returned to Ireland temporarily, but it would not be her home, in the residential sense, until after World War II. Bowen's schooling and then her literary aspirations took her to England, and finally to London. In 1923, her first collection of stories, *Encounters,* was published. In the same year she married Alan Cameron. Despite his substantial career as an educator and administrator, he seems to have been held in contempt by almost all of Bowen's friends. But it proved to be a durable and sustaining marriage.

Her literary output was, especially before World War II, considerable and steady; by 1941 she had published five volumes of short stories and six novels. During most of those years she lived near Oxford, and then in Regent's Park, London. In 1930, on her father's death, she had inherited the family house; but she was at most a visitor there (and during the war, not even that) until 1952, when she moved—permanently, she thought—to Bowen's Court. By then she had achieved some literary eminence, marked by the awarding of a C.B.E. (in 1948) and of an honorary Doctorate by Trinity College Dublin (in 1949). But the economic precariousness of the Bowen estate and the death of her husband darkened her return. After nearly a decade of efforts either to make Bowen's Court self-sustaining or to support the costs of the estate by her writing, Bowen sold the house in 1960 (it was demolished three years later) and returned to England. There she lived the remainder of her life, first near Oxford, and later in Kent. The last (and, sadly, by far the worst) of her ten novels appeared in 1968. She died in 1971.

SEAN O'Faolain (about 1918 he permanently adopted a Gaelic version of the name he was given at birth, John Francis Whelan) was born in Cork in 1903. His father was a member of the Royal Irish Constabulary; his mother, raised on a farm near Rathkeale in County Limerick, took in lodgers. In good Irish fashion, one Whelan son became a priest, another a civil servant, leaving John, "a natural, if mild, rebel" (*Vive Moi!,* ch. 2), to pursue a more individual course. By his own account, his childhood was marked not so much by poverty as by parsimonious sham gentility. His parents were deeply committed to the "rise" of their sons, and O'Faolain enrolled, in 1918, in University College Cork, from which, in due time, he received a B.A. and two M.A. degrees. His education was interrupted—or perhaps continued—by his involvement, from 1918 to 1924, in Irish revolutionary politics. He fought on the rebel side in the Civil War, although most of his service was of a relatively literary sort, including a term as "Censor" of the Cork *Examiner* and (at the age of only twenty-three) a period as Publicity Director of De Valera's IRA "Irregulars." In the brief hiatus between the Troubles and the Civil War he traveled as a

salesman for an Irish textbook company; and after the end of the fighting
he spent one year as a schoolteacher in Ennis, County Clare.

Although it seemed he was headed for an academic career, three years
of graduate study at Harvard—he received yet another M.A. from that
institution in 1928—finally put that aspiration to rest. In 1928 he married
Eileen Gould, who was herself to have a considerable career as a folklorist
and writer. From 1929 to 1933 he taught in England, but he had by then
decided to return from his "exile." His first book of stories appeared in
1932, under the encouraging eye of Edward Garnett; the same year Yeats
arranged his election to the Irish Academy of Letters. By 1933 he had taken
up more-or-less permanent residence in Dublin and the life of an active
and wide-ranging man of letters, which has continued for over half a
century.

By 1940 he had published three biographies, a play, two collections of
short stories, three novels, and a travel book on Ireland; and had edited
a collection of Tom Moore's poems, the autobiography of Wolfe Tone,
and a substantial anthology of Irish verse. In that year he founded the
influential journal *The Bell,* which he edited (and dominated) until 1946,
and to which he contributed until its demise in 1954. The journal quickly
assumed an importance, in Irish literary and intellectual circles, at least as
central as that exerted earlier by Æ's *Irish Statesman.* In its pages O'Faolain
and others waged a constant battle to reform Irish life and culture, a battle
most notably marked by an unceasing attack on the Irish Censorship
Board.[1] His editorship of *The Bell* confirmed O'Faolain's place within
Ireland as the predominant voice of his generation, and the intellectual
godfather of subsequent generations, a role to which his best-known contemporaries, Frank O'Connor (O'Faolain's longtime friend) and Liam
O'Flaherty, were temperamentally ill suited.

Up to about 1940, O'Faolain could fairly describe himself as a novelist
with a considerable interest in political biography. But after 1945, the most
significant part of his work is the short stories; some three quarters of the
contents of his ample *Collected Stories* were published, at least in book
form, after 1945. There were other books, including a "character study"
of the Irish, one more biography (of John Henry Newman, not of a
political reformer or rebel), an autobiography, a fourth novel, and book-
length critical essays on the short story and the novel. The sheer bulk of
his literary output is in itself remarkable. In addition to his career as a

1. His summary of the impact of the censorship and his subsequent doubts about his own
efforts against it are to be found in *Vive Moi!,* ch. 14 (which closely echoes "The Priests,"
in *The Irish*) and ch. 15. As early as 1939, in his enlarged biography of De Valera, he characterizes
the censorship, rather surprisingly, as "really a good idea badly worked."

writer, O'Faolain has been a frequent academic visitor to America, having taught, among other instititions, at Boston College and at Princeton, Northwestern, and Wesleyan Universities. In 1953 he gave a series of lectures at the Christian Gauss Seminars at Princeton, which were later reshaped into his book *The Vanishing Hero*. In 1976 he was awarded an honorary D. Litt. by Trinity College, Dublin.

BORN Michael Francis O'Donovan in Cork in 1903, Frank O'Connor was the only child of a frequently unemployed ex-soldier and a long-suffering charwoman. His early life was markedly poorer than that of his friend O'Faolain;[2] and his education was far more erratic, cut short, at least in the formal sense, in 1917. O'Connor was actively (if, by his own account, rather maladroitly) involved in the political upheavals of 1919–1923, and was ultimately arrested and interned by the Free State government. In 1924 he was released from Gormanstown Prison Camp; the next year he began work as a librarian, eventually in Dublin, which was his usual residence after 1928. It was also in 1924 that, as his biographer puts it, "for reasons of discretion and caution—traits not generally associated with Frank O'Connor—and probably also contempt for his father's family, he adopted [as a pseudonym] his own middle name and his mother's maiden name" (James Matthews, *Voices*, p. 42). Under the sponsorship of Æ and of Yeats, who in 1931 included the relatively unknown O'Connor among the members of his Irish Academy of Letters, he attracted some notice, not only as a writer of fiction but as a translator of Gaelic verse, and then as a playwright and member of the Board of the Abbey Theatre, a connection broken when he was forced to resign in 1939. By then he had published a novel and two collections of stories; and he abandoned his work as a librarian, supporting himself thereafter by writing, reviewing, reading, and lecturing. His stories and his remarks on the state of Ireland and its culture regularly embroiled him in controversy; his books, like those of many other important Irish writers, were often banned by the Irish Censorship Board. In 1945 he sold a story, "News for the Church," to the *New Yorker,* and his stories, as well as the sketches which form the basis of his two volumes of autobiography, appeared regularly in that

---

2. O'Connor at one point describes O'Faolain as "three years older than I and all the things I should have wished to be—handsome, brilliant, and above all, industrious" (*An Only Child*, ch. 15). By the time those words were written, however, the friendship had long since soured. O'Faolain's account of the friendship and of its cooling is in the last chapter of *Vive Moi!* O'Connor appears as "Morgan Myles" in O'Faolain's stories "Falling Rocks, Narrowing Road, Cul-de-sac, Stop" and "How to Write a Short Story."

magazine thereafter, contributing to a considerable American reputation which was capped by the success of *An Only Child*.

He married twice, the first marriage ending in 1952 in a prolonged and acrimonious divorce proceeding; O'Connor's associations, both professional and personal, almost invariably began passionately and turned just as passionate in the eruptions which ended them. His residence in Ireland was interrupted by periods in England, frequently doing free-lance work for the BBC, and (in 1952 and 1961) by teaching appointments in America, at Harvard, Northwestern, and Stanford universities. He returned to Dublin for the last time in 1961, and was presented with an honorary doctorate by Trinity College, a sign of some mellowing (at least on the part of the Irish political and cultural establishment) of the animosities that had marked much of his earlier career. He died in March 1966. Under the editorship of his widow, several posthumous collections of his stories have appeared.

THESE five lives, which cross and recross with varying effect, have a roughly parallel shape, inevitably including a high proportion of what Bowen might have called "dislocation" but involving as well a persistent attraction to the island on which they were born. But to apply the label "Irish" to them is problematic; it is a label that no one can use uncontroversially, especially if he has, by heritage and training, "no rights in this matter," to borrow a phrase from Theodore Roethke. The "Irishness" of Elizabeth Bowen may seem especially suspect; her claims to nationality might be said to have died in the revolution which made of much of Ireland a republic independent of England, and presumptively too independent of the long history of the Anglo-Irish. But Bowen (like Liam O'Flaherty, Kate O'Brien, Frank Connor, and Sean O'Faolain) was born in Ireland, of parents who would have had no qualms about claiming to be thoroughly Irish; and although she would often leave Ireland, she could and did, up until very late in her life, claim a home there. Even if Ireland itself is less centrally a subject and a setting in her work than it is in the work of her four contemporaries, it retains, as I hope to demonstrate later on, a powerful "magnetic" force (the image is hers), as a *locus* of possibly redemptive changelessness. Ireland between about 1925 and 1950 often appeared to be a preternaturally and quite intentionally static place, as the work of all five of these writers demonstrates. Such stasis perhaps inevitably had a far more sinister and claustrophobic look to it when viewed by way of the imagined lives of men and women living within it, than from the perspective of those "English" who predominate in Bowen's fiction.

I call these writers Irish, then, because they were born in Ireland and because they continued to call themselves (not always happily, by any means) Irish. But in one important way, the label is much too broad; for each of the five has an unmistakable link to a specific part of Ireland— speaking both sociologically and geographically. For O'Flaherty, it is the rocky coast of the Aran Islands and the lives of the peasantry; for Elizabeth Bowen it is the Big House culture somewhere in the fertile lands of Cork; for Kate O'Brien, the comfortable Irish bourgeoisie of Limerick, who are fond of summering on the Galway coast; for O'Connor and O'Faolain, it is the world of "provincial" Irish cities that inevitably resemble Cork. The degree to which their fiction can be distinctly *placed* is, I would argue, one of the ways in which it is representative of Irish fiction as a whole, which is almost invariably local to a degree that seems odd to an outsider's eye— odd because Ireland would seem to be much too small a place to sustain such an array of regional identities. That regionalism continues into the present, for instance in the recurrent presence of Ballinasloe (whether by name or not) in the lives of Edna O'Brien's various "country girls" and of Bective in the lives of Mary Lavin's women, of Omagh in the consciousness of Benedict Kiely's garrulous narrators, of Boyle in the work of John McGahern, Galway and the Midlands in that of Desmond Hogan, Celbridge in that of Aidan Higgins.

This intensely local vision is one of the ways in which Irish literature in this century has demonstrated its continuing energy and strength, its continuing ability to generate distinct voices and diverse imaginative visions. And here too the five writers I intend to consider are a suggestive grouping. At first glance, and putting aside for the moment accidents of biography, they seem more disparate than alike. Certainly in point of style there is little to link the almost willfully awkward sentences of Liam O'Flaherty with the Jamesian peregrinations of any paragraph of Elizabeth Bowen or the marvelously voiced manner of a story by Frank O'Connor. They therefore resist any simple categorization of some paradigmatic "Irish" voice or Irish perspective.

Each of these writers produced a considerable bulk of writing over the course of a long career. None of them was exclusively a writer of fiction, but there can be no question that fiction was what they wrote most centrally, most often, and most effectively. Each enjoyed some critical and popular attention; some (especially O'Flaherty) even achieved a certain notoriety. Yet all five are likely now to be ignored, or at best relegated to a peripheral place, in any account of twentieth century Irish writing, lost somewhere in the shadows between Joyce and his artistic sons, Samuel Beckett and Flann O'Brien. In the pages that follow it is my hope to suggest that the loss is considerable.

1

LIAM O'FLAHERTY

A Curious Melancholy Wonder

A READER with a taste for subtle indirections and impressionistic scene painting will quickly find himself unsettled by Liam O'Flaherty's fiction. His story "Galway Bay," for instance, opens with a bitter curse aimed proximately at the Aran Islands, but at all the world as well. It is uttered by an old man, reduced by his age and (so he thinks) by lifetime persecution to the appearance of "a turtle," but still a powerful figure with "wild blue eyes" and the look of "a captured hawk" inevitable in O'Flaherty's fiction. The scene is the ferry from the islands to Galway; the old man—Tom O'Donnell—is bound for the city, to sell his only cow (out of sheer spite, it turns out). But his gaze, and much of his anger, is directed back toward the Arans.

O'Flaherty's stories and novels are full of self-portraiture, both of the man as he was and as he feared or hoped he might be. Tom is nearly thirty years older than O'Flaherty, and unlike the writer he has never really left the Arans. But like O'Flaherty, Tom is a man of great anger: toward his enemies, real or imagined; toward women (though he depends on them, especially on his long-suffering daughter[1]); toward the representatives of the established Irish order (especially priests and policemen); and toward the towns which are the mark of a newer, bourgeois Ireland and take "all the spunk out of" any man who lives there, making him a "gelding." A policeman calls him mad but "not mad enough to be certified"; O'Flaherty, as late as 1934, took a certain pride in the diagnosis of British Army doctors

---

1. In this Tom is much like O'Flaherty's father, as he is described in chapter 4 of *Shame the Devil*, selflessly nursed by and yet bitterly distrustful of O'Flaherty's spinster sister Agnes. The picture of the elder O'Flaherty in that book is in many ways a kind of archetype of the defiant madmen who appear in O'Flaherty's fiction. "I'll show them all . . . that I am still on my feet," the old man cries to the world at large; and in so doing he becomes "a symbol of something too holy for my human understanding. Can one look on God in His nakedness?"

that he was permanently a victim of "melancholia acuta." Old Tom makes much of his own isolation, "without home or company" and absolutely "free," the only one of "the true men of the west" to be found on the ferry, and perhaps in the world. Yet he bristles when a young tourist pronounces the traditional sentimental myth of Aran as "the island of saints and scholars, . . . a galaxy of beauty." "Little you know," he says, "what goes on there."

Contradictory, bitter, misogynistic, Tom transforms his hidden terror of weakness and old age and loneliness into an obsessive condemnation of the world. His railings *are* mad, his bitterness thoroughly in excess of anything that the actual circumstances of the voyage call for. But although Tom is, we are told, not a storyteller, his accusatory and self-aggrandizing voice unmistakably echoes O'Flaherty's. Here is Tom, in full brag:

> All this belongs to us . . . to us, true men of the west. We are a breed by ourselves. We are people of the islands and of all the land that does border on the western sea. We want no foreigners to come interfering with us, putting laws around our necks, like you put a spancel on a wicked goat. We have the spunk in us and we'll take the sway from all comers. We are a breed on *(sic)* our own.

And here—with the language characteristically transposed from the racial plural "we" to the individualistic singular "I," and from formulaic political concern about colonialism and law to heterodox religious imagery of god and devil—is O'Flaherty:

> I have no god, but I have shamed the devil into obedience by an exhibition of inverted pride greater than Lucifer's. I have charted my love, having put love behind me AS THE LUXURY OF LESSER MEN. I sail forth on a sea that has no port of call, no land fall, nor triumphant home-coming. . . . I am a fool, but I am one of the great fools, for my folly is a great concupiscence. I desire first the flesh and then the spirit.
>
> *(Shame the Devil*, ch. 17)

The predominance of negatives in this version of O'Flaherty's creed is altogether typical, and indeed altogether fundamental. His life and the work which dominated that life are in a sense prolonged negations grounded on an effort to set the record straight, to see (and necessarily to explode) the received view of life and of Ireland through the eyes of "wisdom and cunning." If the telling of truth may not in the end be possible, in part because, as *Shame the Devil* insists, all men are born liars, still falsehood can be rebuked and loudly, after the fashion of Tom O'Donnell or of Melville, or indeed of the Devil himself, a creature of denial, a shouter of "No!" in thunder. As his character David Skerrett puts it (with surprising calm), it is no little work to accept the "duty" to "teach what I believe is the truth . . . [and] to fear and despise whoever and whatever is evil" (*Skerrett,* ch. 23).

In his life, that "duty" drove him through an exhausting pattern of resistance and reaction, of involvement with and then bitter rejection of the possible creeds of his time and place. In his work, "the negative or spiritual side of life" ("The Office," in *Two Years*) remains most fundamental. One can, then, read his fiction as a series of obsessive corrections or indeed absolute denials of certain common notions: the nobility (or the pure and stubborn "Irishness") of the peasantry; the coherence and comprehensibility, as well as the controllability, of nature; the long mythic-historical record of Irish resistance and ultimate liberation; the nobility, uniqueness, and complexity of human emotion and the human mind. His immediate targets are almost invariably Irish: weak-kneed intellectuals; disillusioned terrorist True Believers; priests of all sorts, from the avaricious and conniving to the mystically psychotic; gombeen-men and hucksters; arch-conservative peasants and subhuman urban proles. But the ultimate point is only partly, and only superficially, the "reformation" of Ireland. In the end O'Flaherty is interested not in the state of the nation—*any* nation—but the state of the soul. At the center of all his important longer fiction stands a man driven by the resistance of the world and by the prompting of the demons within his own heart to defy all the powers of heaven and earth, even at the cost of nakedness, utter isolation, madness, and death. The quest which that figure undertakes may begin as the pursuit of material, social, political change; but in the end it is a desperate search for mystical insight or absolution.

And indeed, the last, and perhaps most maddening, of O'Flaherty's negations is the denial of his own ideas. The disillusioned rebel who condemns all political activity as futile, and Irish revolutionary politics as especially poisonous, tries to propose, in his very last novels, a tradition of "true" Irish rebelliousness which reaches an apotheosis in the idealized figure of Padraic Pearse, and perhaps of Eamon De Valera.[2] Against the

2. O'Flaherty's apparent (and rather puzzling) affection for Pearse is most evident in *Insurrection;* but one of the grounds of his objection to O'Casey in the 1920s was the playwright's ironic use of Pearse in *The Plough and the Stars*. O'Flaherty directly mentions De Valera only briefly. In chapter 10 of *Shame the Devil,* O'Flaherty recounts a long political argument with several other emigré Irishmen, in which he takes the position of praising De Valera (and Parnell) as the necessary leaders of "enslaved people [who] need, more than anything else, a leader who can be steadfast without violence, stern without arrogance, and

world repeatedly portrayed in his novels, a world of interlocking betrayals, terror and predation, failed or perverted love, and utterly ineffective intentions, he insists upon life, upon human energy, upon the imaginative intellect. The nihilist and anithumanist in O'Flaherty cannot quite win out; the mad mystic who preaches a gospel of love, of aspiration, even of progress to a higher and better state of manhood is the figure likely to have the last word.

AT THE core of his fiction are the peasants. O'Flaherty himself could claim some peasant descent, and the early years of his life gave him ample opportunity to observe them in that part of Ireland where the peasantry was almost universally acknowledged to have survived in its "pure" form. In the hands of any number of Gaelic Leaguers, and especially of the myth-making Pearse and De Valera, peasant purity became a fundamental tenet of the "new" Ireland born in the conflicts of the Irish revolution and Civil War. O'Flaherty's peasants are in a way only one generation of a continuing parade of peasant countertypes, dating back at least to the characters in George Moore's *The Untilled Field* and to the more romanticized Aran Islanders visited by J. M. Synge,[3] and to be followed shortly by the tor-

---

just without cruelty." But De Valera lurks somewhere just beneath the surface of *Insurrection*. In that novel the "saintly" rebel officer Kinsella is not De Valera (among other things, he dies during Easter Week 1916), but he very easily could be: angular, ascetic, an ex-school-teacher (of science, not mathematics). And the battle in which Kinsella leads Bartly Madden is the "battle" of Mount Street Bridge, the one "victory" of the rebellion for which De Valera gained later renown.

3. Moore's book ought, literarily, to have made the case once and for all; it is now often ignored, but to Irish writers (especially earlier in this century) it was accounted decisive in the development of Irish writing, its importance equal to and indeed perhaps greater than Joyce's *Dubliners*. Frank O'Connor's *The Lonely Voice* (p. 205), for example, assigns *The Untilled Field* and Moore's novel *The Lake* equal status with Yeats's poetry. For O'Connor, of course, Moore was to some degree no more than a convenient figure to use to try to diminish the looming shadow of Joyce.

Synge's *The Aran Islands* is, for O'Flaherty, a more directly relevant example; a note on the dust jacket of the first edition of *The Black Soul* announced explicitly that O'Flaherty's novel was a corrective to Synge's book. But a full and careful reading of *The Aran Islands* would reduce the predispositions aroused by Gaelicism and lingering Romantic primitivism. Synge was not much impressed with O'Flaherty's native Inishmore; it was on the (to his eye) more purely Gaelic Inishmaan that Synge found "a simple life, where all art is unknown, [with] something of the artistic beauty of medieval life" and where he could see "a natural link between the people and the world that is about them." But on his second visit he had to admit "I see a darker side of life on the islands"—which is also portrayed in *Riders to the Sea*. See *The Collected Works of J. M. Synge*, ed. Alan Price (Washington, D.C.: The Catholic University of America Press, 1982), vol. II, pp. 58–59 and 107.

The controversy, of course, continues, fought out in part now on the travel pages, where mented souls of Patrick Kavanagh's *The Great Hunger* and *Tarry Flynn* and the comic absurdities of Flann O'Brien's *The Poor Mouth*.

Peasant life is never so centrally O'Flaherty's subject as it would be Kavanagh's; nor is it so laughable as almost everything is to Flann O'Brien. Indeed, even in O'Flaherty's novels set firmly in Galway and the Arans, the peasants (with the marked exception of the Kilmartin family in *Famine*) are more talked about than fictionally present. But neither are they only background; they stand as the instantiation of a central mystery, the observable signs of an inevitable human context. The peasants are what the major characters struggle to escape being or to resist becoming; they are the subject of the "civilizing" hands of the political, the avaricious, and the priestly; and they are in fact the measure of human life when—to use one of O'Flaherty's most persistent metaphors—it is stripped naked. Most of all, they function as a touchstone to the important inquiring minds of O'Flaherty's fiction, which seek out and observe the peasants in an effort to understand the fundamental character both of themselves and of the universe in which they—unhappily—live. The journey of these men is a variation on that made by Synge and by so many others; but with all Romantic ideas of nature radically revised.

For what O'Flaherty offers as the facts of peasant life, one can most profitably turn not to his novels but to his stories. Nearly half of the pieces collected in *The Stories of Liam O'Flaherty* (1956) are direct observations of rural life in O'Flaherty's distinctive corner of western Ireland. The stories are often short (as indeed are O'Flaherty's most effective stories, generally) and focus upon the small, necessary rituals of subsistence: mating, fishing, planting, the care of animals. Some of those tasks are in themselves suggestive of the desperate effort required to live on these hard shores: to wring a life out of the rocks of Aran demands, for instance, the climbing of cliffs to rob wrens' nests.

Two things mark all of this labor. First, it occurs invariably within sound of the sea, a constant reminder of the absolute power, and utter uncontrollability, of natural forces. And secondly, the work is endless. The only things that truly interrupt the grim repetitious effort are disasters, from the small and common ones such as the sinking of a currach in treacherous seas to the cataclysmic, such as those recorded in *Famine*. Small moments of joy cannot withstand the pressure of circumstances; small, inward acts of rebellious defiance are mostly wholly ineffective, and often darkly farc-

---

tales of adorable little Connemara cottages abound. On the other side, a particularly grim view is that of Nancy Scheper-Hughes in *Saints, Scholars, and Schizophrenics: Mental Illness in Rural Ireland* (Berkeley: University of California Press, 1979).

ical. The logical path rebellion can take, given the inequality of the forces involved, is toward mindless destruction, even self-destruction. Patrick Derrane, in "Poor People" (*Short Stories,* 1937), inwardly screams, "God! Why could he not rend and break and destroy everything, instead of being tied down like this by poverty, without power, stricken, helpless, tied, tied, by the great chain of hunger." But to destroy would only further the manifestly destructive forces already at work on his life and the lives of his fellows.

The story "Spring Sowing" is less hopeless, but still typical, both in what it includes and in what its narrator says it signifies. A young Inverara couple, awaking from "the first joy and anxiety of [their] mating," face the task of sowing on a cold February day. It is the first spring of their marriage; the first time, therefore, that they have worked together as man and wife in the necessary if ultimately futile effort "of asserting . . . manhood and of subjugating the earth." The story records, in some detail, the exact nature of that work, which has at least the advantage of allowing the husband to live for a time "absolutely without thought": a condition which many another O'Flaherty character longs for. The wife, however, watches and thinks; and the result is a rapid succession of pure emotions that are utterly typical of O'Flaherty's psychology. First comes fear ("of that pitiless, cruel earth, the peasant's slave master"), then—at a brief moment of rest—a joy that can for a time "overpower . . . that other feeling of dread that had been with her during the morning." And when she sees her husband's grandfather, married fifty years and an exact prediction of what her life will become, she feels anger. But her defiance of "the slavery of being a peasant's wife" is altogether private, silent and "momentary," succeeded by acceptance—of a sort:

> All her dissatisfaction and weariness vanished from Mary's mind with the delicious feeling of comfort that overcame her at having done this work with her husband. They had done it together. They had planted seeds in the earth. The next day and the next and all their lives, when spring came they would have to bend their backs and do it until their hands and bones got twisted with rheumatism. But night would always bring sleep and forgetfulness.

Mary and her husband are, in the context of the whole of O'Flaherty's fiction, more than husband and wife; more even than an instance of the bitter "life of the soil." They are, like Gypo Nolan and Dan Gallagher in *The Informer,* two halves of one being: the brutal masculine body and the watchful, worrying feminine mind. The body, as "husband" and master, must be served, but of course in time will grow twisted and fail. In the end the mind can only hope for—and at the same time fear—self-annihilation, a cessation of its own independent work of seeing and understanding, a long sleep and a complete forgetting.

The predominant force in the peasants' lives is hunger. As the doomed young Michael Kilmartin insists in *Famine* (ch. 2), "What is our life in any case, but hunger and hardship?" The entire course of the novel offers, at grim length, to prove the truth of this assumption. Indeed, the Famine is important in O'Flaherty's fictional world precisely because it is anything but a historical event, or in other words anything but unique; it is rather a clear exposure of the way things always are, a revelation of "that great lash of hunger, the dread spirit that ever haunts the poor, reminding them of the hardship that is to come, deadening the pain that is present" ("Poor People," in *Short Stories,* 1937).

The effect of such relentless hunger is to reduce almost to zero the possibility of mental life. "The very poor," the narrator in *Famine* tells us, "are unable to see far into the future. If they can make provision for their immediate wants, they are not greatly troubled by a remote disaster" (*Famine,* ch. 7). This lack of perspective among other things accounts for their failure to act in that novel in response to the unequivocal signs of approaching cataclysm. They are, however, terribly credulous, as another of O'Flaherty's spokesmen, Raoul St. George, explains in *Land* (ch. 28):

> I don't blame them for their credulity. They have become hysterical with fear. The crops have failed miserably again this year. The vile government is sending troops into the villages. Threats of most repressive measures are being broadcast daily by those on high. It's no wonder that the poor are ready to believe in a sign of redemption, no matter how extravagant and improbable.

Politics, and especially the politics of British colonial rule (it is 1879 when Raoul speaks), have a role to play; but hunger and the fear it produces are the true points of origin.

To this credulity (which makes them especially susceptible to the manipulation of priests, a major element again and again in the plots of O'Flaherty's novels) one must add an absolute refusal to vary from the time-honored ways of wringing a living from the resistant land. The Kilmartins and their neighbors reject altogether the idea of growing vegetables other than potatoes, even as the smell of the blight covers their entire valley; it is not custom, and custom is ordained by God. A century later, the neighbors of Colm Derrane react with exactly the same hostility, and exactly the same invocation of custom as "the law of God and of man," to the outlandish notion of owning more than one cow ("Two Lovely

Beasts"). Nor will they consider leaving the land, even when the life of a peasant farmer is manifestly insupportable. As the stories "Going into Exile" and "The Letter" (the latter in *Short Stories,* 1937) insist, emigration looks, both to those who go and to those who stay, very like death. But to stay risks an equally horrible death-in-life, visible in a Kerry peasant couple who appear briefly in *The Martyr* (ch. 18) and mark the irreducible bottom to which the human animal can be reduced:

> The expression on their faces was a mixture of ghoulish idiocy and diabolical innocence. It was hard to believe that the one had been as far as America, or that the other had once been a girl. The boredom and savagery of their solitary existence on this mountainside had reduced them to a state that was scarcely human.

In O'Flaherty's work Raoul St. George's relative sympathy is much less frequent than is the terror and disgust which that mountain couple arouse. In *Shame the Devil* (ch. 4), O'Flaherty records a visit to his home island in the 1920s and condemns "these people among whom I was born" as "the common herd, slaveling serfs who grovelled before false gods; gods in their own liking [*sic*]; toy monsters without any noble attribute." Indeed, again and again the novels center on an effort not so much to see the peasantry as to understand and define—and thus to try to move beyond—their true nature and significance.

The result of these investigations is profoundly mixed, for something in the life of the peasantry, for all its manifest horror, continues to draw O'Flaherty's mind. One sign of this is the way in which both of his autobiographies overtly announce their contempt for "the common herd" and yet in structure encompass a pattern of departure and return, directly to Aran in *Two Years,* metaphorically to the peasant life of work by way of a sojourn with Breton fishermen and a short story about Irish peasants in *Shame the Devil.* In his recurrent dialogues about the peasantry, the conflict of two divergent views—that the poor are wise and that they are miserably animalistic—is never resolved. What in the life of the peasant might hold such a powerful and contradictory appeal? The condemnation of "the common herd" in *Shame the Devil* offers a clue. We should first observe that what O'Flaherty curses is not something unique to the island peasant; indeed, he draws a direct analogy between the hostile islanders and "the critics who had denounced my book [*The Black Soul*]." In one sense, this is O'Flaherty the thoroughgoing nay-sayer at work, defining himself as utterly outcast both from the world into which he had been born and from the literary "culture" into which he had sought admission in London and Dublin. One thing that keeps him from utter despair and indeed from suicide in *Shame the Devil* is a sense that everyone hates him; which in his moral universe certifies his virtue and gives his life an irreducible purpose: to spite the world's judgment by his mere existence, to live, as Fergus O'Connor says he wishes to, "to be a constant insult to civilization" (*The Black Soul,* "Winter," ch. 1).

But there is more than just self-defensive vitriol at work here. Implicit in the equation of such disparate human groups as Aran peasants and London critics is a characterization of the peasant not as a historical and cultural phenomenon or as representative of a socioeconomic class (despite the use, both by O'Flaherty himself and the more politically active of his characters, of the terminology of class struggle). The peasant, incessantly laboring and yet always starving, victim of inner terrors and outward manipulations, fundamentally and indeed necessarily selfish and wary of anything beyond the immediate needs of survival, is elemental Man. From the cosmic perspective which some of O'Flaherty's characters attain (and it is almost always imagined as a drifting upward and a looking back and down), all human life looks like the life of a peasant, just as the universe itself resembles nothing so much as the rocky Aran coast:

> Suddenly [Skerrett] thought that the earth was a living being, making fun of his defeat. All was so silent and mysterious and unapproachable. He thought how puny and weak was man, wandering haphazard on this cruel earth, pressing its face with his feet, burrowing on its bosom and then passing to his death, when the vain quests of his life have dissolved in horrid annihilation. And it was made manifest to him as he watched this glistening crust of sun-baked rock, beneath its dome of sky, that there was no God to reward the just or to punish the wicked, nothing beyond this unconquerable earth but the phantasies born of man's fear and man's vanity.
>
> (*Skerrett,* ch. 23)

To see life as it is lived by the peasant offers a view into the stony heart of things.

SUCH visions, although likely to occur at least once in any of O'Flaherty's extended pieces of fiction, are in the whole of human life both rare and momentary. Or at least they are rare in the lives of those who think and observe, as opposed to those who incessantly hunger and work; without mystical transport, they have that "queer, unholy wisdom begotten of hunger" which marks the faces of starving children in *Famine* (ch. 4). The educated, the intellectuals, must pursue such wisdom at great cost, only to find that it cannot be successfully sought or intentionally summoned.

But the animalistic side of "the common herd" *can* readily be observed; and the lesson of such observation seems, to O'Flaherty, unavoidable to any truly watchful eye. The metaphor of the herd is strikingly unoriginal, but it is altogether symptomatic of the view he and his characters attain. Skerrett sees humanity "burrowing" like some mole; other visions comparable to Skerrett's reduce human beings not just to the stature but to the very nature of tiny animals, worms, ants. The direction of O'Flaherty's metaphors is always from the human to the animal; and the comparisons must be taken literally.

If O'Flaherty's peasant stories essentially sound the necessary ground note against which all human life must be heard, then his animal stories demonstrate the very tonal system in which all of his fiction is written. There is, I would wager, not a single substantial passage of character-description in all of O'Flaherty's writing that does not rest on an identification between the character and some common animal. Like a medieval allegorist, O'Flaherty defines character in terms of certain basic traits (many of them derived in fact from the traditional catalog of vices and mortal sins: Pride, Lust, Avarice, Despair) and by way of emblematic creatures. Against the victims (often bulls or bears, large and not very intelligent; or timid rabbits) are arrayed the sharp-eyed predators, hawks and ferrets and snakes and ravens and weasels. The common thread is predation, which as O'Flaherty loudly announces to an American woman he meets in *Shame the Devil* (ch. 4) is the grounding principle of existence: "Learn, you foolish woman, that life is an interminable process of one form of life preying on another, from the cow that destroys life in the blade of grass, to the lion that leaps upon a stag in the African forest."

That is certainly one of the common elements in the large number of stories O'Flaherty wrote which have essentially no human characters at all. Their titles almost invariably name the central animal figure. Some are no more than two or three pages long; they center on one moment of struggle and conflict—an eel caught in a fisherman's net, a mother cow searching for its dead calf, a cormorant, hurt by a falling rock, struggling to keep its grip on a cliff face, a butterfly blown out to sea. The animals act out of the same instincts and emotions as do O'Flaherty's people: hunger, fear, jealousy, hatred, the desire to mate, to survive. But the stories are the exact opposite of anthropomorphic: rather than portraying animal life in terms of human attributes, they propose how thoroughly human life is an animal existence. They underscore particularly the way in which the dislike of the outcast, the individual, and the outsider which O'Flaherty regularly observes among humans is a fact of nature. The runt of the litter, the hen more lovely than the rest, the bull more virile than any other, the cormorant now wounded and unable to fly—all are, like the truly thoughtful man, set upon, and most are destroyed, by "the herd."

And yet destruction is not inevitable. Take the tale of "The Little White Dog" (*Short Stories,* 1937). It has really only two characters: a proud young bull, full of the incomprehensible urgings of spring; and a tiny white dog. The bull happens to be near a pump, to which a small boy is sent to fetch water. The bull snorts, charges, chases the boy off; the boy returns with a second, larger boy, who carries the dog under his jacket. All of the battles so far have been unequal, and all in the bull's favor. The arrival of the dog gives no sign of changing that, for it is an absurd creature, "so small and weak that he stumbled over the wet grass," justifiably wary of the bull, but urged on by the boys.

Then the tale turns on itself; the dog becomes the conqueror, the bull the terrified victim. "Predation" is not quite what happened—nothing is eaten, and substantially nothing is changed, except for the mood of the dog, now absurdly "arrogant and fierce," puffed up with his own victory. In one sense the story is no more than a vignette, an anecdote; unlike many another of O'Flaherty's tales and all of his novels, this tale's end has no corpses, no shouts of defiance. Yet without building too vast a structure upon a slight frame, the story can be seen as a small instance of the pattern after which many of his novels are cut. In the animal world, the paradigm of the human, physical strength is—to those who look on—remarkable, even frightening. But physical strength can never win out altogether; and it is especially susceptible to the operations of cunning.

The little white dog, threatened on both sides by a larger and more powerful creature, whether boy or bull, has no choice but to act cunningly. No more does man, with hunger on one side and the manipulations of civilization on the other. A lofty view of "the futility of all endeavor" (the phrase is that of another of O'Flaherty's heroes, the assassin McDara) may permit a knowing laugh and a momentary calmness of soul; but it will not answer the fact of hunger, will not defeat the desire to survive. Observation of elemental peasant man-and-animal nature can, in the end, do no more than describe the circumstances under which one must live; it cannot answer the altogether more pressing question of *how* to live.

ONE cannot even say, either of O'Flaherty's peasants or of his animals, that, like Faulkner's Dilsey, they endure; more often than not they die, and usually in lonely isolation. Yet survival is not out of the question, nor is a certain kind of triumph, like that of "The Hawk" who, although he dies defending his nest, has at least had a moment in which "his brute soul was exalted by the consciousness that he had achieved the fullness of the purpose for which nature had endowed him." The human record is similarly mixed. Even taken in the unprepossessing mass, the peasantry has at times an appearance not entirely hopeless. Here, for instance, is a view of mid-summer bustle in the yard of the cottage of the Deegan family:

> It was a joyous scene. Yet each living thing was hurrying angrily. The beasts and fowls buffeted one another and the human beings bore the dour look of intensity that accompanies fear, greed, and lechery. But the same look accompanies, at times, the acts of greatest heroism, virtue, and creative ecstasy. Here there was the primitive simplicity and beauty of labor, performed with fierce enthusiasm by individuals that worked for no personal reward but through the primeval instinct of the preservation of the family. The lashing of the cows by the sturdy boys, the savage biting and screeching of the pigs, the decrepit grandparents tottering with old age, still moving to their infant tasks, the hard face of the child-carrying mother, were all unified into a single glorious act, when seen as the material and root of human greatness; the struggle for bread and conquest.
>
> (The Wilderness, ch. 5)

O'Flaherty never speaks so credibly of joy or glory as he does of despair and darkness; and even here the reductive eye of Skerrett could find much to work with, most particularly in the prevalence of violent action, in the way man and beast are altogether indistinguishable, and in the way fear and lechery can be stated unequivocally, but heroism and creativity only more tentatively and occasionally. One can still hear in the phrase "the nobility of labor" the stale echo of the rhetoric which O'Flaherty learned (so he says) from James Connolly and an itinerant I.W.W. organizer.[4] But whatever the weaknesses of the style or the distance of the perspective, an irreducible energy is visible here, and an apparently indomitable survival instinct.

"The primeval instinct for the preservation of the family" is a feebly derivative label for this element as it appears in more effective and complex pieces of fiction such as *The Black Soul, The House of Gold, Famine,* "Red Barbara," "A Red Petticoat," and "Two Lovely Beasts." In these works

---

4. O'Flaherty writes of his education by the Wobbly John Joseph Peterson in the chapters "The Lumber Woods" and "The Nickel Mines" in *Two Years*. Patrick Sheeran (*The Novels of Liam O'Flaherty,* pp. 204–216) makes considerable headway in sorting out the exact nature—and the distinct limits—of O'Flaherty's socialism, especially as it derives from Connolly and influences *Famine*.

the result of human effort is not entrapment and lonely defeat but escape, and even something remarkably like success. This "instinct" in fact serves the ends of the individual organism better than of family, and is especially visible in loners, outcasts, eccentrics, strangers. But when accompanied by the love of parent for child (and especially mother for child), it becomes all the more powerful. It seems to derive from, or to draw from, physical and sexual passion—to O'Flaherty more an aspect of predation than a path to salvation. Instinct rejects altogether the usual constraints of morality. Essentially unintellectual and unreflective, it nonetheless has in great measure that cunning which derives from an acute eye for the exact fear which is at the enemy's heart.

Mary Kilmartin in *Famine* is O'Flaherty's most admiring portrait of this survival instinct. She seems at first—both to the reader and to the Kilmartin family, into which she marries—a bourgeois reformer; she brings the supposed virtues of cleanliness and order to the crowded and quite dirty Kilmartin house. In some ways she is no peasant at all. Her father is a weaver, and a prosperous one at that, a man of some education and considerable political wisdom, a self-made "outsider" who is rather proud of his arrival in the Kilmartins' Black Valley with a wagon, a family, a skill, and not a thing besides. Mary has an eye for new ideas (for instance, the growing of green vegetables) and no hesitance about speaking her mind. Young and "a truly beautiful woman," newly married to the passionate elder Kilmartin son, she is clearly a threat to the stability of the family and the power of the older generation, her father-in-law Brian Kilmartin and his wife. To them she represents a principle of inevitable generational change.

Under other circumstances she might have been just that: a woman strong and strong-minded enough to have brought some elements of civilization to the backward valley, to have been (as O'Flaherty's mother apparently was) a humanizing influence within the harsh context of peasant Ireland. But the Famine makes an utter hash of such humanizing and shows how pointless civilization is when confronted with the elemental fact of hunger. Yet the ordeal of famine really does no more than speed up time. For instance, the local gombeen-man, Johnny Hynes, rises even more quickly than he would otherwise have done (for, as we shall see, the flourishing of his kind is, in O'Flaherty's view, if not inevitable then at least terrifyingly commonplace). Hynes's doctor son, half peasant, half intellectual, rushes from debauchery to a kind of fanatical political faith and back again within months. Otherwise, it might have taken him years to fall to pieces and reveal his essential cowardice and division; to traverse, in other words, the path more slowly walked by his fellow-cowards Father

Hugh McMahon (in *Thy Neighbour's Wife*) and Mr. Gilhooley. All around the valley, peasant families die, or suffer eviction, or emigrate: the usual alternatives.

Mary herself ages with great rapidity; and more significantly, she quite literally becomes feral and predatory:

> Her eyes seemed to be searching for something. They were never still. They were fierce, on the alert, suspicious. Her hands, too, were shifty, and it was pitiful the way she now grabbed at her food, tore it greedily with her teeth and looked around in an uncouth fashion while she ate . . . Formerly she used to be so dainty and so restful, as if she were in a delicious swoon of passion.
>
> (*Famine*, ch. 44)

Within a very few pages, O'Flaherty explicitly states the rule of which Mary is one instance: "Under the pressure of hunger, as among soldiers in war, the mask of civilization slips from the human soul, showing the brute savage beneath, struggling to preserve life at all costs" (ch. 45).

But as the animal stories suggest, that struggle is an unequal one, and one in which pure fortune can be decisive. Mary manages, at considerable cost to the probabilities of the plot, to save not only herself and her child but her rebel husband as well. We see them last, in a scene that owes more to wish fulfillment than to any consistency of vision on O'Flaherty's part, on a boat bound for America, armed with the stirring thought that "the fight for liberty must go on" (ch. 54). The falseness of tone of that moment sounds a retreat into the expected pieties of Irish nationalism (or in fact, of its peculiarly sensitive and emotional cousin, Irish-American national-ism). It is partly redeemed by the final chapter, which portrays, much more tersely and persuasively, the last moments in Brian Kilmartin's life. But that same falseness suggests too the strength and the limitation of O'Flaherty's view of the world: examples of what is bad are much more readily at hand and much more realistically convincing, in his fallen world, than are instances of good. Mary Kilmartin is of interest then not because she is herself a fully convincing character (although until very near the end of the novel she is), but because she gives the best possible shading to the survival instinct as it appears more commonly and more darkly in the rest of O'Flaherty's fiction.

A WORLD so dark and predatory seems to cry out for reform. Even in *Shame the Devil*, which is rather dismissive of the political coming-of-age at the heart of *Two Years*, O'Flaherty is still willing to assert what sounds like a reformist creed: "I have a common and universal duty to fulfill, that I must help towards the liberation of the human intellect from the specter of famine" (ch. 14). Yet his fiction—at least up to *Famine*—offers no support for the belief that this duty can effectively be fulfilled. Hardly a single novel is without a reformer, whether political rebel, moral guardian, or social activist. And he comes very close to exhausting the array of possible methods: individual acts of political and moral terrorism; self-mortification and martyrdom; political organization, both covert and overt; mass uprising, whether planned or spontaneous; the application of religious institutions to problems both moral and economic. This is not to mention lesser varieties of moral suasion such as journalism, political oratory, preaching, and schoolteaching, and even—in his very odd satire on the movie industry, *Hollywood Cemetery*—the mass media. All of these have no apparent liberating effect.

The lives of peasants are again a good measure; the cottage of the Kilmartins in 1845 in *Famine* is materially indistinguishable from the cottages of those suffering eviction in 1879 in *Land* or those of Inverara around 1900 in *Thy Neighbour's Wife, Skerrett,* and "The Child of God" or those to be seen in the mid 1920s in *The Black Soul, The Wilderness,* and *The Martyr,* or that from which Colm Derrane starts his rise during the Second World War ("Two Lovely Beasts"). Nor is there any sign of moral or spiritual change which might make those physical conditions more endurable or less powerfully determinative of human lives. So much, then, for the announced agenda of O'Flaherty the reformer. The most visible change in the world of O'Flaherty's fiction is the decay and ultimate destruction of individual lives, almost entirely the work of natural forces such as time and hunger, and manifestly impervious to any predictable human intervention. The lessons of the collapse of church and state and community before the awful fact of the Famine hold true even in more normal circumstances. It is in this sense that O'Flaherty may be said to be, even from the beginning of his career, a historical—or perhaps more fairly a *counterhistorical*—novelist. Because the "new" Ireland which developed after the Civil War, especially under De Valera's leadership, was so rooted in a particular myth of heroism and change, of the rise of a pure and noble Ireland and the throwing off of the yoke of colonial slavery, O'Flaherty's rejection of all forms of heroic action and his refusal to see any substantive change in human lives in general stands as a loud negation of the Ireland of his adulthood.

After the crisis recorded in *Shame the Devil,* that negation seems to have softened somewhat, however. The last three of his novels (*Famine, Land,* and *Insurrection*) are more traditionally historical and attempt in some detail to recreate three comonly accepted turning points in Irish history: the Famine, the Land League agitation of the 1870s, and the Easter Rebellion. Even here O'Flaherty sees much to correct. He is especially dismissive of Daniel O'Connell and his followers in *Famine*. Of Charles Stewart Parnell and Michael Davitt, in *Land*, he is less overtly critical; but a clear argument of that novel is that the real work of political change rests with the obscure and nameless. In *Insurrection* the Easter Martyrs—and especially Padraic Pearse—are accorded surprising reverence; but again O'Flaherty focuses not on them but on the peasant Bartly Madden. (In a way that was not comprehensible to the man himself, or, it must be said, particularly evident to a reader of the novel, he was remade from beast into man by the raptures engendered by an Idea.) In place of the usual roster of martyrs, revolutionaries, and politicians from Wolfe Tone onwards, O'Flaherty offers his own triad—the soldier, the monk or saint, and the poet. In trying, especially in *Land* and *Insurrection,* to make fiction out of what amounts to a theory of revolutionary history, he produces characters with none of the persuasive energy and substance of those in his earlier novels.[5] His three archetypes seem, moreover, oddly derivative; one waits for Tom O'Donnell to snort in derision, as he does when the talk turns to "saints and scholars."

When O'Flaherty tries (especially in *Insurrection*) explicitly to argue that there is, after all, a truly revolutionary thread in Irish culture and Irish history, the details from which he builds that argument stubbornly point in an opposite direction, toward a message more consistent with his earlier work. It seems as if the idealist who now wished to include uplifting visions of the progress of man could not suppress the eye of the novelist, who knows that rebels, like mystics, die alone and largely unrecognized, that most lives are dreary and yet full of a terrified resistance even to changes which might help relieve that dreariness. Those in whose name rebellion is proposed live on, mostly uninterested and certainly not trans-

---

5. Both John Zneimer (*The Literary Vision of Liam O'Flaherty,* pp. 132–145) and Patrick Sheeran (*The Novels of Liam O'Flaherty,* pp. 203–257) treat O'Flaherty's notion of the roles of poet, monk, and soldier more fully, and more appreciatively, than I have here. The greatest problem with these late works is that they can be read seriously only if all of O'Flaherty's prior work is ignored altogether. Raoul St. George's proud assertion at the close of *Land* that he must be at work educating the younger generation sounds silly in the light of *Thy Neighbour's Wife, Skerrett,* and *The House of Gold,* all of which portray the world in which that younger generation will live. Bartly Madden's transformation from beast to hero (conveniently ended by his heroic death) is credible only if one refuses to see that the man, had he lived, would inevitably have become someone terribly like Gypo Nolan in *The Informer* or "Crackers" Sheehan in *The Martyr* or the disillusioned and aimless figures in the political "underworld" of *The Assassin.*

formed. The peasants stay well reined in by the power of the Church and of their own conservatism, as in *Land;* the urban proletarians who figure so unprepossessingly in *Insurrection* change sides whenever evident power changes hands, viewing the "terrible beauty" of the Rising as little more than an elaborate raree show.

Yet O'Flaherty's novels, even before *Famine*, focus on moments which have at least the potential to be historically determinative transition points. They include the period around 1900, when (at least in the distant Arans) the struggle between political nationalism and more conservative economic "progress" led by the priests remains to be fought out; the period near the end of and just after the Civil War, when the exact nature of the new Ireland might be thought to be in the process of formation, and when the defeat of the more radical aspects of the revolutionary programs which had given rise to rebellion was not yet altogether certain; or, much more briefly in several long stories (especially "Two Lovely Beasts" and "The Blow"), the time when the unsettling effects of prosperity engendered by Ireland's neutrality in World War II were still being felt. The absence of anything which might fairly be called progress, even at such supposed turning points, becomes all the more damning.

Instead of development there is a pattern of dreary recurrence, which O'Flaherty imagines in *The Martyr* (ch. 25) as a tired piece of theatre. Looking at a gathering in 1922, near the end of the Civil War, of the Catholic bourgeois leaders of a modest Kerry town, he cannot avoid an apostrophe: "How different and yet how like it had been of old! The old actors had deserted the play, the English colonels and their Irish squires; but these new actors had inherited the stage gear of the old, though not yet as proficient in the word and manner." But in fact in this case the change is more than superficial; the particular transfer of power being acted out here is perhaps the only truly historical transition which O'Flaherty admits, indeed insists on. If his view of the record of political reform and rebellion is, at least until near the end of his career, bleak and unsparing, he is from the beginning convinced that Ireland in the twentieth century is becoming "civilized." Many of his novels record, with particular anger and sharpness, what he rather politely describes in *Skerrett* (ch. 1) as "the infancy" of the Irish "bourgeoisie" as it begins "to detach itself from the peasant stem." Elsewhere he borrows the language of the Marxist dialectic to propose that "the decaying feudal class [is] being destroyed by the rising power of capitalism" (*Land*, ch. 3).

The result seems, to those who live through it, to be "a great change," though the peasants are convinced that because of it "things are all wrong" (*The House of Gold*, ch. 7). Yet in the same novel a priest insists that the central fact in post-Civil War Ireland is that "the peasants are now in power" (ch. 10). The problem with his view (aside from the face that it is the view of a priest, always highly suspect to O'Flaherty), and with the more generalized formulations which O'Flaherty himself gives elsewhere, is that they describe in terms of broad classes a phenomenon which is fundamentally individual. It is not peasants or middle-class capitalists generally who seek and obtain and even dare to use power, but individual men: Father O'Reilly, the "king" of Inverara in *Thy Neighbour's Wife* and his clerical and royal predecessor, "king" Father Harry Moclair in *Skerrett;* Colonel Patrick Hunt, whose (successful) notion of how to defeat the appeal of Republican rebels explicitly admits it is modeled on the behavior of "people startin' a business" (*The Martyr,* ch. 17); Johnny Hynes in *Famine,* who caps his accession to power by manipulating the shrinking food supply, literally growing rich from the starvation of his neighbors' children.

Creatures of unusual single-mindedness, they are the darker and unquestionably more common versions of that "risen" peasant whom O'Flaherty portrays in Mary Kilmartin. Like Mary, they derive a certain freedom of movement from their position as outsiders. Hunt is a total stranger to Sallytown, where he must impose governmental order. Johnny Hynes is the son of an informer whose family was driven out of their native valley and into a hovel in town. Both O'Reilly and Moclair come from the mainland, and are by their role as priests necessarily isolated from common life. But that powerful instinct for self-preservation, which in Mary Kilmartin had the color of sexual desire and maternal love, is in them apparent in the form of lust and avarice—of, indeed, an inextricable mixing of the two. No matter how clever their connivance, they are at bottom creatures not of intellect but of appetite.

And as is the case with appetites, the actions of the power-seekers are clear to see, but their motives are obscure. O'Flaherty can lay out the facts of the matter; can define for each of these men the particular devices they use to consolidate their power. But unlike the cranks—mystics, puritans, terrorists—who occupy the metaphysical center of O'Flaherty's fiction, these men do not really develop. Only once, in the long story "Two Lovely Beasts" does O'Flaherty try to trace, in any detail, the rise of such a man, Colm Derrane; and even there only the general outlines of the process are clearly visible. Part of the formula lies within the man himself: Colm, like O'Reilly, Hynes, Moclair, and Hunt, is a creature of unusual will and stubbornness. Typically, O'Flaherty does not so much analyze this quality as assign it a name—"ruthlessness"—which he can then use like an heroic epithet. But that ruthlessness needs an accident to give it life and room:

in the story a neighbor's cow dies, and Colm is offered the calf. In the usual peasant fashion, he at first reacts formulaically: he has a calf, and the idea of raising two is altogether against custom, and thus impossible, "against the law of God." But such conservatism cannot withstand another, deeper element within him. He calls it "courage," but the narrator calls it an "intoxication," a "frenzy of desire." It lives and works at a level where the usual psychological and moral distinctions—between ambition and love, for instance, or between either of those and the sins of lust and avarice—no longer apply. Once made, the decision (to use a word that implies far too much conscious thought and analysis) becomes a fundamental gesture of self-definition, and of defiance as well. "I'll raise those two beasts if it's the last thing I'll do in this world. Let any man that dares try to stop me," Colm shouts, in the mixed tone of childish petulance and heroism which is the voice of so many of O'Flaherty's central characters.

In many of O'Flaherty's novels, religion and politics operate less as systems of meaning or faith than as languages whereby deeper and ultimately more inarticulable aspirations and insights can be approximately (if often self-defeatingly) expressed. Similarly, Colm in the end translates his instinctive stubbornness and self-assertion into the language of economic advancement: "I want to rise in the world." Inevitably that will demand that Colm step over the line from peasant farmer to huckster: "We are going to open a shop . . . It's only shopkeepers that rise in the world." But such language, in Colm's mouth, seems no more than a belated and inexact metaphor. Colm speaks in terms of "a plan," but the narrator calls it something far less conscious: "such was the power of the idea that possessed him." "Possession"—at least as much demonic as heroic—drives him to beat his wife—who dares to rebel against his singlemindedness—and to force his entire family to go hungry so that the calves can be well-fed. He succeeds, but his rise depends upon circumstance as much as it does upon Colm's own will; the world (outside of Ireland) is at war, and for once there is money to be made.

The story, which tries to anatomize gombeenism, is at least as interested in the response to it on the part of others. Colm's economic rise is accompanied by his changing, in the eyes of his neighbors, from outcast to admired wise man (since his neighbors can explain his prosperity only as a sign of divine favor), and then to another kind of ostracism. At the story's end Colm rides through town in a vast motor car, jeered at by his sometime neighbors, who denounce him (as, a century earlier, Johnny Hynes had been denounced, and justly) as one of "the bloodsuckers [who] are taking the food out of our country." To which talk Colm is indifferent, having achieved a kind of utter independence that shows most clearly in "his pale blue eyes [which] stared fixedly straight ahead, cold and resolute and ruthless." Like the hawk, he has achieved a full expression of that which his nature seems to have intended for him; and if he can be judged, and indeed condemned in the way O'Flaherty clearly means for us to condemn O'Reilly and Moclair and Hynes and Hunt, yet he must as well be admired, or at least taken as an elemental fact.

As we will see, Colm is in his way much like the mystics with whom O'Flaherty has more evident sympathy. He acts when desires are aroused, more or less circumstantially; the very indefinability and near-madness of his "frenzy" is what makes it so powerful, and so insatiable. In turn, it is the continuing lure of the unattainable that marks, in O'Flaherty's eyes, not only the worst of men (among whom he numbers impotent, cuckolded husbands, power-hungry priests, and mindless voluptuaries as well as the avaricious) but many of the best as well. Colm gains, too, by comparison to those among whom—ultimately against whom—he lives: the timid, the fickle, the apathetic; the herd who fear independence, grovel before material success, and jeer at accomplishment.

ONLY once did O'Flaherty put the gombeen-man directly in the center of a novel, in the person of Ramon Mor Costello in *The House of Gold.* As a character, Ramon Mor is a mixture of improbabilities; as Patrick Sheeran remarks (*The Novels of Liam O'Flaherty*, p. 172), from one page to the next it is hard to tell whether to take him as a realistic portrayal, an allegorical "figure" of Avarice, or an Irish Polyphemus in a perverse, nihilistic fairy tale of captive maidenhood. To make things worse, he moves through a plot which, as Sheeran admits (p. 162), is "a piece of hokum." Like Colm Derrane's, Ramon Mor's motives arise in some impenetrable inner place where desires we might like to distinguish—sexual passion, egotistic greed, and the survival instinct—collapse into one black hole the energy of which defies either analysis or resistance. And again like Colm, he gains by contrast to his surroundings, especially to the pale and intellectual figures around him that try to understand, to manipulate, or to destroy him.

The House of Gold is a novel driven almost entirely by O'Flaherty's two-edged anger, at the world and at himself. Ramon's power is both unquestionable and unendurable. Ramon's opponents, like O'Flaherty, have or pretend to have a perspective which allows them to condemn Ramon, but they are wholly self-involved, utterly ineffectual, wavering between belief and skepticism, between disillusionment and passion. At its heart the novel insists on a fundamental conflict of emotional absolutes. In the visible world of human action, individuals driven by their own uncontrollable desires battle, almost ridiculously, over an evil woman and material wealth; inside the individual being, the conflict rages most especially within Ramon Mor, who when he is not some sort of astonishing beast, some lion or bull, is a walking battleground of will and desire, avarice and love, defiance and despair.

In *Skerrett* (ch. 18) O'Flaherty remarks, more restrainedly, on the complex nature of the process of "civilization," which has great "beauty" but which is sadly "stained by the demons which the advance sets loose," among which he explicitly includes gombeen-men such as Ramon. *The House of Gold* extends that demonic image with utter literalness: Ramon is the hellish being that grows when the "germ" of civilization takes hold on a "peasant stem" of sufficient vigor and strength. Yet O'Flaherty at one point almost excuses Ramon by explaining what most frightens, and thus most motivates him: no more than the inevitable "earthman's fears of nature's powers, . . . the fear of death, . . . those animal fears that make sheep bleat when the sky is curtained with dark mist." Against such fear Ramon can do no more, and no less, than call upon will to breed defiance, pride, and then anger, and in the end to escape fear by way of "that deep, deep drunkenness which is conquered only by the arrow of the burglar death" (ch. 11).

As if to emphasize the degree to which Ramon is, for all his nightmarish size and power, no more than an extrapolation of a universal fear, O'Flaherty immediately precedes Ramon's crisis of terror with a vision of chaos, seen through the eyes of Father Michael Considine, a priest driven mad by lust. It can stand as perhaps the darkest of all the visions to be found in O'Flaherty's work, one in which the animal, the human, and the divine dreadfully intermix; in which all distinctions collapse, thus defeating even the path of denial; in which the categories of moral distinction cannot even be turned on their head, as they are in *Shame the Devil;* in which desire is not only the starting point but the desperate last hope of the isolated soul:

> There was God and yet it was not He, for [Considine's] mind had lost the measurements of God's proportions and God became the Devil, on sight, through the confusion of their dual attributes. Neither was evil, that fish with shining scales and a beak of ivory, more evil than good, which was a toothless woman riding on an ass; nor was good evil, since God and the Devil, joining forces, shovelled all the good and evil in the world into one heap . . . Nor did his own senses respond to the urge of memory and register fear against danger, joy against satisfaction, enthusiasm against passion, remorse against

sin . . . [H]e wanted, against wise nature's orders, to embrace danger and to lacerate himself lest satisfaction might make honey with his sap and to look upon sin as the desirable golden woman who walked naked among the stars, beyond his reach. Until at last, Despair, a hunchback with one eye in the center of his forehead, carrying a great flail, flogged God and the Devil and sent them shrieking out of sight, and then, his mind suddenly stopped revolving and he determined to plunge headlong towards the attainment of his one desire.

(ch. 11)

The chaos which Considine sees is what lies beneath the mask of apparently civilized life. Part demon, part animal, Ramon Mor is the creature most visible upon that nightmare earth. The novel intends to strip away the surface of "this ruthless type that was going to put the country on its feet after the revolution" (ch. 1) and to show the terribly unchanged being beneath, "the barbarous consciousness of an animal" (ch. 11). What Colm Derrane puts on, Ramon Mor has torn from him by the combined workings of the connivance of his rivals and the unbearable force of his own inner nature.

THE HOUSE OF GOLD seems at first to invoke, and then wholeheartedly to abandon, any sort of detached social or historical analysis. O'Flaherty dismisses the notion that the purpose of fiction is to provide a representation of real worlds; "the curse of modern literature," he says in the chapter called "Greenwich Village" in *Two Years*, "is that public opinion demands information from it." To try to see the world as it factually is, or historically was, is the mistake many of his characters make (the roster includes an unusually high number of journalists and intellectual social commentators). The initial error may turn out to be productive because the facts of the matter may just be enough to begin to limn the deeper nightmare beneath. Thus in the four Dublin novels (*The Informer, Mr. Gilhooley, The Assassin,* and *The Puritan*) O'Flaherty wrote both just before and just after *The House of Gold,* he is especially scrupulous in using the devices of a pure realist (and especially precision of date and time and location). He does it in large part to explode the whole enterprise of realism, and to arrange a context within which mad visions become inevitable and much more persuasive than the supposedly hard facts of the visible world.

The Dublin of these novels is on one level another version of the "civilized," which once again emphasizes its shallowness and enervation, its reliance upon pretense and self-delusion. But more to the point in O'Flaherty's Dublin, reality and nightmare cannot be, and indeed must not be, distinguished. It is a city of dreadful night—quite literally, since almost all the important action in all four novels occurs after sunset. Its population includes politicians and journalists, both manipulators and victims of a self-serving moralism and religiosity; the "artificers of revolution" who can, however, do no more than grumble and plot. They are joined by intellectuals who are capable of nothing more passionate than irony, priests who believe only in self-protection, cunning whores, vaporously talkative writers, and keen-eyed policemen. Only two forces provide some life and movement. One is—again—the instinct for self-preservation and survival, but all it produces is a web of accusation and betrayal, while denying all charity, all love, all passions more selfless than hunger and lust. The other, and ultimately more important, is a search for, or construction of, an imagined harmony, which may result in visionary madness, but at the price of utter isolation and usually death.

The Informer is the best known, the earliest, and in many ways the most tidily made of the four novels. Almost every chapter, and certainly every important action or turn of plot, is both physically placed and chronologically labeled; O'Flaherty even at one point (ch. 6) creates a series of documentary "sources" to describe The Organization, the particular political splinter group with which all the main characters are involved, and its leader, Dan Gallagher, whose pursuit of the informer Gypo Nolan is the substance of the plot. O'Flaherty here diverges far less than he does in the other Dublin novels from this surface reality; which is one reason why this one has a kind of coherence unusual in his fiction, and why it has been taken (fairly or unfairly) as a nearly documentary record of the terrorist underworld in Dublin in the mid-1920s.

But as John Zneimer has documented from O'Flaherty's letters to Edward Garnett, the novel derives not from observation but from a dream:

> I have envisaged a brutal, immensely strong, stupid character, a man built by nature to be a tool for evil-minded intelligence . . . Elements of cunning, of fear, of struggle that is born of thought, appear in him . . . He is now a soul in torment struggling with evil influences . . . He stands alone, without the guidance of a mind to succor him, seeking an outlet for his useless strength, finding that it is no longer strength but a helpless thing, a target for the beings that press around to harass it. Intelligence, evil intelligence is dominant and supreme, civilization conquers the first beginnings of a man upwards.

(*The Literary Vision of Liam O'Flaherty,* pp. 68–70)

The image, and the novel it engendered, are a short compendium of O'Flaherty's habits of mind and style: the insistent, almost parabolic use of animals as archetypes, the violent and ultimately unequal battle of intellect against physical strength, the central image of an isolated being harassed by everything around, the predominance of the forces of civilization and nature over human endeavor.

The novel has a parallel to the later novel *Land*, which quickly falls victim to a schematization of ideas that is all too apparent behind the characters. In a similar way, *The Informer* seems less to use the pattern of the political thriller to move toward a larger theme than to be a thriller with metaphysical signposts attached. Most of these signposts point insistently toward the centrality of betrayal. O'Flaherty rings almost too many changes on the possibilities of his title; there is not a character of any substance within the novel who is not, in some clear way, an informer. In such a world the only reliable creed is proposed by the odd figure of the crank Shanahan who briefly crosses Gypo's path (ch. 8) and urges a "revolt against every existing institution, habit, or belief." All those false gods having been pulled down, what is left is the keynote of Mary Kilmartin's struggle: "Depend on yourself" (*Famine*, ch. 13).

But "self" is not to be trusted either, because it is invariably incomplete. Gallagher is a creature of pure intelligence; the Organization of which he is both a part and a symbol is "all brain and no body. An intelligence without a body . . . full of plans . . . like a religion, mysterious, occult, devilish" (ch. 5). Gypo is all body—initially, indeed, little more than a vast walking stomach. The two of them are not so much adversaries or even characters as they are two warring aspects of one being. And what both crave most of all is some harmony of understanding and feeling that would explain, if not the nature of the universe, then at least how to live. Gypo, by betraying Frankie, who was always the brains of that partnership, has cut off his own head, and again and again exerts what little intelligence he has to the making or finding of a "plan." Gallagher has a "theory" but it resists even his own efforts to understand and explain it. Gypo needs Gallagher to explain to him his own crime, his own nature; Gallagher needs Gypo to provide at least the opportunity to move from pure idea into a kind of passion, which in his case can only appear as hate, not love.

What O'Flaherty in *Two Years* ("I Become a Hobo") defines as the fundamental conflict in his own life, the "struggle between my bodily senses and my intellect," is thus in *The Informer* acted out on the dark streets of Dublin. The other three Dublin novels do not so readily allow themselves to be schematized, in part because they try to portray the inward struggle as it actually occurs, within the individual soul. Each takes a slightly different angle of view: the puritan Francis Ferriter and the assassin McDara are both similar to Gallagher, creatures, initially at least, more of intellect than of passion, or rather creatures who hope to resist or control passion by means of intellect. The voluptuary Mr. Gilhooley is a genteel Gypo, a man of limited mind but considerable appetite. Ferriter and Gilhooley, in particular, seem to be a matched pair. Each has a system of belief: Ferriter has devised, out of the disappointments of his own life, a variety of ascetic mysticism that undertakes the reform of the entire world by an act of murder but cannot withstand the force of his own passion. As he seems to realize, the triumph of his original system would, like Gypo's suicidal betrayal of Frankie, demand the destruction of a part of his own being. Gilhooley, for all his indulgence in drink and then in sex, desperately holds to a faith in bourgeois respectability and ideal love, both of which collapse under the pressure of a relationship that will not be simplified to fit either. *The Puritan* begins with a woman's murder, *Mr. Gilhooley* ends with one, and the climax of each novel is a vision that explodes each man's initial premises in precisely their own terms. Gilhooley, a creature of the senses with a very limited interest in any deity beyond the immediate needs of his own physical being, reaches an end point of vast nihilism, a denial of all physicality in a view of "the wrecked universe" in which "he himself became nothing" (*Mr. Gilhooley,* ch. 16). With a final gesture he shouts defiance ("I defy everything. There is nothing. Nothing.") and enacts self-destruction (falls into a canal and drowns).

Ferriter seems at least to go a step further; but perhaps that is because he had started form a more *imagined* position, a state of mind which had him from the beginning place less reliance than Gilhooley on "the disappointing reality." Ferriter's vision incorporates the negation of Gilhooley's and builds it into a paradox. Having started with a devout belief in God and a firm conviction of his own predestined role in the working out of God's plans, Ferriter begins questioning: "Does God exist and has man got a divine destiny?" (*The Puritan,* ch. 10). He passionately believes he has found the only answer: "There is no God, but man has a divine destiny. It is the duty of each man to become God" (ch. 19). It might be reasonable to dismiss this as no more than another manifestation of Ferriter's original metaphysical arrogance, the belief that he and he alone is the instrument of God's will. Ferriter is clearly mad; in the novel's last two chapters he has fallen wholly into a delusional state in which he feels "free" but is in fact "entombed." But his words oddly echo O'Flaherty's own:

What, then, is the divine destiny of man? I am convinced that the divinity in man's destiny is his struggle towards the perfection of his species to a state of godliness. And that the most perfect types of manhood are always in revolt against the limitations of man's nature, his position on the face of the earth, and his ignorance.

("I Become a Hobo," in *Two Years*)

Having at least some intelligence, both Gilhooley and Ferriter can follow the *via negativa* articulated by Shanahan the crank, unlike the animal Gypo, who dies bathetically asking Frankie McPhillip's mother for forgiveness. *The Informer* is a disillusioned novel; *Mr. Gilhooley* and *The Puritan* are novels which record the process of disillusionment. But as novels they are in the end—like *The House of Gold*—no better than significant failures. The central characters are altogether too stereotypical; neither the ano-rectic, repressed Ferriter nor the dimwittedly sensual Gilhooley will bear the weight of even their limited mystical progress. The transparent influence on *The Puritan* of Dostoevsky's *Crime and Punishment,* and the recurrent presence in *Mr. Gilhooley* of an ensemble of Joycean intellectuals make O'Flaherty's two novels seem at times like weak translations of a greater original.[6] And both novels are too obviously satiric tours of particular corners of "civilized" Dublin: the Catholic moral establishment in *The Puritan,* pubs full of ranting intellectuals in *Mr. Gilhooley.*

The Dublin of all three novels, and the central figures of the last two, are in the end more objects than subjects to O'Flaherty. And in the effort to explain the intelligent man's disillusionment, these novels are—like *Two Years, The Martyr,* and *Hollywood Cemetery*—just slightly off the main track of O'Flaherty's best fiction, which records what follows disillusionment. Ferriter, Gilhooley, and even the pitiful Gypo experience the stripping away of all upon which they had relied and of all human relationship as well; after that they can do no more than shout and die.

*   *   *

6. All of the Dublin novels date from a period not long after the appearance of *Ulysses,* suggesting at least the possibility that O'Flaherty's Dublin is a kind of rebuttal to Joyce's. There are a number of points of immediate resemblance: the predominance of brothels in *The Informer* and *The Puritan* compares to Bloom's Nighttown; the unscrupulous editor Mr. Patrick Corish in *The Puritan* resembles Joyce's Myles Crawford; the garrulous drunkards MacAward, Hanrahan, Culbertson, and Stevens (the first a "dissolute poet," the last a "student") in *Mr. Gilhooley* compare to Stephen Dedalus and his cronies in both *Ulysses* and *Portrait.* If the echoes are intended, they may be meant to underscore the degree to which O'Flaherty's moral and psychological universe is much more spare and somber than Joyce's, and his distrust both of the learned intellect and of the powers and devices of rhetoric much more unambiguous and explicit.

Just as O'Flaherty's treatment of peasant and animal is significant because it presents the ground upon which his spiritual and psychic quest must rest, the Dublin novels are, in terms of the whole of his fiction, of interest mostly because they develop a picture of the usual world from which O'Flaherty's richer characters justly and necessarily flee. These are Fergus O'Connor in *The Black Soul,* David Skerrett, and O'Flaherty himself in *Shame the Devil,* as well as their less persuasive cousin Lawless in *The Wilderness.* Ferriter, Gilhooley, and the other ultimately damned figures to be seen in Dublin are the devils whom the truly virtuous (which is to say the truly iconoclastic and defiant) must shame into oblivion.

But Michael McDara, the protagonist of *The Assassin,* cannot and should not be dismissed so readily. Of all the characters in the Dublin novels he is the most convincing, and the one who approaches the shape and power of the figures at the heart of O'Flaherty's fiction; just as the novel which he dominates seems to my eye the most effective and richest of the four Dublin novels.[7] McDara from some angles looks like the embodiment of final decadence of political faith; it is likely no accident that he bears the surname of the self-sacrificing rebel hero of one of Padraic Pearse's plays, *The Singer.* But O'Flaherty's McDara is neither fool nor madman; or at least his madness is much cooler, much less melodramatic, and (perhaps for that reason) much more convincing than that of Ferriter or Gilhooley. McDara in some ways is a more fully imagined Gallagher, with whom he shares a seductive intellectual power.

Gallagher has more cunning than intellect; he has "a theory" but he has not "worked it out yet" (*The Informer,* ch. 15). McDara, by contrast, can, if the situation demands it, offer up an intellectual rationale for his intended act of political murder:

> Our business is . . . to create a superior type of human being here. That is the objective of the revolutionary, to create a superior type of human being. Most revolutionary movements make the mistake

7. Even as a "thriller" (the general category under which *The Informer, Mr. Gilhooley, The Puritan,* and *The Assassin* are rather too easily lumped together) the novel works well—especially if one is unaware of the actual assassination, unsolved to this day, upon which it is based: the murder of Kevin O'Higgins, then Minister for Justice and External Affairs in the Free State government, on 10 July 1927. Although he never names "Him" who is McDara's victim, O'Flaherty makes only one significant change in the historical facts: *The Assassin* takes place in March (that is, during Lent), not July, contributing to the atmosphere of sterility in the novel and underscoring the degree to which McDara, for all his atheism, is even at the novel's end still awaiting the birth (or re-birth) of a god in which he could believe. The shift has an additional effect of leaving the plot somewhat in doubt even to those who know "the facts": McDara's plot might very well turn out to be not the successful one but an earlier failure.

of aiming at a change of government, seizing political power and that sort of thing. That is not revolution. It is merely a transposition of the material wealth in a community. . . . When a strong man seizes power, he should be cut down at once. Because the mass feels inferior to a strong man. Each individual loses his initiative. The strong man sucks all power into his own being. The mass become slaves. No progress is made. Until the head is chopped off. Then the mass is free to grope about again. Each individual becomes a living force, groping forward, unimpeded. Do you see?

(The Assassin, ch. 7)

To which the answer is a slow shake of the head, which has been echoed by critics who fault the novel for failing to provide a satisfactory set of motives for McDara.

But that is exactly O'Flaherty's point. The various systems of belief that McDara invokes here and elsewhere in the novel to persuade his co-conspirators are as empty as those upon which Ferriter, Gilhooley, and other Dubliners base their lives; the real motives are not political or religious (in the institutional sense) but utterly personal and psychological. McDara begins at a more intellectually advanced point than does the puritan or the voluptuary; but that merely means he has a less difficult time in stripping himself of some delusions. Having long since exhausted the appeals of formal religion and the more common forms of political action, McDara lives without a creed but inspired by an image, a vision of his own soul at war with the universe.

His purpose has really nothing to do with freeing the masses, but rather with making a "great gesture of defiance" against "the idea of God" (ch. 7). As the deed approaches, all calculations, all intellectual formulations fall away; by the sheer inertial force of his own Idea he is relieved of the necessity of thinking at all. The purpose of his "gesture" becomes far less important than the "furious longing" from which it arises (ch. 17); his motive, it becomes clear, is "revenge . . . on the brutality of nature" to be achieved "by dragging something with him down into the abyss of death" (ch. 13). The nakedness that befalls Ferriter and Gilhooley he actively pursues; and it is, significantly, a nakedness that takes him, in imagination, to the seacoast of the west:

He began to strip off his clothes, uttering fierce words. And he now tranformed himself into a wild fisherman from his native village, a man without subtle thought to disturb and emasculate his virility, dashing his strength against the barbarous cruelty of nature. He forgot his skinny legs, his sunken eyes, his pallid nervous cheeks, the softness of his muscles, and he felt himself towering over the angry sea in a boat, with god-like power, yelling defiance at the gale. He saw, from the rock-bound coast, civilized man afar off and spat at him with contempt.

(ch. 13)

Yet in the end McDara's is a story of failure—ironically, since his defiant gesture of political nihilism succeeds without a hitch. He can, transparently echoing O'Flaherty's own imagination, evoke this image through the power of his own intelligence; he can hold, as a foundation of his own view of the world, an absolute sense of the futility of all endeavor; but he cannot free himself of two demons. The first we might call the devil of intention. Having seen the aridity of political action, McDara still cannot abandon politics as a field of discourse. He still holds to a principle of cause and effect, of intention and result. He is, in that sense, a victim of his own persuasive rhetoric; a true nihilist should know better.

Worse yet, he is altogether a man of mind, dead to any sort of passion, apparently (as the novel ends, he plans suicide) having defeated even that drive toward physical survival which is at the heart of animal man. He hopes to free himself of imagination by way of imagination, to think his way (as he does briefly above) into a permanent state of thoughtlessness. But he is defeated by his own need to believe and to act decisively. Having tied his vision to an act, he suffers from the terrible aftereffect; the act having been accomplished, he must begin again, having circled back to the question to which Ferriter in his madness has the answer: "Is there a God then?" (ch. 22). And although he, unlike Ferriter or Gilhooley, lives to escape Dublin, he heads in a terribly wrong direction: toward England, deeper into the heart of dead civilization, and father away from that barren west where, as his own imagination knows, the sole faint hope of trans- formation is to be found.

ALONG with *The Informer* and *The Martyr*, *The Assassin* is O'Flaherty's fullest exploration of the inadequacy of politics, the emptiness of the political rhetoric he himself had learned, had acted upon, and could still hear so noisily abroad in the Dublin of the Twenties and Thirties. And in both *The Assassin* and *The Martyr* he demonstrates how inextricable politics is from religion; how, in fact, politics (and not just Irish politics) *is* a variety of religion.[8] McDara's inability, then, to escape from political

---

8. Indeed, *The Martyr*—a novel which deserves much more attention than I have time to give it here—is an extended, and mostly convincing, elaboration of the varieties of political

expressions of what are essentially matters of faith and doubt, is thus less surprising, and perhaps less to be condemned. As the continued presence of some elements of political discourse in *Shame the Devil* and the surprisingly optimistic portrayal of political faith and even political action in *Land* and *Insurrection* suggest, O'Flaherty himself could never quite abandon his political hopes.

But what is finally of value in his fiction is not his arguments about politics; it is his analysis of a particular form of mysticism. I have argued that oftentimes O'Flaherty employs the apparatus of pure realism only to exhaust or abandon it; it is equally possible that O'Flaherty grounds his fiction in at least the appearance of a detailed reality to provide some control over, and some way of understanding, the madness which seems the source of his characters' energy and conviction. That madness is the last and only avenue of true understanding, but it is also a path toward the inarticulable. Like many another of O'Flaherty's central figures, McDara achieves—or believes he has achieved—"an extraordinary understanding . . . of good and evil," only to fear that "no one will understand." The context of the real provides for O'Flaherty the writer of fiction a way to diminish that incomprehensibility.

In the voice of a realist observing his own native ground, O'Flaherty defends the centrality of the mad and the visionary:

> There is inherent in our Irish nature a profound respect for those obscure regions of the human soul where mystic phantoms fill the void past reason's limits, so that among us the madness of "holy" men has a somewhat sacred character, as if we understood their brains have grown sick with much labor, seeking the meaning of the all-important mystery.
>
> (*The Puritan*, ch. 3)

At the center of the best (and indeed of some of the worst) of O'Flaherty's novels is just such an approach to "the all-important mystery," some ver-

---

religion, and the ultimate vanity of all. Patrick Sheeran's treatment of the novel, and especially his reading of what he sees as its effort to break the hold of metaphor over the Irish political imagination, is very intriguing (*The Novels of Liam O'Flaherty*, pp. 249–257); and the novel as a whole is more powerful than its total involvement in the political controversies of the Civil War might otherwise suggest.

In the context of the writers considered in the present study, the book bears useful comparison to Sean O'Faolain's *Midsummer Night Madness* (as, perhaps, *The Assassin* does to *Come Back to Erin*). In addition, O'Flaherty's novel contains a bitterly hostile portrayal of a woman very like Con Markiewicz—Angela Fitzgibbon—which can bear comparison to O'Faolain's much more complex biographical view of that important political figure.

sion of the frightening course of McDara's mind. His most central and persuasive characters are intelligent, observant, and hard-eyed enough to see the vacuity of organized religion and especially of the Irish Catholic Church, which has tied its existence to the work of the avaricious bourgeoisie. They are sufficiently experienced in the varieties of "civilization" to know the spiritual deadness of the city and the utter futility of political and social action; familiar enough with the utter bleakness of nature and the peasant life to keep from treading the old Romantic path; reflective enough to know the meanness of their own motives. If they do not start from one, they must reach a dead point of utter nihilism, from which the universe is variously an abyss, a void, a chaotic darkness, a distant anthill; from which all human endeavor looks tiny, erratic, pointless. And yet from that point they derive a sense of possibility, an unflagging energy, rather than the expected lessons of despair. To pursue, by way of understanding, the path—and especially the psychological path—of such figures is the task of his two most central novels, *The Black Soul* and *Skerrett*.

WHAT we have already seen of O'Flaherty's fictional world has made clear some of the basic elements of his portrayal of the psychology of the true and necessary visionaries. Full of questions and intentions, they resist (despite the persuasions of the intellectuals around them) the appeal of detachment and dispassionate observation. They will need and will exhaust great physical strength. And although their minds are often profoundly clouded, and the circumstances and events of their lives complex or at the least very messy, the elements of their minds are in the end quite simple; they feel and act upon a fixed and rather narrow repertory of categorical impulses, many of them painful, most of them violent: fear, anger, hatred, jealousy, shame, disgust. Of that catalog, fear stands as the most predominant and inescapable; and given the hostility of man and nature, fear seems eminently justified, however misdirected it may be in particular instances.

These men act out certain powerful, and ultimately indecisive, conflicts. One is that between mind and body, of course; but that already simplifies the matter a bit too much. Just as the passions (like Ramon Mor's lust and his greed, like sexual passion generally which always must battle fear and shame) are not especially congenial one to the other, so too the mind is divided and at war with itself. Like the narrator of *Shame the Devil*, who engages in long angry colloquies with a "stranger" who is in fact himself, O'Flaherty's central characters are never far from schizophrenia. The elements of imagination, of vision, of creativity, of those acts of comprehension which breed plan and action must somehow come to grips with those elements of doubt, denial, cynicism, of systematization and formulation which breed withdrawal and impassivity. Yet the battle often seems to be terribly simple: the struggle of the instinct to survive against a will to believe, which dares to look upon the nakedness of God and thus to risk destruction.

And as if the inward battles were not enough, there will be the inevitable outward battles: with "the herd" who variously toady to and turn upon the individual characters, as herds always do (whether of peasants, beasts, hucksters, or intellectuals); with women,[9] who at once entice and terrify these men; with priests, not only because they are especially powerful in provincial Ireland, but also because they represent a betrayal into hypocrisy and "priestcraft" of the fundamental will to believe; with nature itself, not so much because, like peasants, the men of vision must wrest a living from the rocks, but because they can see the elemental character of that struggle and are compelled by their own desires to emulate it, as an ultimate test of the limits of the self and as a way of escape from the consciousness that might destroy them.

The plot of *The Black Soul* follows a common O'Flaherty formula: a young man, for various reasons disgusted with both himself and the world, goes to Inishmore (called Inverara in this case) for the general purposes of escape and recovery. The particular circumstances of Fergus O'Connor's life (ex-seminarian, ex-soldier, ex-wanderer) are recognizably borrowed from O'Flaherty's own biography, with one significant difference: O'Connor is not a returning native but a mainlander, whose misconceptions about the life on Aran draw him there (he has in him just a hint of the tired Romantic notion of the "purity" of life among the peasants) and at the same time are something to be stripped away as he moves toward a more universal—and more personal—understanding. Inverara ("Winter," ch. 1) will be the setting for an acting-out of his desire to "get rid of important things, of life." Indeed, his goal is more than anything a search for a kind of living death which the island in winter conveniently provides.

He mimics—indeed, almost parodies—Christ,[10] seeking out a wilder-

9. I leave to the psychologist the question of O'Flaherty's treatment of women in his fiction. With very few exceptions, the roster of substantial female characters is replete with nightmare figures whose sexual passions are voracious and whose minds are sinister and impenetrable—a catalog of snakes, lionesses, vampires, and demons.

10. And—more explicitly—Cain. Both the narrator of *Shame the Devil* and McDara in *The Assassin* apply to themselves a close approximation ("Henceforth I am a wanderer on the face of the earth": *The Assassin*, ch. 22; cf. *Shame the Devil*, ch. 7) of Cain's lament in Genesis 4:14: "I shall be a fugitive and a vagabond in the earth." Fergus's attainment of such a condition occurs, ironically, at the end of the purportedly fruitful season of "Summer."

ness that will mortify flesh and spirit, and that will most of all starve into submission, even to death, the activity of mind; his hope is "to live like a beast without thought." Although he claims to know better than to look for any sort of divinity—"To hell with God," he shouts while drinking in a shebeen ("Winter," ch. 1)—his particular *via negativa* increasingly becomes not an escape from everything but a search for an irreducible "something tremendous and binding, whose meaning he would be afraid to question" ("Summer," ch. 1). But even when he has apparently found it, by way of his sexual passion for Little Mary, he still has some road to travel before it is time to leave the wilderness, "purified," no longer alone or wanting to be alone, having found in the presence of death a continuing desire to live ("Autumn," ch. 2).

But O'Connor's year on Inverara will not reduce itself to a simple linear pattern; nor will his "black soul" act upon or acquiesce to any willful system of self-denial. Although in a proximate sense O'Connor has chosen his exile, in a larger sense he has not chosen the circumstances which drive him to exile, most particularly the war, which has left him with a vision of apocalypse that is altogether too real to be dismissed as mad or to be escaped by way of oblivion:

> He saw millions of dying men, worlds falling to pieces, continents being hurled into the air, while he himself wandered among the chaos, the only living atom in the wrecked universe. He ran faster, trying to escape the vision, but they pursued him, crowding on one another, cries of the wounded, shrieks of the damned, corpses piled mountain-high, races wandering across deserts, chasms opening everywhere, devils grinning, wild animals with gory jaws rushing hither and thither in dark forests, myriads of men talking in strange languages, gesti-culating, shouting furiously, the wails of women, the bodies of chil-dren transfixed on spears. Over all came the noise of the guns, millions of guns, rising and falling and intermingling. Their sound was like a millrace. It made beautiful music that enthralled him and made him want to kill . . . His body was rising into space and flying away, headed for the moon. But there was a great weight tied to the stomach that held it back. His brain began to expand. It covered the earth and then the universe, and then it burst, hurting his forehead.
>
> ("Winter," ch. 1)

The vision, a horrific enlargement of human fear, will not go away, nor can it fully be transcended.

But it will at least recur in a noticeably less all-devouring way; the outcome of Fergus's ordeal is not so much a transformation as an act of translation. The note of music, of harmony, which here seems perverse, becomes a principle of "motion without purpose" ("Summer," ch. 1), which is the one unifying principle to be found in such chaos. The terrible weight of detailed imagery of war and cannibalism will subside into a more abstract "something" (in this novel in particular, a word that O'Flaherty depends utterly upon) that is at least more quiet, a "silence . . . so great," an "emptiness so vast, that one might dream of reading the meaning of the universe" ("Summer," ch. 2). But that very abstraction will have as much of an irritating as a healing effect. To counterpoise, against a terror so specific and so visible, an indistinct "something" that is always just a bit out of reach is not a path of escape. The fear is real and continuing; the relief prospective or episodic and temporary.

Fergus's experience is in the end not so much a series of denials and rejections as a series of exhaustions of apparent alternatives. The divisions within him are echoed—and resisted—by pairings and doublings outside. Fergus encounters two women, the pallid and "highly civilized" school-mistress Kathleen and the voluptuous Little Mary, whom he sees explicitly as a figure of "nature that obeys nothing but the blind instinct to fulfill its function and shatter the tool that has achieved its purpose" ("Summer," ch. 1). And two men counsel or oppose his life on the island. Kathleen's father, Matthew O'Daly, who seems almost a Frank O'Connor character who has wandered into the wrong novel, is full of words and laments, like Fergus a man of the mind, an interpreter and explainer, but with an intellect capable really of nothing greater than genial cynicism, an utterly inadequate defense against the apocalyptic nightmares which haunt Fergus. Little Mary's husband, Red John, inarticulate, impotent, ultimately mad, is a creature who stands for the decadence of the peasantry, and thus is a proof of the falsity of Fergus's notions about the virtue of the elemental life, which seems to produce not insight or purity but corruption. But Red John's devotion to, and fear of, Little Mary exactly parallel Fergus's own increasing passion; and Fergus's sexual potency, his ability to achieve that sexual union the impossibility of which dominates Red John's life, seems only a moderate improvement. Most important of all, perhaps, Red John demonstrates the impossibility of Fergus's hope of living without thought; the mind will not be suppressed, not even Red John's, which seems initially almost not to exist at all.

Fergus has all along carried with him the apparently inescapable notion that there are functional opposites in human life, and that between those opposites choices must be made. But the novel works against such distinctions. Both the civilized Kathleen and the sensual Little Mary fall prey to passion; both the intellectual Fergus and the animal Red John are reduced to fighting like dogs over Mary. Fergus will carry with him from Inverara—it is apparently what to be purified means in this novel—a sense of the necessary dissolution of dichotomies: the world must be seen as inherently oxymoronic, encompassing both "the sadness of joy" and the "ferocity of beauty" ("Autumn," ch. 2). Even that most absolute of dichotomies, life and death, offers not so clear a distinction:

> Nothing in the universe mattered but life itself, purposeless motion. It was perfectly futile to save life . . . One might as well talk of saving death. Death was just as positive, more positive in fact, than life. . . . Why seek anything? What was the use of any effort?
>
> ("Autumn," ch. 1)

That is how close O'Flaherty takes Fergus toward intentional self-destruction; and he even constructs a situation in which self-destruction can easily result from inaction rather than action, from the cessation of effort rather than the exertion of mind or will or body: Fergus need only let go his grip on a cliff face.

In the end it is not understanding or human love or even visionary faith which keeps Fergus alive long enough to leave the island again; it is the assertion, at a moment of great physical danger, of pure and irresistible instinct.

> Going back would mean losing his self-respect. There was no reason for going ahead, but to go back would mean a return to his rudderless floating in a sea of ridiculous theories about life. Instinct urged him forward. Why? It was neither because of honor, morals, principles, religion, or sense of duty. It was merely instinct which said, "Go ahead and you will feel clean. Go back and you will have to keep arguing all your life in order to prove you are not dirty."
>
> ("Autumn," ch. 1)

For the moment, instinct is persuasive. But if the cyclical metaphor announced both in movement of seasons from winter to autumn in the titles of the four parts of the novel and in the recurrences and alternations in Fergus's moods and visions is not to be dismissed altogether, we must recognize the lie in instinct as well. The feeling of being clean will never endure; the need to prove that one is not dirty, not fallen, not accursed, will not be escaped or conquered. What will persist is motion of body and of mind, and the constancy of conflict and argument.

While *The Black Soul* accomplishes no resolution of the vision of chaos within it, it is at the very least a persuasive map of that chaos. True, it offers no particular guide to escape or consolation, but it asserts that the chaos can sustain, even foster, life. The idea of purification seems too simple, too formulaically uplifting to apply to the outcome of Fergus's time on the island; the pattern of the quest, which John Zneimer in particular makes the cornerstone of his treatment of O'Flaherty's work as a whole, is far too intentional, far too articulate, far too linear, to suit more than very approximately any of the more interesting of O'Flaherty's fictions. The result of the inner drama of mind and soul is not the achievement of a full vision of life; it is the adjustment of the whole mental apparatus of inner vision to take into account the paradoxical working of the instincts and body. The mind knows from the beginning that life is terrible; it moves, if at all, only toward a more thoroughgoing articulation of futility; and then it admits that survival, and indeed a defiance of the mind's own formulations, is the last and greatest fact of all.

SKERRETT is, in some ways, a cooler, more detached version of the spiritual crisis so powerfully laid out in *The Black Soul;* possibly because for once O'Flaherty draws his plot and the outlines of his characters not from the nightmares within himself but from the actual history of Inishmore.[11] The later novel also takes a seemingly more satisfactory route to the near-solution of what is probably an insoluble technical problem in O'Flaherty's fiction. The problem is twofold. The first element is the inevitable conflict between O'Flaherty's sense of the universal applicability of certain principles of mind and life and his insistent belief that the most important figures are those who are unlike the rest. All of his characters begin to resemble one another, all of his major characters believe themselves echoed and replicated by those around them, and yet all of those figures who most interest O'Flaherty feel themselves to be unique, as the narrative voice declares them to be.

The second part of the problem has to do with the fundamentally psychological arena within which O'Flaherty's novels take place, and which often makes many of the exteriorizations of the drama into plot, setting, and character seem false: it is as if Fergus O'Connor had imagined Little Mary so that she might tempt him, and Red John so that he might fight him to the death. But O'Flaherty does not quite believe that the mind creates its own world. The minds and states of mind that most interest him are inarticulate, so pure interior monologue is not a way out of his

11. Patrick Sheeran gives a useful summary of the actual conflict between Daniel O'Callaghan, O'Flaherty's schoolmaster, and the local priest, Father Farragher, in *The Novels of Liam O'Flaherty,* pp. 174–178.

dilemma. Given his technical resources (which are not so large) and given his reliance upon a fundamentally descriptive and realistic manner and style, he can in the end only hope that the power and richness of the figure at the center of the novel will compensate for the manifest weaknesses of plot—as they clearly do not in *The House of Gold* or *The Wilderness*, but as I think they do in *The Black Soul* and *The Assassin* and *Skerrett*.

In the case of David Skerrett, the plot is more or less a given: the course of his life on Inverara, his serial encounter with various faiths and adversaries, and his final war with the power-hungry Father Moclair are fact, or very nearly fact. The pattern of stripping away of the beliefs that stand in the way of confronting ultimate futility, and achieving ultimate defiance, does not develop as a succession of states of mind, but evolves as a long series of acts and gestures, all of them in the end defeated. Brought to the island unwillingly by circumstances that have left him little but his anger and an unprepossessing wife, Skerrett undergoes what amounts to a series of seductions—for once not by women, but by systems of understanding and notions of the efficacy of his own will and strength. He remakes his school (although not on exactly progressive lines: he wishes to exert mastery, not to impart knowledge); encounters familial love by way of the birth of a son; undertakes the work of "improving" the lot of the peasants both politically and economically; at first helps the "civilizing" priest Father Moclair and then—realizing the fundamentally avaricious sources of Moclair's supposed concern for the natives of the island—bravely rebels. Every one of these steps ends in failure.

It only remains, then, for O'Flaherty to explore motivation; or rather, to establish at the beginning certain base-points of character in Skerrett that will credibly generate the actions. O'Flaherty makes one important tactical choice: unlike Fergus O'Connor, Lawless, McDara, Ferriter, and the whole line of intellectual figures in his fiction, Skerrett's is a limited mind: "Being essentially a rather stupid man, of very slow understanding, it was vitally necessary for Skerrett to rely on somebody of greater intelligence for a plan of life" (ch. 7). But unlike Gypo Nolan or Ramon Mor or Mr. Gilhooley, Skerrett is neither foolish nor wholly brainless; he has just enough learning, just enough "civilization," and just enough understanding, however slowly it may work, to prevent his being purely a victim of predatory cunning.

Skerrett's relative lack of that powerful interpretive and symbol-making consciousness which Fergus O'Connor identifies almost as a separate self, a "black soul," makes his journey toward and beyond despair in some ways a counterpoint to Fergus's. His is a parable of the resistance which the will to survive may offer to the operations of the intellect which seeks (and necessarily exhausts) belief. Skerrett's is a parable of the indomitability of the will to believe, of the search for some understanding of the universe which will accommodate not only the usual defeat of human intentions and actions but also their recurrence. The end point is nearly the same: a vision of futility, of purposelessness within a hostile universe, but at the same time of life and movement. Lives end, but somehow life does not; dreams derive from and once again become nightmares, but the visionary element within the human organism endures.

Fergus O'Connor's black soul makes him particularly resistant to any human contact; this is why he chooses the barrenness of Inverara. Skerrett's more nearly animal nature, the limitations of mind which leave him aware of the appeal of ideas but unable to formulate them himself, works in an opposite direction, toward other human beings who can provide those ideas and toward those whom he can dominate; this is why his coming to Inverara is a painful banishment. Fergus begins from a point of terror, exposed if not caused by the horrors of the war; Skerrett begins with anger, which in turn derives from or is powerfully doubled by, his own pride. Like O'Flaherty's own life as it is characterized in *Shame the Devil,* Skerrett's life re-enacts Lucifer in hell rather than Christ in the wilderness. He comes with no purpose but soon acquires one: "And so did Skerrett set about to turn the hell from which he realized there was henceforth no escape into his chosen paradise" (ch. 4).

He begins with those limited means he already has: his physical strength and his habits as a schoolmaster. The result, initially, is surprisingly success, even happiness; and a breaking down of the isolating and all-pervasive hostility which he had brought with him. The first of his seductions— and perhaps the cruelest—is love for his son. It produces in him a peculiar and short-lived utopianism: "Life became a hymn to labor and to love of his fellows" (ch. 5). But something will haunt Skerrett, just as much as "something" drew Fergus on: an "unknown power that had [and will again and again] brought disaster on him" (ch. 8). His son dies accidentally, inexplicably. The death reduces Skerrett to the condition of an animal, a "gaping fish"; he cannot speak, cannot even mourn, and ultimately goes out to "hack at a boulder" in a futile battle with the earth itself, a "challenge of his strength to the rocky earth that had struck down his son." All "faith" having "died under the weight of his sorrow," he falls back again upon anger, directed not just at the soil but at the priest Moclair; and he is ready now to hear the persuasive "civilized" wisdom of the local doctor, Melia, who advises "the best thing is to expect nothing " (ch. 8).

The novel will, in the course of nearly twenty more chapters, repeat this cycle: from anger to the dawn of intention to the appearance of success to the crushing intervention of failure to despair to anger again. The motive force in the system is utterly instinctive; just as Ramon Mor Costello is basically a personification of Avarice, Skerrett is a figure of Anger. Anger is pointless, really—that which defeats Skerrett is never susceptible to its operations. But then there is always a target upon which to focus the anger: the school children, a boulder, Skerrett's wife, Father Moclair. Skerrett does not so much defy the futility of his life as he does deny it, displacing his energy of mind and body toward a more particular, if in the end no more defeatable, "enemy." That force of anger and rebellion is ultimately amoral, apolitical: it will use, if need be, the political terminology which speaks of "improving" the lives of men, or the moral (or perhaps only moralistic) terminology which despises drunkenness, or the more or less metaphysical terminology which speaks in terms of some absolute "truth." None of these terminologies prove adequate to account for Skerrett's energy, and all he achieves is an awareness, though not of particular failures and disappointments but of the universality of failure. His vision of "puny man," which we encountered some pages ago, does not, for all its thoroughness, break this cycle, although it drives him to nakedness and a moment of calm happiness; within a few weeks his rage reawakens, and he sets off to defy Moclair yet again. But having now grown old, the apparatus of mind and of body which he so continually re-enlists in the work of defiance finally simply collapses; he goes mad, breaks down, and within a year or so dies, having it seems learned nothing at all about restraint.

And yet he is, for O'Flaherty, an image not of futility or absurdity, but of "nobility": "The nobility of Skerrett's nature lay in his pursuit of godliness. He aimed at being a man who owns no master. And such men, though doomed to destruction by the timid herd, grow after death to the full proportion of their greatness" (ch. 27).

WE ARE back once more to the tone and even to the imagery of the closing paragraphs of *Shame the Devil;* and there is no denying that, even though Skerrett is one of the relatively few major O'Flaherty characters who is not, biographically, some version of Liam O'Flaherty, this protagonist is offered to us as, to some degree, a defense of the life and character of Liam O'Flaherty. The sheer egocentric arrogance of O'Flaherty's novels and many of his stories is unmistakable, and at times unpalatable. And indeed there is hardly a one of his longer pieces of fiction that is not likely, at some point, to prompt an attentive reader to throw it down in disgust, either at the ideas being put forward or at the clumsiness of their articulation into fiction. If the world is as dark as O'Flaherty's characters invariably decide, no matter from what point of intellect or appetite they begin, then any action—and especially the act of writing in so polemically didactic a voice as O'Flaherty customarily does—seems no better than perverse. And if the operation of the human mind is as central, as inarticulate, as wholly a matter of the operation of a fixed palette of fears and appetites, then both writing and reading seem especially pointless.

But there is at least something to admire in the singlemindedness of O'Flaherty's voice and work. That the gods are dead and the universe a vast and apparently purposeless entity are propositions he shares with many. But from those propositions he derives a near-articulation of sheer terror, not merely anxiety. In response to the death of faith (and especially to the emptiness of those faiths in political action or individual heroism which have, to some degree, supplanted older faiths encompasing the more traditional divinities), he adopts a position not of skepticism or Joycean aloofness but of anger and the continuing exertion of energy and passion. The supposed wisdom which Dr. Melia offers to Skerrett—"The best thing is to expect nothing" (*Skerrett,* ch. 7)—is repeated again and again in O'Flaherty's fiction; but it is no more than another of the creeds to be abandoned. And if his ideas seem unsparing, he at least does not try to offer them up in a genial voice (as both Frank O'Connor and Sean O'Faolain are tempted to do) or to embed them in a style whose elegance might conceal weaknesses of logic or flaws of narrative construction, as Elizabeth Bowen sometimes does.

There are times when O'Flaherty's efforts to escape the despairing implications of his own view of the world become transparently unconvincing, when he falls back (as he does in his last two novels) on some vague notion of human progress through the action of political ideas or when he invokes (as he does near the end of *The Assassin* or in the lives of the rebel Tracy in *The Martyr* or of Mary Kilmartin in *Famine*) the hope that somehow human love can conquer all. Those are the points at which he seems willing to engage in the denial not only of the fallacies which he sees all around him, but in the rejection even of his own first principles. They are, perhaps, defensible in O'Flaherty's own terms only as instances of his own effort to pursue what he knows to be unattainable. And in the end, just such pursuits are at the heart of his fiction, and of the world which he intends to portray. His fiction, as I have tried to show, is much more effective in proposing conflict than in providing resolution; it is much more convincing, too, in the projection of images than it is in the construction of narrative or the exploration of character.

The mood that recurs most often and most centrally is one of a distinctive sort of permanent but oddly lively dissatisfaction. An essential component of it is thoroughgoing defiance—Tom O'Donnell on the Galway Ferry; McDara's fisherman, spitting his contempt both at nature and at civilization; David Skerrett one last time marching into town to speak out against the serpentine works of Father Moclair. But such images have another dimension as well. As O'Flaherty puts it: "If we are climbing a cliff, we of the human species, it is surely with our intellects that we are to reach the summit. . . . We are pre-eminent in our power to imagine a state of perfection, which we call God and which we are trying to reach" (*Shame the Devil*, ch. 5). The "if" is only a passing flirtation with manners; like the Aran peasants whose life depends upon it, we too are poised on a cliff, with the forces of annihiliation never far away. And we do—perhaps perversely, given where O'Flaherty sees our imagination leading us—ceaselessly imagine, reshaping both what is and what might be. But, again like the climbing of a cliff, the action of living demands an attention to the body, to the inescapable fear which we constantly try to elude, to the desires which we can either follow (to be disappointed) or repress (to be no less disappointed, and probably mad as well). As O'Flaherty says at the end of *Shame the Devil*, it is a matter both of the flesh and of the spirit, and indeed more often than not of the terrible collision of the two.

Perhaps O'Flaherty's own image of himself as a fool is the fairest accounting for the substance, and even the importance, of his work. Only a fool would be so willing to provoke where another might persuade. Only a fool would be so given to repetition. Only a fool would be so ready to let his own ugliness of mind portray itself. Only a fool would unblushingly proclaim himself Christ and Cain and Lucifer and Jeremiah. But—and this is what makes it impossible simply to dismiss O'Flaherty's work—perhaps only a fool might be willing to follow so far his own demons, to recognize them so often in the minds of others, and, having shown the inadequacy of all human formulations, the weakness of all human intentions and imaginings, to dare to offer up something that calls itself wisdom. Like one vast, loud koan, O'Flaherty's fiction shouts out a paradoxical mixing of utter nihilism with unabashed mystical faith in man: "There is no God. And man has a divine destiny."

2

KATE O'BRIEN

To Be a Free Lance

THE BLEAK landscape upon which O'Flaherty's characters so violently, if ineffectually, loom could hardly seem further removed from the world at the heart of Kate O'Brien's fiction—Catholic (and usually Irish Catholic), "Victorian" (as she often calls it), bourgeois (another of her favorite labels). The two writers, born within a year and within sixty miles of each other are, in all apparent ways, angry opposites. Indeed O'Brien's fiction can be read, in part, as an answer to O'Flaherty's lifelong condemnation of gombeenism; O'Brien's own family history bears more than a little similarity to the life of Johnny Hynes, in particular. But terms of simple contrast do not adequately place the two writers. O'Brien is anything but a sentimental defender of the Catholic middle class; it is the character of mysticism that interests her, as witness her study of St. Teresa. And she is every bit as much concerned with the work of individuation, of self-definition, which O'Flaherty so loudly, if often despairingly, confronts.

Her fiction directly explores the complex interactions of obligation and independence, of home and escape; an exploration recognizably similar to, and yet markedly distinct from, that undertaken by her younger contemporaries, O'Connor and O'Faolain. What she calls, quoting George Santayana, the necessary, even inevitable "*locus standi* from which to view the world" in her work, and the source as well of the "innate passion by which to judge" (*My Ireland*, ch. 8)—is the prosperous Catholic middle class, especially as existed in Ireland in the period from about 1870 to 1914. It was a world of ironmongers, horse traders, vintners, and doctors, a world not far removed in time from its origins in the massive dislocation of the Irish peasantry during the Famine but far enough advanced in wealth and standards to sustain large country houses and the polite education of its children in convents or in such prestigious schools as Clongowes. In one sense, it is the world—only a little to the north and perhaps slightly more comfortably off—of O'Faolain's Corney Crone (in *Bird Alone*), O'Brien's characters dream, often, of something like Corney's radically individualistic escape; as young Fanny Morrow in *The Flower of May* (ch. 6) puts it, "I mean to have no relations whom one loves and to whom one owes the normal considerations of love, and to have instead of them a little secret nest egg—just enough to go off quietly and get some decent education and sort things out." To Fanny, this apparently modest aspiration seems, however, "impossible." Such "liberty," as another of O'Brien's young heroines, Anna Murphy in *The Land of Spices* (bk. 2, ch. 5) realizes, is "an expensive thing"—not only economically, since it requires the maintaining of a household and the costs of an education, but emotionally as well, since it involves at least the attenuation of the bonds of family affection which are of such very great importance in O'Brien's world.

Of all the difficulties which stand in the way of the desire for independence, the greatest is love—familial, sensual, religious. For the intelligent and passionate young women who are at the center of O'Brien's attention, the only immediately available paths (and neither is without its appeal) are marriage and the convent. To be, as the title character in *Mary Lavelle* wishes, "a free lance" without forgoing altogether the roles of wife, mother, sister, lover, is the complex and often unattainable goal of O'Brien's women. The battle is played out in enclosed spaces: the parlor and the dining room of bourgeois life, or the presentation parlor of a convent. And the alternative to these often airless rooms seems to be yet another enclosure; a room of one's own more like a monastic cell than a writer's workshop. Baldly put, the great conflict which generates O'Brien's fiction is that between intelligent detachment and passionate, sensual love; and thus, in broader terms, between separation and freedom of movement, on the one hand, and relationship and obligation, on the other.

But to state the matter in terms of dichotomies represents an essential aspect of the problem; for the great hope is that the embattled individual might somehow manage to encompass both worlds. Such a double, indeed multiple life may be available only to the most saintly and heroic, like Teresa of Avila, who is to O'Brien one of the very few "women of genius" (*Teresa of Avila,* ch. 1). Somehow, in ways that O'Brien's short life of the saint can really only admire, not analyze, Teresa managed to be simultaneously detached *and* impassioned:

It is one of the marks of her genius hardest to convey to those who have not read her that this woman, whose flights into the ineffable and incommunicable might even by us, earthbound, be called crazy, never lost hold of her brilliant common sense, not of her power to stand far back from herself, allowing no facile statement through the net of her self-criticism. It is this exact balance of the scrupulously honest recorder and teacher against the impassionately tortured mystic that keeps Teresa in her remarkable place in human history.

(ch. 2)[1]

It is a high and hard ideal. O'Brien's heroines, no matter how apparently scrupulous in their observance of the rites of the Catholic church, are careful to distinguish between religion—which they accept as a part of themselves—and holiness, to which they make no claim whatever. If Teresa is in her way a representation of what the individual may hope for, the rigors of her life make it clear how very difficult to attain the ideal balance is: "Whatever she won from her vision of life, and whatever she left us, she bought at a price" (ch. 3). And even she may represent a kind of failure, rather than full success; a failure that must be defined, significantly, in terms of love:

It was love, human love and her idea of it, which was the chief enemy between her and her love of God. Probably, like St. Augustine, Teresa was, at her most tempted, always more in love with love than with any fellow creature . . .

(ch. 3)

Even for Teresa, then, and certainly for one after another of O'Brien's heroines, the tension between detachment and love is terribly complicated by the tensions within love itself, and among its various forms and objects.

ALTHOUGH her themes carry over into Belgium (in *The Flower of May* and *The Land of Spices*) and Spain (in *Mary Lavelle* and *That Lady*), much

1. Whatever may be the usefulness of Saint Teresa as a measure of the achievement and as a verification of the intentions of O'Brien's characters, it is worth mentioning as well her importance as a model for the *writer*. O'Brien's brief catalog of women of genius includes Sappho and Emily Brontë (and excludes by name Jane Austen); she diplomatically insists that Teresa's genius was not as a writer, although she accounts her "a formidable writer of prose" (*Teresa of Avila*, ch. 1). But it is through Teresa's writing, and especially her letters, that O'Brien finds and understands her; and it is Teresa's ability to express her own character through the written word that O'Brien repeatedly emphasizes. O'Brien goes so far as to claim that Teresa's mysticism—"a territory that millions would choose never to glimpse, let alone examine" (ch. 3)—has a parallel in the work of the writer: "She believed, from the first thought of her life to the last, . . . in the whole cosmology of Christian doctrine. But her accurate development and expression through herself of what that belief was is analogous to an artist's self-conscious exploitation of his gift."

of O'Brien's fiction takes place in the world in and near Limerick (she renames it Mellick) and the seacoast of Galway and West Clare, where her family spent summers and where O'Brien herself, long years later, chose for a considerable time to live. Late in her life, after she had for the final time established her "home" outside of Ireland, O'Brien nevertheless dedicated her account of *My Ireland* to Limerick, "my dear native place"; and she argues that she necesssarily must begin and end there, in the Irish city to which she had been no more than a visitor for nearly fifty years.

Certainly her fiction begins there, with an extended view of Limerick in the first pages of her first novel, *Without My Cloak*. The city appears there very like a biblical Canaan, lying within the protective expanse of the Vale of Honey, "a wide plain of fertile pastures and deep woods, watered by many streams and ringed about by mountains." The onlooker (his name is Anthony Considine, a name which his grandson will bear in the novel and make into a proud one), is more Jacob than Moses, a fleeing horse thief with no tribes in tow. But he is the progenitor of the Considines; so the promise is real indeed, since that family will within seventy years be large and exceedingly rich and much admired in Mellick.[2]

This is his first view of the world which the novel will explore:

> Villages lay untidily about the plain; smoke floated from the chimneys of parked mansions and the broken thatch of cowmen's huts; green, blue, brown, in all their shades of dark and brightness, lay folded together across the stretching acres in a color-tranquillity as absolute as sleep, and which neither the breaking glint of lake and stream, nor the seasonal flame of woodtops could disquiet. Lark songs, the thin sibilance of dried leaves, and the crying of milk-heavy cows were all the sounds that came up to the man who . . . scanned the drowsed and age-saddened vista.
>
> (*Without My Cloak,* "Prologue")

The ominous sense of a nearly deathlike sleep in part establishes a historical base point; it is 1789, when the Ireland of Anglo-Irish mansions and peasant Catholic desolation, enforced by the Penal Laws, awaits (although it has no way to know it) the birth of a Catholic middle class. But that birth, or rather the bourgeois world which is so born, and which the

---

2. Here is the precise point at which O'Brien's fiction coincides with O'Flaherty's; the rise of Anthony's son "Honest John" Considine from poverty and orphanhood duplicates in its broad outline, the rise of Johnny Hynes in *Famine*. But it is in fact not a point of convergence so much as a point from which the two writers almost irrevocably *diverge*—no Considine bears more than a superficial resemblance to the horrifying Johnny Hynes or the demonic Ramon Mor Costello.

novel describes in great detail, is not so much a change as a continuation. An oppressive sleep of convention and constraint will remain, especially in the lives of women. The wealthier Considines to come will not become the allies of the cowmen and peasant farmers but something very close to their enemies, especially when the peasantry turn Fenian or Land Leaguer. The hard life that shows, if only faintly, in broken thatch and sadness will appear again, nearly a century later, when Anthony's great-grandson, Denis Considine, goes in search of his first love, who lives on a "poor farm" (bk. 3, ch. 9).

The change of which the Considine family are both agent and symptom then is not so much an alteration as an entrance fully *into* the landscape which the first Anthony sees. The Considines will have their parked mansion too, the grand but ugly new house, River Hill, which is the dominant setting of the novel. For all its success, the family never denies its dubious origins. That "their stock was on the upgrade" (bk. 1, ch. 1) is visible in the character and appearance of the younger Anthony; but as his perceptive brother Eddy observes, no matter what the material changes "the root normality and plainness of [that] stock" remains (bk. 1, ch. 6). Anthony the younger learns "the civic virtues" of respectability and responsibility, and accepts as well the apparent price in sadness (bk. 1, ch. 1). But Anthony never loses an "obstinate impetuosity"—of the sort which had, apparently, provoked his grandfather's act of theft and escape.

The pattern of recurrence with variation is played out structurally in the novel. The stages in the plot are marked by ceremonious family parties at River Hill. The whole novel has a certain near circularity, for all the distance in time it traverses. It begins, after a prologue which gives us our only first-hand look at the first Anthony, with a son's unexpected visit to his father, and ends with another son dramatically appearing in his father's house. Both scenes are set—as so much of O'Brien's fiction will be—in prosperous familial rooms; the two places are recognizably the same and yet noticeably different. Honest John Considine's dining room (bk. 1, ch. 1) is, for all the family's prosperity, rather a dark and gloomy place, an old house within the city. Honest John sits alone, his wife dead, his family dispersed (although near enough to be reassembled frequently). His son Anthony brings an invitation to dinner and news of his grand new house, of which Honest John disapproves. Each man, father and son, shows clearly his own form of obstinacy, and the exchange is in its quiet way contentious. Anthony is following, indeed enhancing the expected family course, but not quite in the way his father wishes. But underneath the contention is a bond of agreement. Honest John appreciates change (of a commercial sort) and indeed proves to have rather radical plans for the family business; and he cannot but approve, at bottom, of his son's life—respected and respectable, lovingly married, ready and able to work for the good of himself and of the Considines generally.

The novel's final scene is in one sense an enlargement of the smaller conversation with which the novel's true action begins. The setting is now River Hill, the grand country house; the occasion not a solitary dinner but a grand party in honor of Anthony's son's coming-of-age. The controversy is much clearer; Denis has apparently thrown over utterly the family's, and most significantly his father's wishes. He has refused to accept his place in the succession to the leadership of the family business and has dramatically disappeared into the wild and dark out-of-doors, a place where no Considine seems at all at home. But Denis returns—to the very house, of course, toward which his father, Anthony, had been heading four hundred pages and nearly twenty years before. Far from making one more grand gesture of rebellion, he dances with an eminently suitable (and level-headed) young woman, the daughter of another of Mellick's leading families. As he dances he returns to the paternal love that, only a few pages before, he had been convinced he had renounced: "Anthony stared at his son; his brilliant eyes blazed love on him" (bk. 3, ch. 14). There is just enough ambiguity in the final pronouns to reflect the nature of that love, which is ever-heated and mutual: of father for son and son for father.

Such love, at once natural and unique, is the novel's true subject. Even the stolid, mostly unintelligent, and ever-conventional Considines are full of "inexplicable passion" (bk. 1, ch. 3). Perhaps more surprisingly, given what we are likely to expect within a world that its creator relentlessly calls bourgeois, they are willing to act upon that passion, only to find that such bold action, however necessary or admirable, is hardly a route to sastisfaction.

But the alternative would seem to be the carefully tended life of Eddy Considine, Anthony's brother, a man of great mercantile astuteness and considerable taste and "easy-going urbanity" (bk. 1, ch. 3), who keeps his greatest passion (for his sister Caroline) under necessary rein (and indeed physically at some distance; he lives in London, not Mellick), who is always available to organize a family gathering or help weather a family crisis. Eddy at one point—and just before he advises his nephew Denis to break away from the life planned for him by the family—reflects on the particular costs of his own path:

> What a risk men took who had sons, but what a miser's store they laid up too against these winter-quiet fifties. Eddy gave himself a moment of envying Anthony, but the moment stretched against his

will and took on unsought sincerity. . . . He wrestled now against his stupid, sentimental pain. Life couldn't be everything to every man, and if Anthony had this son and the bright hopes of his manhood to look out at, well, he had known ranges of dream and passion unguessed by Anthony. He had had the life he chose, and it had been good and deep and full. He had a memory now for every hope of Anthony's. Ah, but memories, what are they?

(bk. 3, ch. 1)

Eddy's voice—both what it says, and how it says it—sounds a fundamental note throughout O'Brien's fiction: his mixture of melancholy with passion, of self-analysis (and even self-ridicule) and sympathy, and perhaps most of all the importance he gives not to the attainment of happiness, certainly not to the permanence of any mood, happy or otherwise, but to the making of choices and the acceptance of consequences. What drives most of O'Brien's young women is the desire to attain that point of choice, which is Eddy's by accident of gender and income as much as by force of character. But the life he actually leads (and we never see any of those dreams or passions close-up) seems less an ideal than a warning.

In her first novel O'Brien focuses particularly on the complex action of love within the Considine family, "a highly nervous organism" (bk. 1, ch. 3) whose unity is often, paradoxically, most visible in argument and contention. *Without My Cloak* is very nearly three novels in one; and the first is a capacious family chronicle, a sort of Irish Catholic *Buddenbrooks* or *Forsyte Saga*.[3] O'Brien is at some pains to acknowledge the "arrogance" which is both cause and result of the family's prosperity and to show in particular how unpleasant can be the effects of the Considines' sense of what it is to be "Irish, Catholic, rich, respectable" (bk. 2, ch. 6). The family has its share of fools and hypocrites. The Considines include among their number one nun, who like the O'Brien nuns recalled in *Presentation Parlour,* has renounced the world but who remains "greedy still for the prestige and solidification of her father's house" (bk. 1, ch. 3); and the priest Father Tom, "a vain, hasty, strong-principled man" (bk. 3, ch. 10) whose successful career in the church is soured by "envy," a last vestige of "long controlled, buried . . . emotional fire" in himself (bk. 3, ch. 8). The portrait of Irish bourgeois life is, in other words, anything but purely appreciative.

3. The resemblance of O'Brien's book to Galsworthy's longer saga in particular is sometimes painfully visible—in O'Brien's fondness for large and detailed accounts of family gatherings, like the grand assembly of the Forsytes; or the theme of the thwarting of the passionate woman's attempted flight to freedom, in which Caroline (Considine) Lanigan resembles an older and rather more neurotic Irene Forsyte.

But neither is it satiric; the complex affection the family exhibits—"our terrible family affection" Eddy calls it; "our cowardly inability to do without each other . . . our instinct to be large and populous and united" (bk. 2, ch. 1)—is paralleled by the admiration the narrator has for the Considines, and especially for Anthony, who, as Eddy says, "stands for all the best things that the Considines are" (bk. 3, ch. 1). The energy, the passion, the willingness to act decisively and to take risks, the instinct for the present and the future which Anthony possesses in great measure are what allows the family to prosper so mightily, and without any help from the outside. The story of that success, the substance of the first half of the book, has its moment of full glory in the summer of 1870 when Anthony is elected mayor of Mellick.

From that point the novel begins to look less like *The Forsyte Saga* and more like a *Portrait of the Provincial Artist;* it becomes less the story of the Considine organism and more the story of Denis. His life has a familiar shape, moving from the "gentle brightness" of early childhood to adolescent worship of two heroes, his cousin Tony and his Latin teacher, the troubled young Jesuit Martin Devoy, then to passionate first love for an orphaned peasant girl, Christina, and finally to a crisis on his twenty-first birthday. What faces Denis is, inevitably, a question of choice, of whether and how to take control of his own destiny. Devoy, whose view of Denis is emotional and acute, albeit heavily colored by his own struggle with expectation and vocation, sets the issue in these terms:

Denis won't want the smug and ready-made world of the Considines, all mapped and tidy, with every opinion hall-marked and every action clear-cut in advance! Ah, Denis will want to find life for himself, out of the workings of his own mind, out of his own personality—in reaction from all shades of life. They can't trap Denis, except by loving him too much, by loving him too much . . .

(bk. 2, ch. 11; the repetition is Devoy's)

Denis's sense of himself centers, from a rather early age, on his artistic bent, which begins to achieve definition under the tutelage and example of Devoy, who reveals to the boy "worlds created out of enlightened personality, worlds far flung from this tangible one which, with all respect to God, [Denis] was beginning to think had blundered up in a rather inexcusable mess to its present stage" (bk. 2, ch. 3). But the art which seizes Denis's imagination—the making of gardens—is an especially social and public art, and one which Denis, in common with almost all of the characters in O'Brien's fictive world, defines in recognizably religious, even catechetical terms: "Everywhere and in all times a garden was the outcome of a particular culture, an outward sign maybe of an inward grace, a shot at giving permanence to some essential quality of a mind, and through it, of a race and period" (bk. 2, ch. 1).[4]

Denis's passion for gardens, which portray "man's antagonism to Nature and his subjection to her" (bk. 2, ch. 1) enlarges the hint contained in Shakespeare's Sonnet 34, which gives the book its title. The poem proposes an image of wandering outdoors and uncovered—an apt description of the decisive moment in the first Anthony's life, but hardly suitable to most of the other Considines, who live happily well-dressed and enclosed lives. And gardening as Denis undertakes it stands not as an openness to nature but a playing out upon the landscape of the order and limitation more commonly found in house-building of his father's sort. In Shakespeare's poem, however, the flight "without my cloak" is not a grand assertion of the personal and individual but the sad result of the trials and deceits of love: "Why didst thou promise such a beauteous day?" Nor is the possibility of return a consolation; the pain endures—"Though thou repent, yet I have still the loss." The poem suggests that escape is less an action than a reaction, less a freeing consolation than a necessary physical enactment of spiritual pain, colored—indeed dominated—not by a sense of future purpose but by the memory of loss; and that is indeed the shape which "escape" will take throughout O'Brien's novels.

Denis's formulation of the art of gardening as both the expression of "some essential quality of a mind" and as "the outcome of a particular culture" can serve as the articulation of another fundamental continuity in O'Brien's fiction; one which both defines her view of the character of human life and explains (if not defends) some of the weak moments in her novels. After *Without My Cloak* she would never again undertake a novel with so long a chronological, or so broad a genealogical, scope, but she never lost her expository tendencies. That in part derives from the fact

4. The faint echo of Stephen Dedalus here raises a problematic aspect of O'Brien's choice of gardening as Denis's art, however original and unexpected it may be. It is simply hard to take "I want to make gardens" as seriously as Stephen's literary/cultural aspiration at the close of *Portrait*. But the distance may well be quite intentional, and represents, I think, O'Brien's more restrained view of the proper goal and nature of art, even of literature. Certainly her later characters who include artistic expression among their hopes do so far more tentatively than Dedalus. Some—notably the young actress Angele Maury in *The Last of Summer* and the two singers, Rose Lennane and Clare Halvey in *As Music and Splendour*—find their place in an art of performance, of expression rather than creation. The point is emphasized by the repeated remark that the two sopranos are *merely* singers, not musicians. But even literature has, in O'Brien's lexicon, a somewhat restricted nature. In *The Flower of May* (ch. 12), for instance, Fanny Morrow's wise aunt Eleanor defines the young girl's "gift" almost apologetically: "I suppose her gift can only be literary? I mean, were she mathematically or scientifically or musically gifted—in any considerable way—we'd have noticed by now."

that so many of her novels can fairly be called historical[5]—looking back, for instance, to Victorian Ireland or to the Italy of the 1880s or to late sixteenth-century Spain. Our knowledge of such moments is so limited as to demand some learned information; and perhaps too often O'Brien's novels pause while we are so informed.

But this is not just a fault of style or the lingering aftereffects of O'Brien's education and self-education. Such facts, down to the smallest particular, are part of the crucial historical and cultural context in which her characters live. In a sense the context *is* the character, to a degree which fascinates O'Brien and (often) puzzles the characters themselves. Faced with a dramatic point of decision—whether, for the first and only time in her life, to act upon her own romantic and sexual impetuosity—Caroline Considine Lanigan finds herself poised exactly where O'Brien's protagonists again and again live and struggle, between a cultural and a personal definition of self: "She was bound to be either . . . creature of her Church and of her filial and maternal and herd instincts, a piece of her own setting indeed—or else a woman transfigured out of all that setting by passionate love. She could not judge alone between those two conditions" (bk. 2, ch. 9). Caroline steps back—significantly, in part because of the haunting presence of her dead father—where other O'Brien women go forward, into transfiguration. But those braver spirits discover that even such trans-

---

5. She would no doubt object to the term; her most clearly "historical" novel, *That Lady,* carries a prefatory note that "what follows is not a historical novel. It is an invention[.]" But that has less to do with O'Brien's willingness, there and elsewhere, to set her novels in carefully defined and described moments in the past than with her refusal to claim, in the fullest sense, anything like historical accuracy. So her book on Teresa claims only to be "notes for a portrait" and ends with an apology—"I know that I have failed to do the simple-seeming thing I attempted." Her one venture into personal history, *Presentation Parlour,* likewise demurs at the start ("My recollections are not pure") and apologizes at the end: "They [the aunts who are her subject] elude me yet."

The "historicity" of O'Brien's novels is further emphasized by the way she chooses times just before some radically decisive moment: the final victory of "centralization" and autocracy in Spain in the 1590s, for instance, or the death of Verdi and the transformation of Italian *teatro lirico.* Her apparent intention to record and to preserve a particular moment in the past is visible even in novels set nearer their time of composition, but just at the far side of a similarly revolutionary moment. Thus Mary Helen Archer's return to Belgium at the end of *Land of Spices* is undertaken with full awareness of the imminence of World War I. Similarly, *The Last of Summer,* set in 1939, is dominated by the coming of World War II, which looks to the characters in the novel ominously like the end of the world (the outcome of the war was still very much in doubt when the novel appeared in 1943). And *Mary Lavelle* occurs in the Spain of 1922 but forecasts, very early, that "nine years later a revolution would practically wipe out [Mary's] obsolete and ill-defined profession [of "Miss"]" (*Mary Lavelle,* "Prologue"). As *Farewell Spain* makes clear, that revolution would itself be wiped out by Franco only a few years later.

figuration does not permanently take them "out of" their setting. And no matter how far they go, geographically, they bear always with them, in memory, that "home" which is the seat of the conventions and habits and expectations of their own time and place.

In dealing with the particular impositions of setting and self the element of *self-control*, which can keep both the outer conventions and the uncontrollable inner impulses at a certain distance, is, as we will see, of special value, although it risks rupturing through analysis the lifegiving force that both self and context provide to the personality. Those few who actually triumph manage, by accident or by their own effort, to find a meeting ground of self and setting, where the two can work in unison. For Denis, the most inescapable aspects of the outer world are the figure of his father and the pervasive force of his father's love, ever kind in its intentions (however cruel in its results), surprisingly supple and accommodating (and yet at bottom utterly single-minded and rigorous), enlivening and yet imprisoning.

That love is the substance of the third novel contained within *Without My Cloak* and the element which joins the family saga of the Considines and the intellectual biography of Denis, the artist *in potentio:* a love story of parent and child of a particular force and shape that often turns up as a central element in Kate O'Brien's later novels. This love compels constant analysis but in the end defies understanding; it has the substance and inevitability of a force of nature. Not surprisingly Anthony, by no means a self-analytic man, cannot quite understand what it is that so passionately links himself to his son: "He loved [Denis] inordinately. He loved him with a grave and apprehensive love for which there was no clear reason and which seemed out of place in his forthright character" (bk. 1, ch. 2). The force of such love is "inordinate" even in its resistance to the usual language of relationships; in Anthony, it is "a love which, if it was paternal, would bear no resemblance to the orthodox fatherly feeling inspired by his other children" (bk. 1, ch. 2). Yet it does not overwhelm those other, more nameable relationships; Anthony loves his other children, and loves his wife even more—deeply and with an unwavering force of sexual desire and response.

Viewed from the outside the love of Anthony for Denis is very nearly maddening and even cruel. But the external "objective" view sheds little insight, and even less guidance. An objective view of so thoroughly subjective a force is in fact a contradiction in terms. Understanding might seem to be approachable by way of psychoanalysis. But O'Brien herself has little time for, and less faith in, such an approach; and most of her characters come of age in a world that is chronologically pre-Freudian. Denis's own first appreciation of the world and his father's place in it rests on the language of home and carries an echo of his great-grandfather's first vision of Mellick:

> The house at the center of this world was warm with friendly life, had fires in it and stores of apples, and a long slippery bannister; there were pleasant, gossipy servants there and brothers and sisters with whom to swap things and run races; there was a misty, white-skinned mother, who gathered flowers in the garden and rode in a carriage behind grey horses; there was a bright-faced father who came and went and whom many of the household seemed to fear; a vast man certainly, firm of voice and foot, but in whose shining eyes, that fascinated him, Denis never saw anything but the assurance of happiness, happiness that would last and was everywhere.
>
> (bk. 2, ch. 1)

The ensuing decade or so of Denis's life inevitably complicates that view; yet those years do not force him to revise his first impression but to see fully its accuracy. His father *is* vast and frightening, most powerful when most loving. His father does wish only his happiness, and is willing to risk the wrath and antagonism even of his family to ensure it. His father's house remains busy, and (with Denis's help) grows in a literal way even brighter and more lovely. And when Denis returns—having taken the one step that, he is certain, will "free" him from his father—he enters a River Hill crowded with relatives, full of music and flowers, where he will once more find a place under those very eyes which, at the novel's end, "blazed love upon him" again; or, more accurately, *still*. What that final moment leaves moot is whether Denis, dancing in the arms of the girl who will surely in due time be his wife, under the proud eyes of his father and his prospective father-in-law, has returned to Eden or to the most delightful and inescapable of prisons.

It is impossible to miss the Biblical shape of Denis's vision of home— the rich pastoral landscape, the father whose nature consists of light and power and who offers the promise of eternal happiness, the mansion which has, both literally and figuratively, so many rooms, so many places of human contact and of rest. We recall O'Brien's hypothesis that St. Teresa saw an inevitable conflict between human love and the love of God; and certainly other of her characters (not Denis, who seems on balance to have little religious passion) will feel that conflict. But the incomprehensible, inescapable, provocative and yet sustaining love which her characters find at the heart of their often somewhat heterodox, but nonetheless persistent, religious faith is exactly similar to the love which they feel for others, especially parents and lovers. Good Catholics all, raised in the catechism and schooled usually by clergy, they may simply be confusing the human and the divine, or taking over the given language of religious devotion as a way of articulating to themselves the shape and character of passion directed at human objects. Like the God these characters seek or recall, but from whom they fear they have fallen away by "sin," the people they love are often absent—dead, or dying, or far distant, or cut off from them by marriage or duty. But human distance does not dispel human love, any more than the incomprehensible distance O'Brien's people feel from the God to whom they were taught as children to pray diminishes their sense of the continuing necessity of their own kind of religious observance, whether they be dutiful nuns or "fallen" women.

I HAVE not spent this long with O'Brien's first novel because it is her best—it assuredly is not. Aside from its interest as a historical and sociological record of a particular place and time and class in Irish society, it is of importance in the way it lays out at unusual length the particular dilemmas which are at the heart of the rest of her fiction: the demands of "personality" in a world of relationships; the approaches to (and limits of) a self-control that will still allow the radical escape from the self through love; the effort to find any point of balance among the various conventions which surround the individual, and especially between the "terrible" affections arising from family and religious faith and the shock of sudden romantic involvement; the search for a place that is home but not prison.

In many ways O'Brien seems to have used her first novel as a way of learning what not to do again. Denis's wandering without his cloak represents almost the last moments in which the exterior world is of any significance as a field of action. In their reliance on one or two well-defined and carefully furnished interior settings, in their acceptance of a chronological span much smaller than the nearly twenty years encompassed by the main action of *Without My Cloak,* in their continuing use of family dinners, weddings, funerals as major elements of the plot, O'Brien's later novels often resemble well-made plays. The apparent orderliness of the novel itself is not solely, perhaps not even primarily, a structural decision on O'Brien's part; the lives she studies *are* orderly, or at least hope to be so. To be a young woman in Victorian Ireland is to be a creature of drawing-rooms and parlors; and the only customary escape is into another set of rooms, either a husband's house or a convent, which in an eerie way echoes the domestic world. For convents of the sort which O'Brien describes (and where two of her aunts lived their lives) have many parlors and are—like many a household—dominated by mothers and sisters, with fathers who are officially powerful but actually rather an intrusion.

In the best of her fiction the lives of women attract O'Brien's most imaginative attention. They unfold, in Ireland or in Spain or Belgium or Italy, within a fully developed, powerful, and resilient set of conventions. The very shapeliness of so many of O'Brien's novels, their refusal to go, even by way of imagination, far outside of the parlor, suggests that she too was a piece of her setting, an instinctive conservative. It must be admitted that in her books on Spain and Ireland she has at times rather a Tory voice, which decries what the contemporary world thinks of as civilization as "humanity's abominable monster" based upon "the unavoidable mass supply-and-demand thing" (*My Ireland,* ch. 2); which speaks of science as "the universal dictator" and decries "the forward marchers" (*Farewell Spain,* "Adios, Turismo").[6] As if still in the grip of a lingering Victorianism, O'Brien retains, early and late, a sympathetic interest in those for whom renunciation and obedience, not passion and self-expression, are the great and necessary ends.

Insofar as her novels propose any sort of program, it is probably that laid out by Eleanor Delahunt to her niece Fanny's friend and schoolmate Lucille in *The Flower of May*:

> For me the point is that when the young have ranging spirits, their spirits should range . . . I'm not supposing either you or Fanny is a genius of any kind. Only I think it would be a good thing if two like you could try out your brains. For your own sakes—and because of the pleasure it might give us to see you at it.

(ch. 12)

6. The tone here is less reactionary than it might seem; the "forward marchers" are not liberals or suffragettes but Fascists. The one avowedly New Woman in O'Brien's fiction— the suffragette Miss Robertson in Book Two of *The Land of Spices*—attracts the admiration both of Anna Murphy and of her godlike brother Charlie.

O'Brien's distaste for politics, like many of her "detachments," was not, apparently, complete. One of her first jobs was as secretary to a group put together by the newly established Irish government to obtain financial support from the United States. However little appeal she may have felt in Irish nationalist doctrine, in *Presentation Parlour* she finds it easy to ridicule in passing one uncle's loyalty to the British imperialist regime in Dublin Castle, and easy to admire one aunt's loathing for the Tans. With regard to political developments in Spain, *Farewell Spain*'s final chapter, "Arriba España," has hard words indeed for Franco; and despite her unwillingness to accept the name or the platform of the Communists, O'Brien manages to see a link between Communism and "the old, old generosity and decency of a few of the world's saints"—most notably her great heroine, Teresa of Avila. In *Mary Lavelle* O'Brien has Juanito de Areavaga lay out a political program, at somewhat greater length, it must be said, than can be justified purely on the grounds of narrative necessity. There, Communism takes its place as a sort of immediately necessary evil, but one which will need to wither away quickly if the real work of change is to occur.

Earlier Eleanor has rather surprisingly defended her just dead sister Julia, who had spent her adult life tending to the wants and eccentricities of her rather silly husband, and whose marriage left Eleanor with the task of caring for their father: "To look as she does tonight you have to have lived, I think, by the highest claims of whatever your nature happens to be. In any case you have to have lived by some discipline which can be saluted" (ch. II). The advice is, at bottom, paradoxical—for surely the "highest claims of your nature" are, more likely than not, at odds with "discipline," especially the demands of family or the rule of an enclosed order.

O'Brien's novels demonstrate how the apparently simple question asked of Denis—"What are you going to do with your life?"—turns much more complex when it is asked of young *women* of good family and conventional upbringing. Indeed, simply to *ask* the question is shocking; even more so to do as Eleanor does, to ask and then to listen for an answer. O'Brien's young heroines attempt to find a point of observation, a separate place from which to reflect both upon their own natures and upon the disciplines and emotions all around them: to think, to choose, and to find a way to act upon that choice. Individualists but not rebels, they are nonetheless women of intelligence and passion.

O'BRIEN's second and third novels can be taken almost as two variations on one theme. One—*The Ante-Room*—stays indoors, almost claustrally so, and takes up with even greater intensity Denis Considine's dilemma: his duty to, and of course his affection for, his family, clashing with his sense of himself, his desire to be free, to "range" as Eleanor Delahunt puts it, which becomes nearly overpowering when he falls in love. The other, *Mary Lavelle,* moves abroad (to Spain) and outdoors (if only to gardens, patisseries, and city plazas). It too is a study of obligations which come up against the unavoidable force of passionate and sexual love. Agnes Mulqueen (whose mother is in fact a Considine)[7] is the dutiful second

---

7. Agnes is Denis Considine's cousin; her mother, Teresa, is one of Anthony Considine's sisters, whose devotion to her charming but mysteriously ailing son Reggie is noticed several times in the earlier novel. Agnes appears there too, but only in passing. Of all the various Considines outside the immediate circle of the Mulqueen household, only Father Tom appears in *The Ante-Room*—recognizably the same (Agnes sees him as "unimaginative . . . prudish") and yet, as the clergyman called to his dying sister's bedside, considerably less meddlesome and sinister than in *Without My Cloak.* Although *The Ante-Room* is set in 1880, three years after the dance with which *Without My Cloak* concludes, we are given no news whatever of Denis—no clue, in other words, as to whether his return to River Hill is a triumph or a defeat.

daughter (or, as a rather hostile observer puts it, the "dutiful machine" [*The Ante-Room*, bk. 1, ch. 2]) who has stayed at home to bring order and good sense to a household where her mother is dying, her father is (and always has been) ineffectual and unintelligent, and her brother Reggie is a pathetic invalid. Mary Lavelle, another Mellick girl, has managed to find a way out of her familial household only to stumble into another. The journey is just far enough to let her see what "detachment" might well involve, for a young woman with neither great education nor particular talent. Both women mask a troubled and passionate nature with an appearance of self-control and good manners; both find it hard to sustain that mask in the face of an insistent and yet impossible love—for Agnes, her love for her sister's husband; for Mary, her love for the adored (and married) son of the Spanish family by whom she is employed.

Both, then, are novels of awakening, and in each case the power of sexual attraction is a primary force. But in neither is sexual awakening *per se* the point. Both Agnes Mulqueen and Mary Lavelle seek some independent sense of self, which must necessarily incorporate the "reality" of human passion but also resist the tendency of such passion utterly to submerge and dissolve the self. That search has, in each case, the shape of melodrama; particularly that variety of melodrama which juxtaposes restrictive circumstances against forbidden love. But neither novel accepts the formulaic endings of melodrama. For Agnes and Mary, marriage or dramatic escape with the beloved or tragic death are not in the cards; each instead must continue with what O'Brien calls "the errand of keeping alive" (*Mary Lavelle*, "Prologue").

Like many another of O'Brien's novels, *The Ante-Room* is haunted by the death of a parent.[8] The few autumn days in 1880 during which the

---

8. Given the centrality and power of the relationship between parent and child in *Without My Cloak*, O'Brien's reliance on this archetypal moment of the final interruption of that relation is understandable; but it must as well draw strength from the lingering shadow of the early death of O'Brien's own mother. In any case, it occurs in almost every one of her novels. The deaths both of Honest John Considine (Denis's grandfather) and Molly Considine (Denis's mother) are major turning points in *Without My Cloak*. The death of Julia Morrow, the protagonist's mother, dominates the second half of *The Flower of May*. Even though Mary Helen Archer has long been estranged from her father, his death is a central moment in *The Land of Spices;* so too is the death of the redoubtable Mother General of the Company of the Sacred Family, who has been in all significant ways except the biological, Mary Helen's parent. Angele Maury's mother's death is somewhat more in the past, in *The Last of Summer;* but it occupies her mind still, as does Angele's desire to be the actress her mother never quite managed to be. The death of Pablo de Areavaga in *Mary Lavelle* not only delays and complicates Mary's departure from Spain, but colors as well her "sinful" love for Juanito with an additional note of guilt, their one night of sexual fulfillment having occurred on the night Pablo dies. The death of her beloved grandmother is, for Clare Halvey,

novel occurs (including, as the novel reminds us, the feasts of All Saints and All Souls) are the last days in the life of Teresa Mulqueen, and are full of the duties and rituals necessarily accompanying that death. Teresa, like a near-parody of her brother Anthony Considine, is obsessed by her son—not a passionate and at least potentially creative young man like Denis, but a diseased and very nearly helpless individual. One plot of the novel—the major one, in Teresa's eyes—addresses the problem of what is to happen to Reggie: who will make a home for him, tend to him, humor his sentimental egotism, admire his inept piano playing. If it is a new version of the story of Anthony and Denis, it is a dark and even pathetic one. To use Agnes's term, it is "hideous" and founded on "the vast exactions of the sentimental" (bk. 1, ch. 2).

But Teresa's focus on security, love, and home is only a counterpoint to the main concern of the novel, a love-quadrangle involving Agnes, her beautiful sister Marie Rose, Marie Rose's "demigod" husband Vincent deCourcy Regan, and the family doctor, William Curran. Agnes loves Vincent (indeed, as *Without My Cloak* [bk. 3, ch. 13] tells us, she always has); but she also loves Marie Rose. Marie Rose's marriage has decayed to the point that "hatred stood, almost declaring itself, between her and her husband" (*The Ante-Room,* bk. 1, ch. 3); and so she depends all the more on what remains of the childhood devotion of Agnes to her. But even if Marie Rose does not clearly love her husband any longer, she still "wants" him (bk. 3, ch. 1). Curran, "a Victorian bourgeois, rationalist in the idiom of his mind, Catholic in tradition and practice, a man eager to harness feeling into usefulness" (bk. 1, ch. 5), nonetheless suffers an "un-conditional love for [Agnes] which was to be the state of all of his life" (bk. 2, ch. 2). Teresa's last illness places all four within the same house; indeed, within the same room much of the time.

The almost operatic symmetry of the four characters is undercut by the impossibility of any satisfactory division by two; the relations between individual characters simply will not, cannot co-exist with the field of relationships among all four, and between these four and the outsiders, like Teresa, Reggie, and Nurse Cunningham, Teresa's attendant and Reggie's ironic suitor. The novel is much concerned with order and with formula. The literary formulae of "novels" seem, to Agnes, to offer an

---

the final break with her physical home in *As Music and Splendour.* And in many ways the death of Ana de Mendoza's husband, Ruy Gomez, in *That Lady* has the power and contour of a parent's death; for she is much younger than he, and he exerts a kind of formative pressure upon her that seems parental rather than husbandly. But as Mary Lavelle comes to realize, the roles of father and husband are often chillingly similar; a realization shared in a way by Pablo, who imagines his son acting in his stead in loving Mary.

order and unity in the lives of characters which she cannot find in her own. "Polite literature" provides the model upon which Marie Rose can base her pretense, her role as "the classic feminine," beautiful and married (bk. 1, ch. 7). The shabbiest drama, the "barnstormer's play" which arrays its characters so as to "exemplify to an excited gallery that love is the lord of all" seems to Vincent to be precisely what he and Agnes are engaged in (bk. 3, ch. 1). The Church stands as "an aged principle out of which a million million patterns and formulas could rise, but which spans and covers all" (bk. 2, ch. 1); but perhaps because it can encompass such variety, it offers no specific and lasting relief to the troubled Agnes. Most significant of all, the habits and patterns and pretenses of customary family life are able, if only for a time, to deny that a son is syphilitic, that a daughter's marriage is crippled, that a mother is dying. For all their apparent falsity, formulas offer at the very least a kind of respite from the usual stresses of living; especially for Agnes, who dreams of being "part of a formula. What was required of her was to be accurate in moving with the formula. Accurate, regular, and cold" (bk. 1, ch. 6).

Later in the novel, Vincent (who has seen his "barnstormer's play" collapse) charges Agnes with a "mania for tidiness"; to which Agnes replies, "I'm sick of the mess of things" (bk. 3, ch. 1). "The mess of things"—not just the disarray of the Mulqueen household—is one of the larger realities to which Agnes finds herself returning, especially by way of self-examination (bk. 2, ch. 3). Curran sees it as well: "Nothing was too silly or wasteful to be a fact. Nothing was too destructive to be true" (bk. 1, ch. 10). Here Curran is very close indeed to O'Brien's climactic insight at the Altamira caves:

> The sentimentalist—I speak for myself—always comes out of that cave in a condition of broody inertness, a condition bordering on pain of some kind. Feeling unsociable—like a homeless, evicted troglodyte. Pondering the accidents and blisses of initiative and genius, and the arrogant irresponsibility of the processes of life and time.
>
> (*Farewell Spain*, "Romanesque and Neolithic")

Amid the cosmic mess, home is one possible safety, as it is for Marie Rose, "the only place . . . where she was taken, with the ease of love, for granted. This house, with Agnes now the kindler of its warmth for her, was her one safety—and it was dying" (bk. 1, ch. 9).

A safe and familiar house with a loving and comforting (and more often than not female) figure within it—the great good place—is, if not always dying, at least always under siege. The comfort is of course not just spiritual, as the hardheaded Nurse Cunningham can see; she knows from experience "the poverty of life outside these walls, . . . the bleak years and her defenselessness" (bk. 2, ch. 5) that make even marriage to Reggie look like a haven. In one sense, then, the issue is one of the messiness of human passion against the fragile but necessary order of conventional life; and indeed Agnes's decision not to act upon her love for Vincent is founded upon her wish to protect the safe home her sister seeks and her refusal to betray the certainty which her sister finds in her. Whether it be a bourgeois mansion, a Castilian country house, or a convent, "home" takes much making and protecting; and much energy and vigilance and discipline as well. That those who seek home (and especially, it must be said, the men) are often egotistical, rather shallow, even a little silly, is really beside the point; for in all those ways they demonstrate not their triviality but their humanness.

The force that both binds and threatens home is love; and the real battle is not between love and duty but between love and love, as even Vincent can see. "You love [Marie Rose] more than me," he says to Agnes (bk. 3, ch. 1). Agnes will not engage in comparisons and in the quantification of love they imply: "I never thought about how much I love her." But it is certainly the case that her love for Vincent is much messier, much more threatening, not only to home but to Agnes herself, than is love for Marie Rose. The lovers' last kiss (bk. 3, ch. 1) is anything but healing. To Agnes it demonstrates "her sentimental mistake" and "her own innocence"; it offers neither "pacification" nor "freedom," but instead "anguish, with the worst of it that its moment must pass, that there must be an end of the pang of insatiability." And for Vincent it brings "a poisonous vitality" which at the same moment proves both the "rightness" of his feeling and the impossiblity of its enactment.

Agnes and Vincent are, in a sense, opposing principles. He embodies utterly self-involved human passion which—oddly enough, given its narcissistic impenetrability—finds its expression in sexual attraction to another. He believes that there might be a love which is "central and explanatory" (bk. 1, ch. 7). She has lived in a state of "neutrality" (bk. 1, ch. 1), which makes her look "coldblooded" (bk. 1, ch. 3). But at least she tries to understand the multiplicity of her own nature, and if she cannot live a life which causes no harm or pain, she learns to measure with some accuracy what damage (and to whom) her actions will cause. For Vincent, such detachment and order are fatal symptoms of the abandonment of life. Even for Agnes utter detachment is impossible: "It was all very well to fold hands before the spectacle of character working out its fate—but was there no help anywhere?" (bk. 1, ch. 10).

But the fact of the matter is that Agnes is immeasurably more complex and various than Vincent. In his selfishness and his devotion to his mother he is more than a little like the pathetic Reggie: an outsized child, able "to keep a film of incredulity between himself and the final absurdities of his romanticism" (bk. 3, ch. 1) and very much "in the habit of having what he wanted" (bk. 3, ch. 1). Agnes does have some of that romantic childishness, which underlies both her devotion to her sister and her refusal, even in the face of the evidence of his behavior and appearance, to abandon altogether her impression that Vincent is a "demigod" (bk. 1, ch. 3). Her "neutrality" then is an effort to encompass even the regressive and demanding side of herself; and at the same time to acknowledge that convention, tradition, and the habits of affection are not external forces but "at least half of herself" (bk. 1, ch. 6). Her renunciation of Vincent derives from an awareness that the "ghost" of her sister represents an element of her own nature, "this withering blast of fact, this discovery of the residuum of herself" (bk. 3, ch. 1).

Her "detachment"—tested against the death of her mother and the persistence of her love for Vincent—must at the very least take on a new depth and complexity, as she realizes while she comforts her bereaved father:

> Then in that half-hour, which stretched to be an hour, of sitting still and talking gently, of patting her father's hand and making indeterminate sympathetic signs, of being filial with every jaded nerve, she saw life telescoping back from her into a new perspective of remoteness. So that what she was experiencing now, of compassion and helplessness, seemed remembered rather than felt, and what she remembered of last night, the long unhappy torturing dialogue and the kiss that ended it—was not a memory but the narrative of some dream.
>
> (bk. 3, ch. 2)

Such remoteness distances but does not defeat emotion and passion, and has the capacity to bring comfort to others if not to oneself, offering only the prospect of being "middlingly content." But even that contentment lasts only briefly; the memory and dream which had seemed to offer respite become in themselves painful: "Oh, idiotic unrealities, which cannot be trusted to keep their character, but from hour to hour assume and abdicate a senseless power!" Against the background of that pain, even the saddest of family rituals has its healing force; and so Agnes turns for the time being from her anguished remoteness to "family reality."

She has made a choice, has tried however approximately to know her own nature and to act upon its complex, even contradictory claims; what is not clear is how she will now live. Indeed, she is tempted to think that she will *not* live; our last glimpse of her finds her crying out (but only inwardly: there is no one in the room to listen): "They are all alive, even Mother [who in fact has just died]. But I'm dying. Vincent, if I could only die—oh, Vincent, darling—" (bk. 3, ch. 1). The unsteady balance of detachment and passion can as yet take her no further. Vincent—whose knowledge of the ways of the mind and spirit is really no more trustworthy than Anthony Considine's—insists to Marie Rose that "There'll be great sadness for a while and then it will be over . . . Anything that ends misery is bearable for a while" (bk. 3, ch. 2). But the life of emotions, continued beyond experience through memory, has in the novel seemed more persistent than that; and certainly there is no evidence that either sadness or misery are soon to be ended for Agnes, for whom the final price of her insistent sense of responsibility and renunciation may well be spiritual death.

Agnes never leaves home, never follows passion into disorienting foreignness; her way is that of detachment and renunciation, although in her own way she resists the imposed choice between wife and nun, which at its best involves a choice between human love and divine, and between the acceptance of passionate relationships[9] and the saintly solitude of the monastic cell. Agnes is neither a romantic and sexual egotist, like Vincent, nor a saint; and she at least is wise enough to realize that. The case of Mary Lavelle is to some degree the opposite of that of Agnes—an escape from home, both literally and figuratively, an acceptance of passion, a continuing intention to be not the comforter but the "free lance." But Mary too faces the twin prisons of the parlour and the nun's cell, and the results of her particular choices are no more certain that those of Agnes or of Denis Considine. If her story is, like Agnes's, a vision of the actual through the melodramatic (or a reformulation of the melodramatic by way of the actual), it too refuses to conclude with the finality that is one of melodrama's greatest appeals. Both Mary (with brave intentions but few concrete prospects) and Agnes (with apparent desperation mixed with resignation) are left alone and not at the end but at the beginning of a life story.

Mary bears some resemblance to Agnes: a younger child, intelligent but

---

9. It is important to note that O'Brien is not convinced that sexual passion falls necessarily somewhere between home and the convent; the marriages she describes, however "Victorian," are not inevitably sexless. Indeed, Anthony Considine's marriage to Molly is if anything too full of sexual desire and response; given the conventions of the age and the facts of medical practice, this means frequent childbirth and ultimately Molly's death. Marie Rose's marriage to Vincent retains its sexual passion long after it decays into "hatred"—indeed, Vincent's rebuff to her sexual overtures is a great shock (*The Ante-Room*, bk. 1, ch. 11).

mostly self-educated, a mixture of individual personality and the routines and conventions of her place and time. She is—and remains—a "well-trained Irish Catholic . . . somewhat Jansenistically instructed" whose knowledge of human nature, human passion, and sin is both definite and, lacking experience, necessarily abstract (*Mary Lavelle,* "Candles at Allera"). Her life seems settled; engaged to a respectable young man, she defends even her surprising decision to take up a job in Spain as being necessary to teach her to be "a good wife" ("Three Letters"). Her more individualistic hopes are, significantly enough, definable at first only in terms of a space between conventional roles, and are laden with a self-condemnation that demonstrates to what degree her training has taken hold, how much hers is, at the outset at least, "a life deflected, reformed, reshaped against the will"[10] ("Don Pablo"):

> To be alone for a little space, a tiny hiatus between her life's two accepted phases. To cease being a daughter without immediately becoming a wife. To be a free lance, to belong to no one place or family or person—to achieve that silly longing of childhood, only for one year, before she flung it with other childish things upon the scrap heap.
>
> ("The Children")

To achieve this, she takes on the job of "Miss" or children's companion—a job which partakes of the roles of wife, daughter, and mother and is less an escape from life in Mellick than an extension of it:

> These women [the other "misses" whom Mary meets] came, undoubtedly, from impoverished wings of that not easily definable section of society, the Irish Catholic middle class. . . . In Mary's own family, impoverished as she always remembered it and simple as its habit was, a tradition of formality and quietude prevailed. . . .It appeared to [Mary] that the *sine qua non* of becoming a miss was not so much that one should be genteel by birth as that the veneer of gentility should have been sufficiently lacquered on by education in a good-class convent school.
>
> ("San Geronimo")

10. The narrator applies this description not to Mary herself, but to Pablo de Areavaga, whose life is a particularly rich and problematic study of the sources and effects of "detachment." But as I argue just below, Pablo's role in the novel—like Agatha Conlan's—seems primarily to be as a point of reference by which the reader can understand Mary's own struggle with "neutrality."

Such a life promises—to use Mary's own images for it—"invisibility" ("The Children") or (and this word is Agnes Mulqueen's, as well) "neutrality" ("San Geronimo").

Neutrality is another form of detachment (that word is just as predominant in *Mary Lavelle* as it is in O'Brien's other novels). It allows her "time to observe and meditate" ("A Corrida") and thus to try—with increasing difficulty, it must be said—to "keep the inner and the outer world at equal distance, and give sanity a chance" ("A Hermitage"). As detachment becomes harder to maintain, the need for external rituals, for routines and disciplines and duties and habits, for what Mary calls "living outwardly" becomes all the greater:

> By living outwardly for long enough and with determination, all would be restored . . . The exercise of self-evasion did create a fundamental sense of strain—a vague feeling of exhaustion . . . But she supposed that practice would make it easier, and that after a while there would cease to be any need to fly from real thoughts.
>
> ("Candles at Allera")

To this point Mary has, although in different and apparently more "free" and less enclosed circumstances, traversed much the same ground as Agnes: from neutrality to passion to renunciation to "detachment" with which she hopes, however futilely, to keep emotion at bay by the diligent exercise of duty and ritual. Confronted fully by her "desire" for Juanito, the only Areavaga son, a promising politician and (to outward appearances) a brilliantly and happily married man, she chooses to "forbear." Again like Agnes, she acts out of a sense of obligation to others: "for Juanito's sake, not for hers" (*Mary Lavelle,* "A Hermitage").

But Mary has at least one advantage, one bit of experiential education that may help her avoid misplacing her passion. Mary has in a sense already left a Vincent behind, in the shape of her father, older than Vincent but no wiser: "a man of great beauty" and "of indolent squireen stock," but "lazy" and worse yet "in his heart defeated, inefficient, and bored," a man who has outgrown or exhausted even that element of passion which may be Vincent's one saving virtue (*Mary Lavelle,* "The Children"). When Mary encounters her own demigod, Juanito—another rather spoiled young man—he is at least better than the best that could be hoped either of Vincent or Dr. Lavelle.

And for Mary the results of forbearance are too visible to be ignored. The misses have to some degree detached themselves, at least from their home place; but without apparent happiness. More significant is the perception of the enigmatic Pablo de Areavaga ("Don Pablo"), who has "learnt, among a million lessions, that the isolation of the self is not only inescapable . . . but that it is to some spirits essential," and who—his admirable and orderly political inventions having been interrupted by "the malady of love" for his wife—lives where "the imperturbable loneliness of the heart becomes love's devil and mocker, no matter what capitulation love may win." Yet in the end he is anything but imperturbable. The perturbation (a fatal one) is the arrival of Mary, a creature "mythical, innocent, and shameless . . . virginal and pagan" to his eye, which still retains the knowledge of "the buried dream of ideal love."

Pablo never breaks his silence; his example is thus largely opaque to Mary. Such is not the case with another of the misses, Agatha Conlan, an oddly unsettling figure, "very hungry-looking," with "a pale, fanatical face" and "a too mobile, too bitter mouth" whose severity is belied by her eyes, "deep blue and full of light" ("San Geronimo"). Agatha's room, like Pablo's, is "immaculate and impersonal as a monk's" ("San Geronimo"); and her detachment is so extreme as to allow her to announce that "It isn't Spain I loathe—it's life. Anywhere" ("Candles at Allera"). But Agatha's stiff, even fanatical self-isolation is no more lasting than Pablo's; she too falls in love with Mary, and goes Pablo one further by admitting the fact.

Detachment, even when bolstered by the firmest conventional taboos, simply will not bear up under the inevitable intrusion of love. Mary, as much from an understanding of her own nature as from her reading of the lessons to be found in Pablo's and Agatha's lives, will not stop at renunciation; she acts (quite literally) by demanding and receiving from the resistant gentleman whom she loves a physical consummation of their love.[11] The result, articulated in the chapter called "The Good Basque Country," is in part an escape from the self into "a brilliant light of sympathy." But that yields no loss of consciousness, or of self-consciousness; even as she embraces Juanito Mary thinks "of school and home, of John [her fiancé], of God's law and of sin, and did not let herself discard such thoughts."

The enactment of love is in its way the final, true detachment; and as such it derives not only from passion and intuition but from a carefully meditated, "clear-eyed" ("The Good Basque Country") sense of self, aware of risk and aware too of gain:

11. O'Brien's young heroines, well-reared as they may be, retain a power of choice and action even in sexuality; the man may think he's in charge, but he is not—whether he offers only a kiss, as in *The Flower of May*, or an affair, as in *That Lady*, he is, as the narrator describes it, the seduced, not the seducer.

She had cast her lot. Not with Juanito, whose fate was shaped already, in Spain and Spain's future, and with his wife and child. But merely because of him, of what he made clear about the remarkably distinct and sweet sensation which underlies the relationship of love. For the purchase of this accidental knowledge, for this brief hint at a theory which she might never test, she was beginning to suspect that she might have to sell the orthodox order of her own life, and the present happiness of another . . . She was risking loneliness for herself, and almost certainly undertaking to cause pain and humiliation elsewhere.

("A Hermitage")

Loneliness is, it seems, inevitable, whether one renounces or accepts love.

Mary ends up not distinctly happier than Agnes or even any more self-aware. What Mary had known all along—"she had read in her time of all those regrets and griefs and misunderstandings which are, in fiction, the certain flowers of love" ("A Hermitage")—has been borne out by her own experience; and yet deepened, darkened as well:

There were truths that were indefensible, truths that changed and broke things, that exacted injustice and pain and savagery, truths that were sins and cruelties—but yet were true and had a value there was no use in defending . . . That was the fruit of her journey to Spain. Anguish and anger for everyone and only one little, fantastic, impossible hope. Yet there it was—a real story.

("A Matador's Cape")

Like those other fictions Mary has read, the "real story" bears only an approximate (if nonetheless powerfully formative) relation to things as they will be, just as the guidebooks she reads bear only a faint resemblance to the Spain she encounters. What has happened to Mary is perhaps no more—and no less—than a realization of what her wish to be a "free lance" in a world of relationships and obligations will demand. She returns home full of intentions; we are left to wonder whether they work themselves out as peculiarly and unexpectedly as did those which brought her to Spain.

BY THE time *Mary Lavelle* appeared, O'Brien was herself nearly forty, had tried and abandoned the role of wife, had established a career as a writer of fiction and a life well outside of Limerick—had left home and childhood and the decision point both Agnes and Mary encountered some years in the past. The conflict of order and passion, of intention and routine, of individuality and relationship did not disappear from her fiction, however; both *The Last of Summer* and *The Flower of May* approach the same moment of decision, the first by way of an "outsider" (as Mary Lavelle is in Spain, and as Angele Maury is in Ireland), the second by way of a dutiful daughter (as Agnes Mulqueen is, with sad result, and as Fanny Morrow is, but with the help of the nearly angelic intervention of her aunt). Neither novel has the force of *The Ante-Room* and *Mary Lavelle,* although both (and especially *The Last of Summer*) are more shapely and economical. But all four novels in a sense beg the question which they seem to address: what will you do with your life? Or rather, they answer it only prospectively, by launching their young heroines into the first moments of adult life.

What makes *The Land of Spices* and *That Lady* stand apart from the rest of O'Brien's novels is the presence, indeed the centrality in each of a woman who has long since formed her intentions and tried to live them out. They again are contrasting figures: Ana de Mendoza wordly, sensual, and powerful; Mary Helen Archer ascetic and aloof; the one a wife, mother, and lover, the other a nun. If they do not necessarily resolve the choice between the world and the nun's cell, between passion and renunciation, they at least show what Kate O'Brien believes might be the shape and character of a life of continuing decision supported, however unsteadily, by a sense of self in which both emotion and detachment find a place.

These two lives demonstrate the degree to which the apparent dichotomy of wife and nun is in fact anything but simple. If the wife seems to be the one who accepts the obligations of relationship and family, one must observe as well that the nuns in O'Brien's fiction (and the two nuns, Aunt Mary and Aunt Fanny, in her own family) are also creatures of obligation and relationship. They are teaching nuns and part of large and complex communities, not saintly isolates. And if the nuns seem to be those who have chosen renunciation and obedience over all else, it is equally true that the role of wife involves greater "acceptance" of the customary "muddy road." To be a wife, a young girl (even a remarkably plain young girl like Teresa Considine Mulqueen) need only await and acquiesce to the inevitable offer of marriage; while to be a nun is an act of conscious, willful choice, and one that meets—in the lives of O'Brien's aunts, of Mary Helen Archer, and of Josie Kernahan—considerable shock and resistance from the affectionate prison of home.

The ambiguity shows up in the life of Ana de Mendoza (*That Lady,* "Prologue") before we first encounter her. The daughter of one of the richest of Castilian families and an heiress in her own right, then the wife of the king's most trusted minister, and the object of the king's odd (and, so O'Brien would have it, celibate) passion, Ana has from the beginning power that neither Mary nor Agnes can hope to attain. But by her own account that has left her "nothing to do" (part 2, ch. 3). Her power is at best implicit and invisible, to be exercised only in closed drawing rooms. Her marriage was arranged, and although it became affectionate it remained largely passionless; her husband was more father than lover. Now a widow, she has achieved, by the force of her own nature and by the educative force of her life experience, a state of detachment; what she awaits is the moment in which she may act. The novel records in great detail a whole series of her moments of decision and action. The first is abortive, and only remembered—her effort, when first widowed, to become a nun under the redoubtable Teresa of Avila, a decision which arises from her "great sense of waste," her conviction that "all her life had been like an athlete's training for a course never to be run" (part 1, ch. 4).

The second decision (the numbering is her own [part 1, ch. 1]) is the motive for action of the entire novel: her seduction of the man who has replaced her dead husband as the king's indispensable minister, Antonio Perez. Like many another man who attracts an O'Brien heroine, he is a mixture of man and boy:

> She liked the light, boyish cut of his face. Not his handsomeness, which was only too obvious, but its alert suggestion behind the charm, its hint of an anxiety that might almost be taken for innocence. He's odd, she thought approvingly; he's himself.
>
> (part 1, ch. 1)

And he proves to be both a passionately adept and a surprisingly faithful lover. With him Ana enters the world of passion which Mary too—but so much more briefly—had entered, and from which Agnes has drawn back; only to find it no more satisfactory a resting-place than the detachment and relative isolation which was its precursor and seemed to be its opposite: "There must be a reason, Ana thought, for being oneself, and this is not it. Suffering perhaps, or conflict or faith or an argument or a test of some kind" (part 1, ch. 2).

As they did for Mary Lavelle, to Ana the usual routines of life take on an added force and importance:

> Passion, after all, love-making, cheating and the counting of money; prayer, fear of death, the desire to know God and to have children—all these things, perilous with traps for the hasty, lay privately within the gentle, obvious surface, for every actor on that surface. If they did not the routine would have no meaning; and perhaps it derived

its apparent grace, and its heavenly grace too, from the fact of underpinning dangers, private shames and snare. Sin, after all, was a commonplace; and perhaps others too felt sometimes that the most idiotic part of sin is our failure to understand our own motives within it. But a part of self-disgust must be, she thought, that we bear it alone; we have to learn to live with it in silence, and simultaneously go on being the people our fellows know and work with.

(That Lady, part 2, ch. 1)

The particular mixtures of language and mood here are characteristic not only of Ana but of O'Brien's voice throughout her fiction—a language of selfhood and self-disgust, of sinfulness that does not drive out faith; and most of all the final insistence on going on. As Ana will ultimately formulate it, the catalog of necessary virtues is simple enough to lay out, and yet terribly hard to live: "honor and love and goodwill and seeing things through when you started them" (part 2, ch. 4).

And religious faith is necessary as well; of a particular kind, which is likely to be called by more orthodox Catholics Jansenist or even Protestant (*The Land of Spices,* bk. 1, ch. 2), since it is grounded in a belief in the inevitability of sin, and even (although nowhere does O'Brien put it in these terms) in something like a belief in a Fortunate Fall. Ana's own faith can be defined most fully in terms of what it is not—she is "not religious-minded" and "no mystic" but nonetheless "it was as natural to her to be a Castilian Christian as it was to have nails at her finger-ends, or an appetite for dinner" (*That Lady,* part 1, ch. 4). That faith, in other words, is as inherently a part of her fundamental self as is the passionate being awakened by Antonio. This is why her decision to act on that passion is only the first of the decisions motivated by the desire to be—and even more to *do*—"something of my own" (part 3, ch. 1).

The novel follows the sequence of such decisions: to turn away from the sexual expression of her love for Antonio (a decision signaled, significantly enough, by her moving into a bedroom that resembles yet another monastic cell); then to defend the continuing power of that love by defying the king, not once but several times; and climactically to see the now fugitive Antonio one last time. The end result of this course of action and resistance, of self-expression and self-defense, is yet again "detachment" (part 3, ch. 5), enforced not only by her own long-standing "self-control" (part 2, ch. 1) and austerity, but by the action of the king, who seals her into a single room in her own house. Ana increasingly comes to believe that more than self-expression or self-discovery is at work in this long course of actions and renunciations. She sees in it as well the defense of an absolute "principle" of individuality and privacy (part 3, ch. 1), to which the centralization and autocracy imposed upon Spain by Philip II are the greatest threats in her time, as in O'Brien's in the 1930's, in Spain and elsewhere (*Farewell Spain*, "Adios, Turismo" and "Arriba, España"). Ana's defense of that principle, however high the cost, is anything but perverse; it allows her alone among O'Brien's fictional characters to encompass within one life the roles of wife and nun, and of passionate "free lance" as well, and to act both "outwardly" and yet in deep awareness of and "accord with the inner ranges of her spirit . . . guarded by her worldliness and her will to feel, enjoy, and behave according to her natural law" (*That Lady*, part 2, ch. 2).

IN A DISTANT way, with due (which is to say considerable) allowance made for effects of time and place and class, Ana is what Mary Lavelle may hope to become. By this I do not mean that Mary should look forward to the utter isolation which is Ana's final fate; only that to live a life well off the muddy road, she must be willing to accept that much risk. Mary Helen Archer, O'Brien's one large-scale portrait of a nun, bears a similarly analogic relation to Agnes Mulqueen, who has chosen not to act upon but to step back from the urging of her passionate nature. Mary Helen, Reverend Mother of an Irish convent of the Company of the Sacred Family, presumably within the see of the Bishop of Mellick,[12] becomes a nun for reasons the novel long chooses to keep a mystery, but which amount to a disgusted reaction against human love. Mary Lavelle, loved both by Juanito and by Agatha Conlan, had come to a belief that in a sense all love is "fantastic and perverse" (*Mary Lavelle*, "Good-bye to the Cafe Aleman"); but Mary Helen—at least at the age of eighteen—cannot manage such a tolerant view.

The object of her devotion—and the cause of her flight into the convent—is her father, once a Fellow at Cambridge, then a resident of Bruges, where he lives a life of gentlemanly penury, while pursuing his scholarly interest in the English devotional poets of the seventeeth century. The devotion of the young Mary Helen to her father parallels the relationship between the young Denis Considine and his father, but is if anything more singleminded. Her childhood, like Denis's, is dominated by a house—not the ample River Hill but "a narrow, modest house, detached, like each of

12. For once, O'Brien leaves the precise location unclear; but the Bishop with whom Mary Helen deals is distinctly like the Bishop of Mellick who appears in *The Last of Summer* and indeed like the actual Bishop of Limerick whom O'Brien recalls in *Presentation Parlour*.

its neighbors, in a narrow, leafed-in garden" (*The Land of Spices,* bk. 2, ch. 3). That house enacts and represents a kind of ideal of safe enclosure yet of neighborliness, of detachment but also of settlement within a human context. The context—the old, shabby city of Bruges, and especially the "old slanting square, Place des Ormes" just around the corner from her father's house (bk. 2, ch. 3)—is, as both Mary Helen and her father believe, "accidentally perfect," a place in which "beauty, the necessary root of the matter," is present "in particularly good, unassuming form." Within that beauty, the narrow house; within the house, the godlike figure of the father: "In childhood she thought her father beautiful." That beauty is enhanced by his role as her teacher: "he poured imaginative knowledge all about her; he gave her an individualistic, sunny access to life." His existence, his treatment of her (both before and after the death of her kind but altogether more shadowy and less important mother) makes God almost superfluous; trained in a convent school, she considers a religious vocation but puts it aside, since it involves a choice "between [her father] and the only thing that measured up to him in her mind—the religious ideal. But all her *feelings* gave victory to him."

The revelation[13] which destroys that Eden involves human love and sexuality; the shock drives Mary Helen out of her home—but only just around the corner, into the convent of the Company of the Sacred Family. The rest of Mary Helen's life will be, in one sense, a long and permanent exile from home, to places as far away as Poland and Ireland. Yet it is at the same time a continuation of home, in enclosed spaces with gardens. The convent in the Place des Ormes centers on a "wide cloister" with a "holy well" (bk. 1, ch. 1) and has at its heart a sheltering room and a comforting figure: the "little study" of the redoubtable Mother General (bk. 3, ch. 1) who becomes Mary Helen's new parent, mother-God in place of the fallen father-God, her protector, teacher, and ideal.[14] To Mary Helen, her father—especially after his "fall"—retains an unsettling mixture of innocence and sinfulness; and Mother General too is a striking mixture of apparent opposites, both "businesswoman and saint." The dichotomous nature of both women is significant; Mary Helen is when we first encounter her likewise "divided within herself" (bk. 1, ch. 1) as her very name suggests by yoking the divine and the worldly ideals of femininity and beauty.

In the long run, the novel accounts for Mary Helen's own growth into

13. I avoid making that revelation explicit neither from impishness nor a desire for euphemistic avoidance; it simply seems unreasonable to deprive the novel of the suspense, the "mystery" it wishes to construct.

14. She reappears in *The Flower of May,* where she demonstrates at first hand the wisdom and good sense Mary Helen attributes to her.

someone who becomes worthy to take Mother General's place, both in
the life of the order and in the individual life of Anna Murphy, a student
in the convent school who lacks both home and satisfactory parentage.
The Irish convent where much of the novel takes place, and where Mary
Helen is Reverend Mother, is too a place with a beloved garden and a
sheltering room, her study, where the novel ends, and which becomes
over time Anna Murphy's haven. All the places in the novel remain oddly
the same (although early on, at least, the Irish convent seems to Mary
Helen an altogether strange and foreign place); what must change is Mary
Helen herself.

   That the necessary inward journey may, however, find its fundamental
expression in exterior spaces is supported by the two poems to which the
novel repeatedly refers. Henry Vaughan's "Peace" was Mary Helen's father's favorite poem and is the set-piece the young Anna Murphy, coin-
cidentally, recites to Mary Helen. The other is George Herbert's "Prayer
(I)," from which the novel takes its title. Both are poems of spiritual
aspiration; both speak—as does Shakespeare's Sonnet 34—of journeys and
wanderings—to "a country / Far beyond the stars" (Vaughan), a "pilgrimage" which is also a "plummet sounding heaven and earth" but which
in the end seeks and finds "The land of spices" (Herbert). But both poets
in the end counsel the abandonment of journey in favor of settlement.
"Leave, then, thy foolish ranges," Vaughan insists (as if speaking to Denis
Considine!). Each poem expresses the religious ideal in imagery of safe
enclosure ("Thy fortress and thy ease" [Vaughan]), of gardens ("There
grows the flower of Peace" [Vaughan] and "spices" [Herbert]), and especially of home ("the church's banquet" and a return to "birth" [Herbert])
and of a comforting, sheltering figure within that home ("One who never
changes, / Thy God, thy life, thy cure" [Vaughan] who offers "Softness,
and peace, and joy, and love, and bliss" [Herbert]).[15]

   Ana de Mendoza went from the world to the cell, from passion to a
kind of detached wholeness that at the very least *knew* well what it was
that had been renounced. The shock which drives Mary Helen out of her
father's house, and in a sense which begins her life (what had gone before
having been in very nearly a literal sense a dream) is particularly a shock

---

15. The two poems stand in the same sort of precise analogic relation to the events and
aspirations contained in the novel that *Don Quixote* does to Mary Lavelle's desire to be "a
free lance"; and that three operas—Gluck's *Orfeo,* Bellini's *I Puritani,* and Verdi's *Otello*—
do to the plot and the basic conflict of romanticism and austerity in *As Music and Splendour.*
It is not just a matter of vaguely Modernist allusiveness, however; or even of learned cleverness
on O'Brien's part: the texts are those found and encountered and then used as vehicles of
understanding and expression by the characters themselves.

to her feelings, and it produces a "self-control" which is a kind of madness (*The Land of Spices,* bk. 2, ch. 3), searching desperately for "lessons of elimination, detachment, and forgoing for which . . . her hurt spirit craved somewhat hysterically" (bk. 1, ch. 1). Mary Helen's journey is one of escape from self-enclosure; not literally (she will not leave the order) but figuratively, by way of her maternal love for Anna Murphy. Her love, like Anthony's for Denis, undertakes "the difficult task of protection" even "at long range" (*The Land of Spices,* bk. 3, ch. 1) and, again like Anthony's, rests on a power that can be, indeed often must be, silent "the best of its goodness often being, to keep still" (bk. 3, ch. 4).

Mary Helen, continually self-analytic, can fairly measure how far she has herself come. She defines her progress (bk. 3, ch. 4) in terms of an escape from enclosure and of movement into spiritual worlds from which she had once hoped to flee. The course of that movement is determined by her willingness not only to acknowledge the "messiness" of outside circumstance, even the hard lesson which her father's life seemed to teach, that "sin" is not only commonplace (as any skeptic might argue) but indeed all-pervasive (as the Jansenist or Protestant puritan would insist). And more to the point she must accommodate the division within herself. Her "compromise" with human feeling is a compromise with that part of her nature which had loved her father so thoroughly and which she had, for long years, tried to make "obedient." That, in its turn, forces her to recognize that detachment—however much a part of her it is, however necessary and even admirable it may be—is, pursued at the cost of human connection, "something deadly" (bk. 1, ch. 5).

O'Brien counts Mary Helen as being "that kind of nun . . . who will always have to wrestle with obedience" (bk. 1, ch. 1); it shows in an inability to control the nervous movement of her hands. Early on, Mary Helen connects obedience with "negation" (bk. 1, ch. 2); but it comes equally (and especially painfully, given her desire for escape and isolation) to involve action and obligation—to Anna Murphy and to the order. She is well aware of that part of her that most resists such connection; it is her capacity for judgment, which is sound enough to see, in the young Anna, someone who will need help and to whom she will find connection; but dangerously full of conviction, especially when it considers her sinful father. Mary Helen's final advice to Anna is not only a summation of what the nun believes she has learned but also a statement (like Eleanor Delahunt's advice to her niece to "range" and like Ana's catalog, "honor and love and goodwill and seeing things through") of the human truths which O'Brien intends to be the heart of her fiction; and it involves a careful balance of self and other, and a careful restraint (but not denial) of judgment.

You will make what you must of the life for which we have tried to prepare you. And you have gifts for life. Spend your gifts and try to be good. And be the judge of your own soul; but never for a second, I implore you, set up as judge of another. Commentator, annotator, if you like, but never judge.

(bk. 3, ch. 4)

It is advice, too, which might lead Anna to become a novelist of a kind remarkably similar to Kate O'Brien.

I HAVE considered *The Land of Spices* as if it were wholly and entirely Mary Helen's story; but it is as well Anna's. Even at the age of six, newly arrived in the convent school from a sorely troubled home, she displays her nature—the attentive, observant watcher. Her life balances Mary Helen's almost too symmetrically; for her, the convent is from the beginning a shelter from her "home," which is anything but Edenic. She too has a problematic love for her father, but the difficulties of Harry Murphy's nature require no sudden revelation; the "excitement and racy violence he stirred up" (bk. 1, ch. 3) are open and apparent, both appealing and dangerous. That more singleminded and idealistic love of Mary Helen for her father is reflected, however, in Anna's love for her younger brother Charlie. Like Mary Helen's, it is suddenly and irrevocably interrupted, and Anna flees back to the convent, to consider a religious life and to become detached and cold (bk. 2, ch. 4 and bk. 3, ch. 3). But Anna's road—like Mary Lavelle's, like Angele Maury's, like Fanny Morrow's—leads not into the nun's study but through it, toward life and particularly toward a university education. We last see her, as we last see so many of O'Brien's characters, at the start of that road, having at last found "her dual purpose—escape from grief and direction, in some sense, of her own future" (bk. 3, ch. 3). What the lives of Ana de Mendoza and Mary Helen Archer suggest is the full complexity of that passing qualification, "in some sense." Even to start on the road has taken the forceful intervention of the Reverend Mother, who proves her ability to be a good and powerful mother by outmanipulating Anna's grandmother, who would have the girl return home and refuse the university scholarship she has won.

The novel, then, approaches the "division" within Mary Helen between detachment and feeling from two chronological and circumstantial perspectives, which meet, if only temporarily, in Reverend Mother's study, from which each woman will soon depart into the world—the university in Dublin, the convent in the Place des Ormes. Throughout O'Brien's fiction duality and compromise are played out not only within characters but between pairs of characters—Anthony and Denis; Anna and Mary Helen; Fanny Morrow and her school friend Lucille de Mellin; Angele Maury and Josie Delahunt. And between physical settings as well, especially the parlour and the bedroom or study cell, the communal and familial place against the private, isolated place.

The division is especially clear in O'Brien's last novel, which must be accounted a rich and characteristic failure. *As Music and Splendour* stumbles in part over the challenge it sets itself, to portray fully and in detail its own particular, now gone world of Italian opera in the later nineteenth century. The documentary recreation of that world makes demands on the reader; most particularly it demands a passion for, and a knowledge of, opera. But even without them one can find interest in the novel; and especially in the almost paradigmatic contrast of the two central characters, Rose Lennane and Clare Halvey, both born into the impoverished end of the Irish Catholic bourgeoisie.[16] Both are well aware of the bitterness of home, but both are persistently homesick. Both are the recipients of help of the sort offered to Anna Murphy by Mary Helen Archer, and to Fanny Morrow by her Aunt Eleanor; each has her training supported, and is thus considerably burdened by a debt which is both economic and spiritual. Both are sopranos, become *assolutas* of some renown, and at an early age encounter passion and sexual involvement, yet accept the conflicting demands of their artistic discipline. Both seek a room of their own—the same room, in fact, first rented by Rose and then by Clare. In it each woman acts out detached meditation and passionate human connection.

What particularly strikes Kate O'Brien about her own aunts, who share so many circumstances of environment and upbringing, is that nevertheless "they were individuals" (*Presentation Parlour*, "Introduction"). However much this may frustrate her task as a memoirist, it is yet another proof of the power of individual "personality" to work even within the forming (and deforming) pressures of family, class, and culture. Similarly, the two sopranos prove to be surprisingly different. Rose is, for all her excellence and training as a disciplined musician, a creature of instinct and passion; and a woman with a sense of purpose not unduly swayed by self-doubt. She survives the end of two love affairs with sadness but not permanent injury; we last see her setting off to that land of the perpetual present, America.

Clare is another matter altogether. Her "song" is both of the more austere past (Handel's "I Know That My Redeemer Liveth") and of the

16. Rose is clearly derived from the actual Catherine Hayes, "the washerwoman's child who was to sing at La Scala" whom O'Brien mentions briefly in her tour of Limerick in *My Ireland*.

ambiguous future (a difficult new cycle of songs composed for her by a fellow-student and devoted, if Platonic, lover). Her talent as a singer has less to do with expressiveness and emotion than thought and discipline. Even in love she is different; her passion is for another woman, but unlike Agatha Conlan she comes to speak of it openly and enact it physically, in an affair which retains its power even after she realizes that her lover will not prove faithful. Her last word is not a hope for the future, however, or a sense of contentment: it is "sin."

Each woman finds a compromise between the detachment and isolation of an operatic career and the passionate love they encounter, never quite when or where they expect it. They enact the parallel "journeys" which we have seen so often before in O'Brien's fiction in a way that is altogether too programmatic to let the novel come fully to life. But the combination of intelligence and affection, of judgment and feeling, which O'Brien brings to bear in the imagining of these two lives is too powerful to let the novel decay altogether into schemes and lessons. What this last novel lays out, even if in less-than-wholly-satisfying terms, is the conflict at the heart of all O'Brien's work between sentiment and skepticism. That conflict is visible even in the plots of her novels, which never stray far from the outlines of the melodramas of love (Pablo de Areavaga, for one, would prefer to call them romances) but resist the closure and tidiness of melodrama. She has learned well, perhaps from Henry James,[17] that if the events of life often appear melodramatic, then the inward drama of consciousness, which coexists with and complicates those events, is not so easily categorizable; and that novels, to reflect life, must be willing to stop at a point of continuing action rather than to end with a climactic gesture. And the conflict appears as well in O'Brien's willingness to admit affection into her characters' bourgeois world without therefore omitting to see and to record its cruelties.[18]

At two important points O'Brien—who offered no extended apologia

17. That he is perhaps her mentor is suggested by passing references: in *The Ante-Room*, to *Washington Square;* in *As Music and Splendour,* Clare Halvey is said to be an avid reader of James, and the character Silas Rudd is an explicitly Jamesian "American" who resembles both Christopher Newman and Lambert Strether. Mary Helen Archer's last name is possibly a nod to James as well.

18. And especially its cruelties to the "retainers" who make it possible; O'Brien's portrait of Dotey, Hannah Kernahan's dependent and tool in *The Last of Summer,* shows the dark side of such relationships, as do Nurse Cunningham in *The Ante-Room,* the Countess de Mellin's servant Seraphine in *The Flower of May,* and Signora Buonatoli's servant (and virtual prisoner) Assunta in *As Music and Splendour.* One of the points at which O'Brien's novels seem to me to gain by comparison with Elizabeth Bowen's is in her ability more effectively and convincingly to look upon such lives and to understand their not especially happy connection to the more prosperous lives which are her—and Bowen's—major focus.

for the principles on which her fiction is based—allows herself or her characters to discuss the nature of art. The first instance is in *Mary Lavelle,* at a bullfight. Mary has not yet met Juanito and so has much to learn. Still, her instincts have been sound, and the sheer force of her response to the *corrida* is in itself a measure of credibility:[19]

> Death, so strangely approached, so grotesquely given and taken, under the summer sky, for the amusement of nonentities, death made into an elaborate play . . . There it was, she had seen it, the tawdry bull-fight, and all that she had known of herself was shocked, as she expected it to be, by its indefensibility, its utter, cynical cruelty. There was no escape from that and even now, in this moment of detachment from herself, this moment of queer dreaminess, its truth knocked and she admitted it . . . Burlesque, fantastic, savage, . . . but more vivid with beauty and all beauty's anguish, more full of news of life's possible gain and senselessness and quixotry and barbarism and glory than anything ever before encountered by this girl; more real and exacting, more suggestive of wild and high exactions . . . Here was art in its least decent form, its least explainable or bearable. But art, unconcerned and lawless.
>
> (*Mary Lavelle,* "A Corrida")

The sheer proliferation of O'Brien's favorite words—beauty, self, detachment, exaction—argues for the centrality of this moment. So too is the insistence upon death, which is ever-present in her novels (as it is in those of Elizabeth Bowen), and present usually in one of its most problematic and painful guises, the death of a parent. But what Mary seems to discover is the presence of glory and beauty as well, even in ordinary routines, even—no, particularly—in exactly repeated rituals. The "art" may be unconcerned but it evokes a response both detached and powerfully emotional.

That the circumstances are unfamiliar to Mary, and that her response is to some degree formed in advance, based on what she thinks she knows, makes the moment all the more striking in its apparent, and surprisingly mixed, significance. It may be why O'Brien continually sets her novels in worlds which are on the one hand well-known by way of stereotype (the

19. That Mary is speaking for her creator is made clear by O'Brien's own remarks on bullfighting in *Farewell Spain,* especially in the chapter entitled "No Pasarán." O'Brien inevitably (and approvingly) invokes Hemingway. But her interest in bullfighting seems much less focused on the bullfighter himself than is Hemingway's; and in general less upon the meaning of the fight itself than on its significance as spectacle. She sees it not as a fundamental test of human nature but as an art-work of a particular (and indeed rather shabby) sort.

bourgeois parlor, the convent) and yet in their particulars, and thus perhaps in their meaning, are unfamiliar, displaced in time and context from the world of her reader, who knows Victorian Limerick only by the vaguest of reputations, and Ana de Mendoza, Princess of Eboli, only perhaps by way of the misrepresentations of Verdi's *Don Carlo*. Within those settings we rarely encounter bullfights, but we continually encounter matters of life and death, cruelties and polite barbarism alongside quixotry and glory. It is a world in which God is visible only as "ironist" (*The Land of Spices,* bk. 1, ch. 2), but there is always someone to argue that God is love (*The Land of Spices,* bk. 1, ch. 2): an irony in itself, given the disarray which love produces, even when it seems to offer comfort. It takes the sentimentalist to see, and to speak of the love; and the skeptic to account for the irony.

In *My Ireland,* O'Brien, trying to account for what is most striking and most important in old Irish poetry, quotes Daniel Corkery and enlarges the point to apply to "the best of Anglo-Irish writing" generally:

> "A sense of reality, a grip on the life of the human land, a certain hardness of vision . . ." says Corkery. ". . . the mind in the grip of the vision . . . precise and hard-edged will be those sudden and unpremeditated words . . ."
>
> (*My Ireland,* ch. 7)

It is such a mixture of detail and detachment with something unpremeditated, even visionary perhaps, but certainly always emotionally charged, that is the great intention, and to an admirable degree the accomplishment, of O'Brien's novels.

3

ELIZABETH BOWEN

Squares of Light in the Hungry Darkness

A TOURIST might easily confuse the ample houses in Kate O'Brien's novels with the indoor world of comfortable houses and mannerly (indeed, often mannered) urbanites that is nearly universal in Elizabeth Bowen's fiction. But neither the houses' inhabitants nor their creators would make that mistake. To Bowen, O'Brien's bourgeois world would almost certainly appear hopelessly vulgar, hopelessly caught in a tired respectability and an impenetrably conservative religiosity. And indeed, for all that Bowen's characters cling, with a grip born of desperation, to elements of cultured civilization on which O'Flaherty's Michael McDara contemptuously (and with his creator's hearty approval) spits, Bowen's fictional universe is rather closer to O'Flaherty's than to O'Brien's. Beneath the radically disparate surfaces of *Skerrett* or *The Black Soul* and *The Death of the Heart* lies a shared sense of the immanence of chaos, of the near and probably inescapable presence of what David Skerrett calls "horrid annihilation." It is not so much in their perceptions of the fundamental nature of what *is* as in their answers to the question "What then—if anything—is to be *done?*" that the two writers diverge.

On an airless, very rainy September afternoon, the question of what is real confronts two young men in Bowen's story "Human Habitation." They "had made friends toward the end of the London University session" and now find themselves lost while on a walking-tour of "the canals of middle England." The atmosphere is more than a little disorienting. All that is, and has been for some time, visible is, paradoxically, "nothing." What looms "ahead of them, along the tow-path" is no more distinct— visually or verbally—than "the sense of just a possibility that something might approach them." The surrounding uncertainty begins to have a great effect on the consciousness of one of the two men, Jeffries.

Jeffries felt sundered by a world from the now almost invisible Jameson . . . He thought dimly, "If I lose consciousness of myself, shall I leave off being? I don't believe in Jameson, I don't believe he's even there; there's just something against which I should fall if I fell towards the canal sideways . . . . There was once a man called Jameson, who asked a man called Jeffries to walk with him for years and years along a canal, and—they walked and walked till Jeffries forgot himself and forgot what he had ever been. What happened then? I can't remember . . ."

Inner loss—of identity, of the story-making imagination, of any sense of rhythm or order, even of memory and emotion—exactly parallels an increasing sense of outward loss. But this is not only a projection of the self out onto the weather. Rather it is a darkly synergistic interreaction between landscape and soul, a distinctly Beckettian[1] inversion of the Romantic intersection of self and nature. And the result is nearly a complete loss of any defining reality, inner or outer: "He had begun to believe vaguely—the thing took form in his brain nebulously without any very definite mental process—that they had stepped unnoticingly over a threshold into some dead and empty hulk of a world drawn up alongside, at times dangerously accessible to the unwary." Suddenly, there is relief: not an empty hulk, but a little house, with a garden, and inside a waiting woman, like "all the women of the world, hailing them home with relief and expectation." She is not, of course, waiting for them; she awaits a mysteriously absent Willy. Nor is she alone in the house, which also holds within its "lighted, hidden room" another woman, "very stout elderly . . . immobile."

To Jeffries, for whom the outside world was a universal disorientation, this house was an equally universal sanctuary: "Here was a Wife . . . an Aunt . . . a Living-room—*home*." But that relief, that welcome, begins to dissipate. The woman is in the grip of an unceasing "expectation"—where *is* Willy? Jameson begins to talk with college-student grandiosity[2] of "that

1. To speak anachronistically; this story of Bowen's, which might well be called "Waiting for Willy," was published a full six years before the appearance of *More Pricks Than Kicks*.

2. It will not do, however, to excuse either the substance or manner of Jameson's program as some pardonable youthful enthusiasm. Bowen's political views, when they surface at all (as they do in her defense of the importance of property in the "Afterword" to *Bowen's Court*) have a distinctly eighteenth-century air; she does not pretend to hide their roots in Edmund Burke. Like Burke, Bowen has a clear dislike (indeed, by the end of her life, a distinct dread) of "enthusiasm"; and Jameson's dream of a new world is no more and no less than the dangerous inversion of Robert Kelway's statement of his faith in *The Heat of the Day* (ch. 15), which announces his readiness to accept and work for "the next thing," which in his

new Earth which was to be a new Heaven for them, which he, Jameson, and others were to be swift to bring about." Jeffries finds his companion's hopes incomprehensible and comes to a conclusion of his own about the nature of things: "After all, it all came back to this—individual outlook; the emotional factors of environment; houses that were homes; living-rooms; people going out and coming in again; people not coming in; other people waiting for them in rooms that were little guarded squares of light walled in carefully against the hungry darkness, the ultimately all-devouring darkness."

Jeffries has by now demonstrated a certain fascination with the very word "living-room"—which to Bowen means both a room in which to live, and a room which has a life, a history, a shaping (or a deforming) power. But the living room is, in this instance, no resting place. The accuracy and broad applicability of Jeffries's metaphor—for Bowen's world is full of "squares of light walled in carefully against the hungry darkness"—rests in part upon his awareness that the metaphor simultaneously encompasses security *and* fragility. Jeffries cannot long ignore the fact that this particular house is not his home, or even a place where he has a role to play, since he is not the one waiting or the one waited for. He and his friend are intruders, a threat to the "queer unity" of the wife's life. Indeed the presence of the two men in the house is more than just an intrusion; it is "horrible, something is being violated."

The unity which Jeffries believes he sees in the house is not altogether benign; it "had created and destroyed [the young wife]." Still he finds it hard to leave: hard to re-enter "the cave of darkness beyond the threshold." When he and Jameson do continue on their way, the puzzling "something looming ahead" which had so bothered Jeffries has been replaced with an equally puzzling immanence behind—the "queer house," the lonely women, and the unanswerable question of Willy's fate. The incident has been only a transient moment in a continuing—perhaps endless—journey; the story ends with "no answer" and with the two (whose friendship has revealed its uncertain footing, its likely end) seen as they "stumbled forward in the dark with tingling minds."

"Human Habitation" appeared in the second of Elizabeth Bowen's story collections, *Ann Lee's and Other Stories*. I have rehearsed it at such length because, whatever its youthful flaws as an independent piece of work, it

eyes is Fascism. What that "next thing" might be is in part the concern of Bowen's one pure fantasy, the dystopia-story "Gone Away." Whenever in Bowen someone (usually young) announces the need for change (as does, for instance, Maria in "Sunday Afternoon"), Bowen is careful to have someone nearby who, like Henry Russell in that story, is willing to announce "I still want the past"—especially in preference to some "ideal" future.

is very like a conveniently small map of Bowen's fictional world. Darkness and dissolution always threaten it, and usually triumph; houses (and their cousins, hotels) stand as small, fervently (if in the end ineffectually) defended places of sanctuary, especially to the relative strangers whose comings and goings most of the stories record. The "accidental" contact between wandering travelers and mysterious settlers is powerful but never easy; the important, healing, unifying word is one that is never quite spoken, indeed never quite thought. Human contact is often dominated by an emotional and psychic "presence"—a ghost, whether actual or imagined; an absent lover; a missing parent. Somewhere near the center stands—quite literally—a young woman, who watches and waits.

The narrative is likely to be full of comings and goings; but the fact and meaning of travel is vastly complicated by the degree to which points of origin and intended destinations are uncertain, even unimportant. To put it another way, while the terms "departure" and "arrival" are predominant, the words refer only to a particular place which is no more than a way station. To arrive is to find shelter, to seek help, to have moved toward, but never quite reach a desired but usually ill-defined goal. But to arrive in a "habitation" is to intrude, with a violence demonstrated not by any action of the characters, who are all more or less mannerly, but by the language of battle and near-rape describing the passage across thresholds. To depart is to be launched once again into uncertainty, to return from a temporary "here" into a prevailing "nowhere." But it is also an escape, a release from something distinctly like entrapment. As Bowen is careful to point out in the first chapter of *Bowen's Court,* she spent a part of her early childhood not far from Spenser's ill-fated Kilcoman Castle, in "*Faerie Queene* country." And for all their recognizable modern detail, the places upon which travelers happen in Bowen's fiction are places of magic, even of enchantment. The enchanter is, most commonly, a woman who could, viewed in the proper light, be Duessa in modern guise.

One could say that Bowen spent an entire career expanding and complicating Jeffries's sense of what "it all came back to." Some forty-four years later, in "The Move-In," the first chapter of the novel *Pictures and Conversations* Bowen was working on at her death, the reader will find yet another scene which includes a lone house, featureless landscape, shelter mixed with threat, accidental (but irreparable) arrival, the observing, judging young girl. The novel would, had Bowen lived to finish it, have shown clearly its kinship to *The Last September,* to *The House in Paris,* to *A World of Love,* to almost all of Bowen's stories and novels, in fact.

*   *   *

RECURRENCE of this mix is a demonstration of the sheer repetitiousness of Bowen's work, or to put it more positively, of its reognizable, indeed unmistakable consistency. In terms of style, of the arrangement of individual sentences, there is a whole battery of Bowenisms—a taste for inversion and for stating things in the periphrastic negative; a fondness for polysyllabic adverbs and generally for the language and manner of oblique, well-schooled, "polite" conversation; a devotion to the words "something" and "nothing" that can, in weaker moments, become almost comic in its insistence. Certain images reappear throughout her work: misdirected letters; mirrors, bubbles, and glass domes; windows that seal out or seal in the world; jigsaw puzzles; dancing classes; gardens, caves, and grottoes.

Her characters tend to fall into categories or "Bowen types," of which Sean O'Faolain[3] has provided a useful and witty, if not quite complete, catalog: "the dreaming but recusant girl . . . emerging, awkwardly for herself and for others, into womanhood"; the "clever but ineffectual" young man and his near-cousin (but moral opposite), "the near cad"; "the demon child"; the "upright, well-meaning, refined couple." To them one must at the very least add Hermione Lee's "powerful Machiavellian older women" (*Bowen: An Estimation,* p. 100), although I believe magic is more relevant to their natures than is political calculation; and also (perhaps as a subcategory of the "refined couples") a train of rather baffled husbands and suitors, all of whom display a proportion of passion to good sense that is noticeably out of line when tested against those whom they love and/or marry.

What unifies many of these types and constitutes something a good deal more substantive than mere repetition or habits of style is the quality that Bowen variously calls "displacement" or "dislocation" or—more rarely—exile. Bowen's major characters find themselves oddly *between,* historically and chronologically. Many are around forty, no longer young enough to fit adequately the role of romantic hero or heroine, not yet old enough to be willing or able to abandon love altogether. Like Henry Russell in the story "Sunday Afternoon," in a social environment they are likely to feel themselves to be "between two generations," the energetic young and the civilized old. Another large group consists of women just beyond adolescence but just shy of adulthood, uncertainly facing a world of love and marriage (or as it usually turns out, love *or* marriage).

Bowen clearly intends this discomfiting, Arnoldian middle ground to be more than a fact of individual lives. Increasingly as her career proceeds, Bowen parallels the lives of her protagonists to the "life" of the century

3. *The Vanishing Hero,* pp. 146–169.

in which they and she exist. The connection is especially clear in the case of Stella Rodney in *The Heat of the Day,* who must live in the "tideless, hypnotic, futureless day-to-day" (ch. 5) which is London during World War II. Stella, "younger by a year or two than the century," understands herself to be a creature—or a representation—of her generation, "which, as a generation, was to come to be made to feel it had muffed the catch. The times, she had in her youth been told on all sides, were without precedent" (ch. 2). And as the condition of her life deteriorates, the power of that connection between self and history increases: "the fateful course of her fatalistic century seemed more and more her own" (ch. 7). There is of course an element of self-aggrandizement, even of self-pity in this tendency to project the situation of the self out onto the cultural and historical landscape; those occasions when Bowen seems most intent upon building up such equations are often moments when her fiction shows strain and mannerism. But to Bowen the equation, and the dark terms in which it must be couched, are fundamental facts.

The novelist herself was of course chronologically a child of the century and felt herself to be such spiritually as well: it was a radically unsettling condition. Even before the start of World War II, she and her characters seemed, in their own eyes, to be living in an interim between cataclysms. For Bowen, World War II came not so much as an apocalyptic shock or a betrayal (to borrow one of her favorite words) as a confirming enactment of the way things had always been. As Stella Rodney observes, "War, if you come to think of it, hasn't started anything that wasn't there already" (*The Heat of the Day,* ch. 2). Writing in 1951, and accepting again the centrality of the connection between the individual and the century, Bowen asks:

> What is the matter with us . . . that we cannot acclimatize ourselves to our own time—to the days in which we are called upon to live? Does our century fail us, or we it? . . . Are we to take it that our own time has been, from the point of view of its inhabitants, irreparably injured—that it shows some loss [or] vital deficiency? What fails in the air of our present-day that we cannot breathe it; or, at any rate breathe it with any joy? Why cannot the confidence in living, the engagement with living, the prepossession with living be re-won? One must have the life-illusion.
>
> ("The Bend Back," *The Mulberry Tree*)

That battery of questions implicitly dominates Bowen's literary consciousness from the very beginning. And so too does the particular context within which the life-illusion must be found or defended. Bowen derived

the title of her novel *A World of Love* from Thomas Traherne, whose words
she quotes as an epigraph: "There is in us a world of Love to somewhat,
though we know not what in the world that should be . . . Do you not
feel yourself drawn by the expectation and desire of some Great Thing?"
To which most of Bowen's characters might answer yes; but with an ever-
growing sense that such expectation is illusory and more likely to bring
pain than fulfillment. The mere existence of a world of love—which as
Traherne suggests must be an inner world—is increasingly in question,
as the century and Bowen's career proceed; and to live at all such a world
must engage in a struggle to the death with outer worlds of darkness,
dissolution, and war.

"ALL-DEVOURING" worlds are ever-present in Bowen's fiction. Her stories
and novels are full of epigrammatic reminders that existence occurs within
a "disproportionate zone of emptiness" where "things . . . seem to be closing in" (*The Last September,* ch. 3). And these frequent and despairing
propositions are supported by the very topography within which her fictions are set. Here, for instance, are Fred and Lilia Danby, long married
but only now metaphorically entering a world of love, more literally walking in a garden:

> Over everything under the tree lay the dusk of nature. Only car-tracks
> spoke of ever again coming or going: all else had part in the majestic
> pause, into which words were petering out. This was not so much a
> solution as a dissolution, a thinning-away of the accumulated hardness
> of many seasons, estrangement, dullness, shame at the waste and loss.
> A little of redemption, even only a little, of loss was felt . . . Impossible
> it is for persons to be changed when the days they have still to live
> stay so much the same—as for these two, what could now be their
> hope but survival?
>
> (*A World of Love,* ch. 8)

It is a characteristic instance of what Bowen herself called "the Bowen
terrain" ("Pictures and Conversations," part 2), where even the visible
world is full of, indeed defined by absence, waste, and loss.

In Bowen's fiction the predominant time is evening or full night (especially in *The Heat of the Day* and the stories set in wartime London).
The predominant season is autumn, a time not of mellow fruitfulness but
of loss and impending death, a season which looks toward but never
beyond the arctic desolation of winter. If the more promising movement
of spring to summer is included, it is likely to be placed well in the

irretrievable past; and its promise is further undercut by the frequency with which the arrival of summer signals sudden death and separation. Thus individual acts of suicide occur in early summer (*The House in Paris*) and manslaughter takes place in June (*Eva Trout*). Historical forces are unleashed in that season, like the Troubles which burn down Danielstown in *The Last September* or the two world wars, the immanence of one darkening the beach party in the center of *The Little Girls,* the other complicating the spring of new love which seems to be the end-point of *A World of Love*. Spring's promise is thus either illusory or extremely short-lived, or indeed both. Better far, in terms of the reality of things, to have an eye of winter.

To evening and seasonal barrenness should be added a prevailing wetness and a fondness for seacoasts. Like Jeffries, or like Eva Trout, looking out on a beach not far from the house where she intends to make her own "home," Bowen's characters often seem to look at the fragile edge of the known world:

> The eternal shingle skeined with eternal sand was strung and clotted with dunglike seaweed; bedrabbled seaweed slimed some exposed rocks proceeding outward like stepping-stones to nowhere. A last-summer's child's bottomless bucket, upturned, could have been jettisoned by expeditionaries from some other planet. A colorless haze was gathering out at sea.
>
> (*Eva Trout*, ch. 7)

Given the proximity and centrality of such landscapes, it is no wonder that Bowen so insists upon the word *dissolution*.[4] One might more accurately speak of *dissolutions;* for the effects are various and all-encompassing. What dissolves is not just the world of visible signs and landmarks (although, for Bowen's characters, so often traveling, that is a fundamental

---

4. There is a paradox at the heart of Bowen's sense of the nature of things and the kinds of plots she devises to enact that sense. The fragility and darkness she sees are all-pervasive; they are the usual and ordinary conditions of life. Yet to represent them she is, more often than not, driven to draw upon an apparatus of the melodramatic extraordinary—suicides, murders, spies, improbably confused genealogies—and a style which, in its insistence on loomings and incomprehensibilities, seems at its worst an unhappy mix of Poe and Conrad. It may be that only in *The Last September* and *The Heat of the Day* she has, at least in the setting, a directly "real" way to enact the threat which she always sees. Both the Troubles and the Blitz provide a body of precise and historical detail; the constant and extreme threat which the outside world contains—indeed, which *is* the outside world—in those two instances alone requires no "working up." But of course they are both extraordinary circumstances, distinctly recognizable historical moments; and thus again even in those instances the ordinary can only be represented by the extraordinary.

problem). Memory and imagination, and even language itself begin to dissolve, since they have no visible materials to work upon, to be prompted by, and to be tested against. The greatest threat of all seems to be a return to that child-like condition in which the very limits of the self, and the continued existence of those who are out of sight, are absolutely in question.

Surrounded by, and fully aware of "that general threat to life that is ever present" (*The House in Paris,* ch. 11), Bowen's characters necessarily experience "the feeling that if you stopped for a moment you'd go out" ("Sunday Evening"). Indeed, when in a Bowen tale motion is interrupted, as at the conclusions of *To the North* and *Eva Trout,* the results are almost inevitably tragic. In part for that reason, Bowen's characters are all travelers; and many of them are set in motion by forces against, or outside, their will. One can with considerable ease trace this to the dislocations of Bowen's own early life, reflected in the number of children in her stories and novels who are "sent away," supposedly for their own good. Travel is, however, just as common among those who are fully grown; no doubt in part as a function of the time, place, and class in which Bowen's fiction almost invariably occurs—the well-to-do English during what Paul Fussell has characterized as perhaps the last great age of travel.[5]

The motives for such travel are, predictably, mixed. The desire to move is partly a desire to avoid the "crude intrusion of the actual," and especially the actualities of contemporary English life. Put in a more positive way, travel may be an effort to gain time and perspective so as more fairly and satisfactorily to answer the question of what to do with one's life. There may be secrets to flee, especially but not only in Bowen's ghost stories. And invariably there are things to be looked *for,* especially the name and apparatus of a social self.

But the fact of movement is so commonplace as to make questions of motive almost irrelevant; and as we shall see, Bowen places no great hope in the efficacy of any human intentions. To Bowen the real movement is in any case interior and psychic:

---

5. Paul Fussell, *Abroad: British Literary Travelling Between the Wars* (New York: Oxford University Press, 1980). Fussell mentions Bowen not at all (although the travel agency which Emmeline Summers runs in *To the North* might at least have warranted his passing attention). But the suggestions he makes for the importance of travel—as a response to the dislocations and horrors of the First World War and as an expression of distaste for the England of the 1920s and 1930s—might be fruitfully applied to Bowen's various travelers; certainly to the tourists who make up the entire cast of characters of *The Hotel,* to the restlessly wandering Cecilia Summers in *To the North* and Karen Michaelis in *The House in Paris,* and perhaps as well to the Quaynes in *The Death of the Heart,* who try to escape the observations of Portia by dashing off to Capri.

Someone remarked, Bowen characters are almost perpetually in transit. Arguably: if you are to include transitions from room to room or floor to floor of the same house, or one to another portion of its surroundings. I agree, Bowen characters are in transit *consciously*. Sensationalists, they are able to re-experience what they do, or equally, what is done to them, every day. They tend to behold afresh and react accordingly. An arrival, even into another room, is an event to be registered in some way. When they extend their environment, strike outward, invade the unknown, travel, what goes on in them is magnified and enhanced: impacts are sharper, there is more objectivity . . . I may, too, impart to some of my characters, unconsciously, an enthusiastic naivety with regard to transport which in my own case time has not dimmed.

("Pictures and Conversations," part 2)

Although the fundamental journey is strictly personal, the world of physical travel within which it commonly occurs is anything but solitary. That in turn makes for the inevitability of encounters (the title of Bowen's first book) and their seminal importance. Even moments of relatively insignificant contact, such as a conversation between Karen Michaelis and a nameless young Irishwoman in *The House in Paris* (part 2, ch. 3), have a resonance of meaning and some deeper understanding of the self. At the same time the exchange emphasizes the inadequacy of the very language by which we usually try to orient ourselves within human experience:

[Karen] thought: She and I belong to the same sex, even, because there are only two: there should certainly be more. Meeting people unlike oneself does not enlarge one's outlook; it only confirms one's idea that one is unique. All the same, in the confusion of such encounters, things with a meaning ring, that grow in memory later, get said somehow—one never knows by whom . . .

Even the smallest and most ordinary of such accidental encounters can generate whole novels. All of *To the North* derives, for instance, from the accidental meeting of a young English widow and a London lawyer on a train leaving Milan. All of *A World of Love* points toward an encounter between Jane and the improbably named Richard Priam at Shannon Airport. The two men who dominate Stella Rodney's consciousness in *The Heat of the Day* enter her life more or less accidentally. Bowen's stories and novels are full of meetings at house parties, over lunch, at people's weddings, at Sunday teas or during aimless walks in the park; their commonness, and even their apparent triviality, should not mask the degree to which they define lives.

"We're instruments of each other's destinies" says an older woman in *A World of Love* (ch. 9), attempting nonetheless to deny responsibility for the character of the lives around her. Her premise is, it seems, one which Bowen shares, even if the reasoning she builds upon it is self-serving. Any human encounter, then, has (in its effects if not in its appearance) something fatal about it, in several senses of the term. Even love itself can be construed in terms of travel and encounter; it may be, as is the case with a pair of wandering lovers in the wartime story "The Mysterious Kor," that love is "a collision in the dark."

Some of the richest stories focus on just such moments of collision within a world of human particles, each of which is following—so he or she hopes—a unique path of transit. Consider, as one example, the story included in *Collected Stories* under the title "A Love Story: 1939." It opens with another soggy and threatening landscape:

> Mist lay over the estuary, over the terrace, over the hollows of the gummy, sub-tropical garden of the hotel. Now and then a soft, sucking sigh came from the water, as though someone were turning over in his sleep. At the head of the steps down to the boat-house, a patch of hydrangeas still flowered and rotted, though it was December. It was now six o'clock, dark—chinks of light from the hotel lay yellow and blurred on the density. The mist's muffling silence could be everywhere felt. Light from the double glass doors fell down the damp steps . . . . Inside the double glass doors, the lounge with its high curtained bow windows was empty. Brilliantly hotly lit by electric light, it looked like a stage on which there has been a hitch.

The conflict between heat and mist, between light and dark; the mixture, perhaps even a temporary equilibrium, of persistent life and evident decay; the ominous time of day and' year (and of course, of history—to be represented a few lines later by "a voice announcing the six o'clock news"): all tell us we are unmistakably in Bowen country. The hotel, somewhere in the west of Ireland, may seem a haven where "there was nothing to dread"—although a "tinder-dry turkey carpet" is dangerously close to a fire in an "immense tiled fireplace."

On this "stage"[6] three pairs of players enter and encounter one another.

6. Bowen had a hand in at least two stage pieces—an apparently forgettable play, *Castle Anna*, on which she collaborated with John Perry, and which William Heath sees, along with the story "Happy Autumn Fields," as a kind of preliminary to *A World of Love* (*Bowen: An Introduction*, pp. 124–126; see also Glendinning, *Bowen: Portrait*, p. 180); and a Nativity Play, performed at various times and in various forms, most importantly at Derry in 1970

Each pair is linked by love of a kind: the collisions, in that sense, have already occurred. One pair is a mother and her grown daughter; their familial relationship is complicated by the dominating absence of Teddy, the mother's lover, just killed in the war. The mother, Mrs. Massey, in a sense pursues Teddy's ghost; they had come together to this hotel, although the Masseys live almost within sight of the place, in a "sweet . . . lonely" house called Palmlawn just "through the woods." Teddy was, unsettlingly, the age not of the mother but of the daughter, Teresa. Teresa has an angry air about her—to one onlooker she is a "tiger cat"—but her mother accuses her of having "no feelings" at all. In any case it is not clear if she has come to help her mother or because Mrs. Massey has somehow coerced her.

Another of the pairs in the story, the recently married Polly and Clifford Perry-Dunton, have a similarly complex connection. She, like Mrs. Massey, is an older woman, but with "childish, hard will." She can (together with a "ring of technicians") make herself look "fourteen." Her marriage to the younger Clifford, who is, or would like to be, a writer, is peculiarly described as a "rape . . . . Her father had bought him for her." But there is, at least on her side, considerable passion; perhaps even a minimal kind of fruitfulness: "Rain—a little rain, not much—fell on her parched nature at Clifford's tentative kiss." Now they represent—more to the point, they impose upon their surroundings—a "static, depleting intimacy" which "deaden[s] the air around them." At least their reasons for having traveled this far are clear: they are avoiding the war, which Polly has managed to personalize into "a masculine threat" to their marriage.

The relationship of the third pair is truncated in its own way. Major Frank Mull (his rank dates from "the last war" but as he is quick to say "I'm not in this one, thank God") and the woman he calls his "cousin," Linda, are in fact lovers on a regretfully brief weekend holiday. To the (apparently slim) chance of Frank and Linda's having a quiet time together, Mrs. Massey is largely an interruption—"something is always happening," Linda thinks. It is Frank's good nature and curiosity that get in the way of their intimacy.

(*Bowen: Portrait*, pp. 233–4). Neither suggests that she had much talent for theatrical writing; but there is something clearly "theatrical" in her work. It appears first in her preference for clear stage-settings—carefully described drawing-rooms, for instance; or, more significantly, the "public" rooms of houses and hotels (an ante-room in *The Last September;* yet another glassed-in lounge in *The Hotel*), full of doors to provide for entrances and exits. Her penchant also shows up in the predominance of dialogue in all her works, at least down to *The Heat of the Day,* and in the tendency to define chapters, like the scenes in Restoration comedy, in terms of the entrance or departure of a character.

The story has little or no plot; the one dramatic action involves deciding who will drive the "dazed" Mrs. Massey back to her house. Although, in speaking of the novel, Bowen calls plot "essential . . . the pre-essential" ("Notes on Writing a Novel," in *The Mulberry Tree*), in her stories she often avails herself of plotlessness, of a narrative in which situation, character, and "impression" rest upon no more support than small-scale incident. The story is in fact not so much a love *story* as it is a representation of the fact that—at least in 1939—love cannot have a story, cannot that is have shape, pattern, durability. The couples, so various in terms of their lives, natures, and human connections, arrange and rearrange themselves into parallels and opposites. Taken as a whole, the three love affairs represent an unprepossessing set of alternatives. That of Teddy and Mrs. Massey has been reduced entirely to memory. That of Polly and Clifford exists in an unnaturally "timeless" present that is, in its way, a sort of death-in-life. That of Frank and Linda seems more "normal," more human in its shape and emotion; but it is extremely temporary and constantly interrupted by its collisions with other lives. Still, the geniality of Frank Mull (for all that it tends to encourage, rather than to resist, those forces which, at any moment, try to interrupt love) has considerable appeal. Unlike the rather unappetizingly saintly mother of Thomas Quayne, who with baneful effects preferred "to do right" rather than "to do good" (*The Death of the Heart*, part 1, ch. 6), Frank acts helpfully, enthusiastically, warmly, charitably. That warmth almost leads him astray: at the last he sees Teresa, and "thought, calmly, of Linda wondering where he was, and [he] wanted to go, and wanted to stay." His choice—to go—is quickly, and even easily made; but not in terms of right: "in love there is no right and wrong, only the wish." By that standard, even the dreadful stability of Polly and Clifford may, without apology, be called love.

And there is this too in defense of the kind of love Frank Mull has and offers: it seems to be able to resist, with apparent success, the deforming effects of human "collision." That makes "A Love Story" rather stand out in Bowen's work in contrast to more violent intersections elsewhere, most famously perhaps the encounter between Mrs. Drover and the title character in "The Demon Lover."

The image of collision is developed fully (or perhaps only insistently) in *To the North,* a novel that contains almost an extravagance of variations on the ideas of travel and encounter. It is one of the few novels by Bowen without anything like a good place, whether real or imagined; indeed, the usual house, which stands within the Bowen terrain as the one hope of stability and resistance to change, enters this novel by way of a metaphor of profound loss:

When a great house has been destroyed by fire—left with walls bleached and ghastly and windows gaping with the cold sky—the master has not, perhaps, the heart or the money to rebuild. Trees that were its companions are cut down and the estate sold up to the speculator. Villas spring up in red rows, each a home for someone, enticing brave little shops, radiant picture palaces; perhaps a park is left round the lake, where couples go boating. Lovers' lanes in asphalt replace the lonely green rides. . . . After dark . . . where once there was silence, a tree's shadow drawn slowly across the grass by the moon, or no moon, an exhalation of darkness—rows of windows come out like lanterns in pink and orange; boxed in bright light hundreds of lives repeat their pattern . . . .

(To the North, ch. 12)

This is, as we will see, a shocking inversion of Bowen's customary language; "home" and "radiance" seem altogether ironic, shelter is a matter not of drawing rooms but of boxes, love must find its place on asphalt, and "pattern"—which may in the end be Bowen's last hope—becomes undifferentiated repetition.

Lacking any place on which to stand, much less any home in which to rest, all of the characters in the novel move insistently. Cecilia Summers no sooner returns from Italy than she begins planning a trip to America. Her "aunt," the meddlesome Lady Georgina Waters, dashes back and forth between London and Gloucestershire; Julian Tower, who hopes, in a rather indefinite way, to marry Cecilia, wanders around London, with side trips to oversee the schooling of his niece and ward Pauline. Most of all, Emmeline Summers rushes here and there (she runs a travel agency whose peculiar motto could reasonably serve as the theme-note of the entire novel: "Move dangerously")—to see Lady Waters, to her lover Markie's flat, to a cottage near Devizes, to Paris. The major collision takes place between a "not quite angelic," even "a shade perverse" Emmeline and Markie. It builds to a climax during a trip by motorcar in the dark of night (ch. 28), with Markie persistently crying out "Stop for a moment." When they do stop, there is a moment of calm:

Emmeline looked through the night that like grey water clearing let her distinguish the folded country and hanging darkness of woods. Through this not-quite-oblivion . . . their headlights sent unmoving arrows that died ahead. This breathing outline of earth, these little mysterious woods each aloof from the other and molded like clouds in the air brought to her desolation a healing stillness that had eluded her happy and living, so that she touched for a moment the chilly hand of peace. A sense of standstill, a hush pervaded this half-seen country.

If this is "peace," it is a state somewhere between sleep and drowning; and it lasts in any case only a moment, until once again "Speed . . . began to possess Emmeline" and she achieves a new kind of standstill, as she sits "fixed immovable with excitement" behind the wheel of the speeding car.

At the last, the only relief is in the speed of leaving it all behind, with "the traveller alone with his uncertainties, with apprehensions he cannot communicate, seeing the strands of the known snap like paper ribbons" but "sustained and more than himself on a great impetus" and willing then to let go even of love "with its unseen plan, its constrictions and urgencies" so that it may "[drop] to a depth." The novel ends with one more (and ironically misdirected) desire for stasis, companionship, and home; Cecilia, waiting in London for the return of the doomed Emmeline, says to Julian "Stay with me till she comes home." Such understandable human desires cannot overcome the "immense"—and indeed, fatal—"idea of departure" which has overtaken Emmeline, and which seems throughout the novel to be the prime motive force in the visible world.

Travel, and the encounters it produces, are not always so clearly destructive to life and to love, but to move is inevitably dangerous. As one character remarks in "Sunday Afternoon," "There is only one journey now—into danger." It may be worse than that; the only journey may well be that envisioned by Gavin Doddington in "Ivy Gripped the Steps," and that is "a tour of annihilation" made all the more striking by the action of memory. So is Dinah Delacroix's journey in *The Little Girls*—a trip both in place (from Somerset to the seacoast) and in time (from her adult life as widow and matriarch back to her school-girlhood). Such trips are death threats to the self.

It is perhaps not surprising that the voyage out, toward "an after world" (*To the North,* ch. 1) and away from the comfort and stability of home, should offer so many dangers. But even the journey toward a more attainable goal has its dangers. In the story "Summer Night," for instance, a woman (her name, Emma, and her reckless driving both recall the central figure in *To the North*) leaves behind "an obscure country house" populated by her puttering husband and her two daughters. She knows where she is headed; the house of her lover, Robinson. Still, it is a journey deeper and deeper into darkness, at least until Emma can step from that night-scape into the "living-room." To make such a trip inevitably engenders doubt—"have I been wrong to come?" And to be safely indoors is to suffer the interference of the life of the room: "She could not have said . . . how much the authoritative male room . . . put, at every moment when [Robinson] did not touch her, a gulf between her and him."

For all of her apparent sense of purpose, no sooner does she enter than she exits. Physically she moves only out to the lawn and garden. Still, there is a larger journey—an "adventure even, [a] pilgrimage"—in her mind, toward the ghost or ruin of a nearby estate:

> "What are all those trees?" "The demesne—I know they burnt down the castle years ago. The demesne's great for couples." "What's in there?" "Nothing, I don't think; just the ruin, a lake . . ."

It is not altogether clear whether the absence which so dominates Emma's sense of locality represents a note of loss or of good sense: "she thought for a minute he had broken her heart" by "head[ing] her off the cytherean terrain," but "she knew now he had broken her fairytale," and perhaps therefore offered her "not poetry but a sort of tactile wisdom" deriving from a renewal of contact with the physical reality of things. One can wonder, however, how likely a love affair is to prosper without "poetry." The story leaves the two figures together but still outdoors, in "dry, tense, translucent darkness."

But it does not in fact end there; and in rather the same way that "A Love Story" demanded that Frank and Linda's affair be understood in terms of at least two other love stories, the long-awaited collision of Emma and Robinson is encompassed by other examples of love and its rupture, the experiences of a brother and sister, Justin and Queenie. The examples serve as much to complicate as to clarify; much of the body of the story before the moment when Emma arrives is taken up by a conversation between Justin and Robinson, centering on Justin's belief that "we should have to find a new form . . . for thinking and feeling," but marked as well by Justin's powerful if not quite explicitly sexual "anxious, disturbed attraction" to Robinson; and culminating in Justin's angry feeling of "dissonance" and his re-enclosure within "his small, harsh room" which exactly matches "his constriction," from which he can see "no crack of outlet." Even the bleakest of outdoor settings seems less airless than that.

Justin's sister Queenie is profoundly deaf, and thus at liberty to create and inhabit her own worlds of memory and imagination without the intrusions of the present. Her image of human connection contains a nameless lover from her past who becomes Robinson and takes her on a walk which is much like the "pilgrimage" or fairy tale which Robinson had denied Emma. Alone in her room Queenie recaptures the past and fuses it with the present and the ideal:

> This was the night she knew she would find again. It had stayed living under a film of time. On just such a summer night, once only, she had walked with a lover in the demesne . . . . They had gone down walks already deadened with moss, under the weight of July trees; they had felt the then fresh aghast ruin totter above them; there was a moonless sky . . . the subtle deaf girl had made the transposition of this nothing or everything into an everything . . . Tonight it was Robinson who, guided by Queenie down leaf tunnels, took the place on the stone seat by the lake.

Hers is recognizably a "life-illusion"—illusion which has both the shape and emotional force of life. But it is still *illusion,* without any but the most modest and decorous human contact, and even so containing an abundance of omens: darkness, deadening, a tottering ruin.

Even this is unavailable to Emma. She does not have the advantage of a solitary and self-enclosed life. Her actual relationship with Robinson will inevitably take place somewhere outside a fairy tale, in a world which must include as well the judging world Emma tried to leave behind her, at home. The voice of that world speaks through Aunt Fran, left in charge of Emma's children. In a tone of Old Testament religiosity it reaches a solemn vision of the apocalyptic present, couched in terms of place, of fragility, and of dissolution that are recognizably similar to Bowen's own view of things:

> The blood of the world is poisoned . . . The solitary watcher retreats step by step from his post—who shall stem the black tide coming in? . . . There is not even the past: our memories share with us the infected zone; not a memory does not lead up to this. Each moment is everywhere, it holds the war in its crystal; there is no elsewhere, no other place.

BOWEN'S insistent sense of the individual facing "the black tide coming in" seems no more than short step from pure deterministic nihilism. But she is never quite willing to abandon individual intention and individual will as the basis for human artistic *resistance* to the conditions of the age, as the starting point of the search for "life-illusion." Her characters—not always happily of course—continue to choose, to act upon obligations, especially the obligations of love.

It is possible, sometimes, to wonder why. The "fact" of the inevitably sad end of things[7] is demonstrated amply by the plots of her fiction; and especially by the plots of her novels, which characteristically show love affairs broken off short. Some marriages live on, demonstrating perhaps nothing more admirable than a certain sturdiness; and in a world of all-devouring darkness sheer duration is something like a cardinal virtue. Yet even the apparently stable marriages are ill-proportioned unions, with at least one haunting ghost, at least one inescapable direct example of the painful discords of love, the memory of a particular death, a particular separation against which stability can be measured, but which as well looks like an omen of inevitable breakdown.

If love, then, were a matter of sense, even of calculation, it would simply not occur in Bowen's fiction; but occur it does. Indeed it is fair to call just about every one of Bowen's published pieces of fiction a love story, and usually—in broad outline—of the traditional sort involving one man and one woman. Love is not so much the subject of Bowen's fiction as it is the inevitable condition under which life in that fiction exists. It is certainly not solely an emotion, although Bowen's characters often talk of it in those terms, especially when they confront the sort of connivance Stella Rodney meets up with in *The Heat of the Day,* on the part of the sinister Harrison. Such calculation proves not to be love's opposite, how-ever, but at worst its "distortion," and quite possibly no more than one of love's powerful variant forms. The question, as it is framed by a character in the story "Summer Night," seems so simple—"what's love like?" But its answer proves so very nearly impossible to find or to articulate.

Love is certainly *not* easy; nor is it altogether clear that its force in human life is, even in the broadest sense, positive. The notion offered in *The House in Paris* (part 2, ch. 11) that "love is obtuse and reckless" finds ample verification elsewhere in Bowen's fiction. Love is, to Bowen's people, something like the "primitive need" discussed with apparent irony in *Eva Trout* (part 1, ch. 12). It is "devouring" (and thus oddly parallel to the outer world as Jeffries had seen it, so long before) and can be "balked" only "at peril." If so, for all its disruptive and threatening power, it offers at least one standard of order and predictability: that of the "narrow and fixed compulsion" which can be deduced or observed "inside the widest range of our instability" (*The Last September,* ch. 13).

Or love is a condition of being, a disposition, what Traherne calls "an

7. Bowen suggests that this is in part a racial predisposition when she argues for the importance of the Shelbourne Hotel as perhaps the only Irish "antithesis" to the "distress, miscarried projects, evanescent dreams and romantic gloom" which are more endemic to Ireland, or at least to the "reputation" of "we Irish" (*The Shelbourne Hotel,* ch. 1).

expectation and desire." Oddly enough, its force does not depend on the finding of a worthy object. It is thus that Bowen can say (quoting *As You Like It*) in the final words of *A World of Love,* "They no sooner looked but they loved." This is not because "they" (Jane Danby and a young man whom she has never met, and hardly even heard of) know or understand one another (although Bowen's lovers, like many another, are fond of the word and the notion of "knowing" the beloved fully), but because they— or at least Jane, whose mind has been a central focus of the whole novel— have "loved" all along. Desire, in other words, long precedes its object. That is one reason why love, especially in Bowen's novels, is so resistant to common sense; why so many of her lovers (especially the "innocent" Emmeline Summers in *To the North* and Portia Quayne in *The Death of the Heart*) fall for and remain in love with self-evident, indeed self-announcing cads, or with those with whom they are manifestly incompatible; even, like Stella Rodney, with villainous deceivers.

Love does not conquer all—far from it. But it takes on the character of "a very high kind of overruling disorder" which can outdo all other attributes of mind and soul. And thus its absence, the inability of a character to feel love, represents a distinctly painful condition of standstill and exclusion. Particularly love tends to override almost all of those realistic "readjustments" of mind and heart which, as Lady Waters proposes in *To the North* (ch. 8), constitute life, especially a sociable and social life.

In short, Bowen can say with a certainty only that love *is,* and is inescapable and immensely powerful, a defining element. To speak of it, to try to understand it, usually involves a language of human categories built upon standards of relationship, of friendship, and of passion. But applied with rigor, that very language falls victim to its own inherent confusions. Love needs no seeking (and indeed, if the experience of Sydney Warren and Lois Farquar is representative, it won't be successfully sought); it may even be so powerful as to need not defense but the effort, however ineffectual, of control, of reining, caging, housing through the work of memory and imagination. That is, perhaps, why the "world of love" so often enters in by way of a ghostly echo of the past; why, in other words, the work undertaken in *A World of Love* is more of an exorcism than it is a recovery of the past or even the imaginative union of past and present in which Queenie and Robinson walk in a timeless demesne.

"NOTHING can happen nowhere," Bowen announces, in a notebook entry included in part 2 of "Pictures and Conversations." Oddly enough, it seems that love can; or perhaps must. Especially in her fiction of the late 1930s and 1940s, Bowen's lovers again and again find themselves in the terribly homeless condition of Edward and Janet in *Friends and Relations* (part 3, ch. 4): "there is nowhere for us to be."[8] Especially amid the overcrowding and destruction of wartime London that placelessness is a literal fact; there is no privacy whatever to be found. In a trio of stories ("A Walk in the Woods," "Mysterious Kor," and "I Hear You Say So") dating from just before and during the war, the "displacement" is actual and lovers must wander abroad in public, where their paths cross those of a random assortment of others. The placelessness of Stella Rodney and Robert Kelway in *The Heat of the Day* is equally clear, albeit both more willful—they chose not to live together—and much less geographic than emotional, historical, and cultural.

Still, whenever Stella Rodney walks outside, she courts danger, most notably when she approaches a hellish "bar or grill"(*The Heat of the Day*, ch. 12), an establishment that seems to be utterly removed from both place and time: it "had no air of having existed before tonight," and it leaves Stella utterly lost ("I have no idea where we are!"). In that she resembles so many of Bowen's characters, often seen indoors but having no real "place": illicit lovers forced out of doors or into out of the way hotels; orphans temporarily in the care of relatives; visitors or tenants-at-will on large country estates; travelers, widows, divorcees, refugees whose very nationality is, like Bowen's own, contradictory and uncertain.

Such uncertainty makes "places loom large" for Bowen's characters, as she admits in part 2 of "Pictures and Conversations." By places Bowen certainly means houses, preferably (after the custom of the gentler classes in England and in Ireland) houses with names. One might again catalog types, each with its correlative in the various homes in Bowen's own life—Big Houses like Bowen's Court and its neighbors; seaside English villas of the sort where she and her mother lived; ample London houses in Regent's Park, where Bowen lived through the war. There is as well an array of London flats and country cottages, a scattering of vicarages, and

8. The idea, and perhaps the stories which enact it, has produced at least one step-child: Eudora Welty's fine story "No Place for You My Love," in the collection of stories, *The Bride of the Innisfallen and Other Stories,* which Welty dedicated to Bowen. Welty's story offers an intriguing variation on Bowen's theme. It deals with two "refugees" (northerners adrift in New Orleans) and describes a long (but on the whole rather genial) car-trip into the country south of that city. Like Bowen's stories, it is at some level "about" love; but just as the landscape is much more eccentrically lively than Bowen's usually is, so too the relationship between the two characters, while hardly clear-cut, is not so fraught with portent and pain as is so often the case in Bowen's work. The title story in Welty's collection—which has an Anglo-Irish setting and again concerns travel and love—also bears comparison to Bowen's work.

one or two English country places of various sizes. Any house built after about 1900 is more than likely not quite up to the mark, and complete modernity—the whole world evoked, with hostile irony, by the title of the story "Attractive Modern Houses"—is just about the absolute of un-livability.

Only one type of dwelling truly matters to Bowen; it is an Irish place, appearing most recognizably as Danielstown in *The Last September,* Mon-tebello in *The House in Paris,* and Mount Morris in *The Heat of the Day.* Many of these places do not exist physically at all. Montebello has been burned down in the Troubles; it lives only in the memory of one character, Karen Michaelis's affable Uncle Bill Bent. Similarly, the evocative house which dominates the consciousness of Mary in the story "The Happy Autumn Fields" is in effect entirely a structure of her imagination, the happy life she dreams there having been interrupted in part by what may be her own psychic visitation.

The places that *do* exist are girt around with danger; Danielstown, when we see it, is in its last year. Outside is the Troubled Irish society which will, on the abrupt last pages of the novel, burn the house down. Mount Morris is, as anyone can see, a white elephant, as likely to blight as to adorn the future life of young Roderick Rodney who unexpectedly inherits it. And it can be reached only rarely and with great difficulty, given wartime restrictions on travel to the "neutral" Irish Republic. Moreover, amid the apparently all-pervasive destructiveness of war, its future (like that of every-thing else) after 1942, when the novel mostly takes place, is very much in doubt. That very fragility may be a kind of virtue, especially in contrast with the horrible solidity of such places as Robert Kelway's Holme Dene, a "man-eating" house which cannot be sold or given away (*The Heat of the Day,* ch. 14). But it makes the good houses highly unreliable as homes— and indeed, for the characters nearest the center of each novel, they are not home at all, but only places that can at most be briefly visited.

But however distant, however much they endure only in memory and imagination, they work powerfully as reference points; all other places exist only as echoes, as replicas or conscious reconstructions of these Great Good Places. The imitation may be roughly successful—both Corunna Lodge and Batts Abbey in *Friends and Relations,* seem able to sustain human life and human love, to provide a habitation for kinships and affinities. But often the scene of family life is more like bitter parody, as at Holme Dene; or at Farraways in *To the North,* populated by a collection of rather sinister and certainly self-involved derelicts; or among the household of the damned who come together in a vacant mansion in "The Disinherited."

For good or ill, houses are alive; hardly a one ever appears in Bowen's fiction without being given a face capable of expression, eyes capable of watching. Even individual rooms have an eerie capacity for animate existence and for more than animate power. A room indeed has "a life of its own" ("Joining Charles")—and in a world of threatening death, that is part of the powerful magnetism of houses. But that too can be a problem, at least if the sibylline Matchett in *The Death of the Heart* (part 1, ch. 6) is right: "Unnatural living runs in a family, the furniture knows it, you be sure. Good furniture knows what's what." As that novel demonstrates, it is hard enough to be watched and judged by one's "innocent" wards; how much worse to be judged by one's furniture!

Sydney Warren (*The Hotel*, ch. 10) has a similarly unsettling thought when she imagines the possibility of looking inside such powerful "shelters": "I have often thought it would be interesting if the front of any house, but of an hotel especially, could be swung open on a hinge like the front of a doll's house." Sydney's image takes her into a world in which the structures which individuals seek as a way of escaping the surrounding darkness prove to have a terrible power:

> One could see [the inhabitants] so clearly, as living under the compulsion of their furniture—or the furniture they happen to have hired. It would seem very doubtful, I daresay, whether man were not, after all, made . . . for beds and dinner-tables and washstands, just to withstand the obligations all those have created.

It is a sardonic version of the notion raised more seriously in *The Death of the Heart* (part 3, ch. 1), when Bowen says of the Quayne house in Windsor Place that it is an "ideal mould for living." That apparently virtuous power may well be fatally at odds with the human, which rarely can stand up to the test of ideality. Or the power may simply be ineffective; certainly the lives of the Quaynes show clearly how mightily the human material can resist molding.

What houses may provide, if circumstances allow, is a locus of time, a place with a past (and with things which communicate that past) and thus with the promise of a future. One test of their virtue is the degree to which they have stayed consistently in the hands of one family, and therefore the degree to which they are the structural enactment of patterns of family and relationships, for however complex and even dangerous they may be, they are at least durable. But virtuous or not, houses in Bowen country have a powerful, nearly irresistible attractive force; they are each, like Danielstown in *The Last September* (ch. 8), "a magnet for [human] dependence." The most interesting of them, and those in which Bowen usually sets the bulk of her narrative, are places of complex enchantment.

In her essay "The Big House," reprinted in *The Mulberry Tree,* Bowen puts this element in its most positive light:

> When I visit other big houses I *am* struck by some quality that they all have—not so much isolation as mystery. Each house seems to live under its own spell, and that is the spell that falls on the visitor from the moment he passes in at the gates. The ring of woods inside the demesne wall conceals, at first, the whole demesne from the eye: this looks, from the road, like a *bois dormant,* with a great glade inside . . . [Having entered that glade] one takes the last reach of avenue and meets the faded, dark-windowed and somehow hypnotic stare of the big house . . . [which], in its silence, seems to be contemplating the swell or fall of its own lawns.

The note of possible threat, which is present even in eminently good places, is all the more predominant in the less ideal houses where Bowen's characters actually live. As we know, the *bois dormant* is a dangerous place, and the houses share the ambiguities of danger and meaning which haunt fairy tales. Or perhaps, if we want to look for a more purely literary ancestry, they derive from the Bower of Bliss which Spenser describes at such length in the twelfth canto of Book II of *The Faerie Queene:* "A place pickt out by choice of best alive, / That natures worke by art can imitate."

Bowen would surely reject the "lavish affluence" which Spenser sees in the Bower; as she is at pains to remind her readers, both in "The Big House" and in *Bowen's Court,* the houses she loves are not in fact so large, and are rarely prosperous enough to maintain even comfort, much less extravagance. But other aspects of the Bower recur through Bowen's fiction: the complex sense of enclosure, which involves both defense against external forces and the risk of exclusion of life; the fragility of wall and gate; and the mixture of seductive appeal with a sense of dangerous temptation.

It is fairer, in the end, to take these houses not as metaphors or settings but as active characters. One relatively short and self-contained example is the title story in Bowen's 1941 collection *Look at All Those Roses,* in which a "house in a sheath of startling roses" catches the eye of two lovers, Edward and Lou, who are on their way "home [to London] for the purely negative reason that there was nowhere else they could as cheaply go." The house sits in a peculiarly empty landscape: "There was nobody on the roads; perhaps there was nobody anywhere." The two lovers are, typically, rather mismatched. He is a married writer with a need for sociable environments. She is anxious, particularly about the risk of "displeasing Edward too far"; but something of a romantic as well: "Lou saw life in

terms of ideal moments"—of which, however, she "found few . . . in their
flat" in London.

Again exterior emptiness parallels exactly the inner landscape. This relationship, while it does technically have a place to be in a shared London
flat, is proceeding without any clear sense of destination. Like the "summer
country" seen from the road, the affair is "relentless, pointless, unwinding."
The oppression of time, weather, season, and travel all contribute to a
sense of imminent doom which is in fact an element of their affair, not
of the landscape. Lou and Edward live just at the edge of a "future [which]
weighed on them like a dull burden." So—for all the unpleasantness of
the long drive—they choose to "extend today," to keep moving.

But the car breaks down; the house becomes not just a striking visual
oddity, but a place where help might be found. From a nearer vantage
point, its mysteries only deepen:

> There stood the house, waiting. Why should a house wait? Most
> pretty scenes have something passive about them, but this looked like
> a trap baited with beauty, set ready to spring . . . . Each side of the
> path, hundreds of standard roses bloomed, over-charged with color,
> as though this were their one hour. Crimson, coral, blue-pink, lemon
> and cold white, they disturbed with fragrance the dead air. In this
> spell-bound afternoon, with no shadows, the roses glared at the
> strangers, frighteningly bright . . . . The blurred door was propped
> open with a bizarre object, a lump of quartz. Indoors was the dark,
> cold-looking hall. When they had come to the door they found no
> bell or knocker: they could not think what to do.

The very fecundity of the roses seems suspect; while the elements—"life,"
"cool," "darkness," so appealing on a hot, bright, dead summer afternoon
have gone just too far: from life into overripeness, from cool into cold.

Still, because of force of circumstance and because of the seductive
beauty of the house itself, the house must be entered. That entrance feels
very like an "intrusion"; but the two strange figures the couple meets
(mother and daughter, again) overcome even that sense of the proprieties.
The older woman—at first she seems "a moron"—welcomes them, but at
a more fundamental level ignores them. Like the deaf Queenie, she has a
personal world, an "occupying inner life" into which no intrusion is possible. The effect of this reintroduces the problem of place: "She must have
lost contact with the outer world completely: there was now nothing to
'place' her by."

Of course we are seeing all this through Lou's eyes. The mother, if we
judge only by her behavior rather than what Lou's distorting anxiety makes

of her, seems not so sinister. She offers advice and "unexpectedly clear directions" to the nearest village (Edward will have to walk the three miles). Politely but clumsily she invites Lou to stay: "Leave your wife here . . . Then she can have tea." For Lou, the courtesy is doubly problematic: she is not Edward's wife, and (like some anxiously possessive child) she "seldom let [Edward] out of her sight—her idea of love was adhesiveness." But there is really no way to say no, and the remainder of the story finds Lou alone, with her hosts.

She soon encounters "the nerve and core of the house": the daughter, Josephine, a cripple who lies "flat as a board, in a wicker invalid carriage." Her immobility links her to many of Bowen's most powerful and witchlike figures.[9] Here the possibility of magic is raised only by way of a joke; Lou laughingly accuses the girl—who admits that Lou is "the first new person I've seen for a year"—of having put a spell on the car. The girl has, however, an acute sense of what Lou most fears: the total loss of the now-absent Edward. The talk turns, necessarily, to moving and staying, volition and compulsion:

"When people go away they sometimes quite go," [Josephine] said.
"If they always come back, then what is the good of moving?"
"I don't see the good of moving."
"Then stay here."
"People don't just go where they want; they go where they must."
"Must you go back to London?"

9. For instance, Mme. Fisher in *The House in Paris* and Dinah Delacroix at the end of *The Little Girls*. In both cases the notion of witchcraft is made explicit. Karen, in a long interior monologue during her time with Max, accuses Mme. Fisher directly: "She is a woman who sells girls; she is a witch" (*The House in Paris,* part 2, ch. 9). *The Little Girls* is littered with references to *MacBeth,* and near the end of the novel Clare angrily if confusedly shouts at Dinah, "You enchantress' child!" and just a few lines later "Circe!" (*The Little Girls,* part 3, ch. 6). As with Bowen's ghosts—who have, on the whole, attracted more critical attention—the list of Bowen's witches and magicians is considerable and varied; a representative sampling would have to include Miss Murchison ("Daffodils"), the Lennicotts in "The Parrot"—a story which, like "Look at All Those Roses," seems at least indirectly indebted to "Goblin Market"); Ann Lee ("Ann Lee's"); Maria ("Maria"); Maximilian, who lives on "Medusa Terrace" ("No. 16"); the crippled Francis in "The Girl with the Stoop"; and both Mrs. Varley de Grey and her evil niece Ethel ("Hand in Glove"); as well as such figures in the novels as Mrs. Kerr (*The Hotel*), both Matchett and Anna Quayne (*The Death of the Heart*); Nettie, whose name suggests her potential for entrapment (*The Heat of the Day*); Antonia, Maud, and Lady Latterly (*A World of Love*); and Constantine Ormeau (*Eva Trout*). All have considerable power; all have a certain unavoidable appeal; all have distinct "places" within which they live and operate; all endeavor to influence and even to control the lives of others; all have a certain ability to talk persuasively (and often, by way of telling "the true story," narratively).

Elizabeth Bowen 113

"Oh, I have to, you know."
"Why?"

To which there is no real answer.

But to stay seems so dangerous, so questionable too. The parlour seems "gutted by too-intense living." The whole house is a place irrevocably marred by the past, for Josephine's no-longer-present father was in some unexplained way to blame for her paralysis. It is "an unlucky place" and "lonely," a place of utter entropy and negation: "Nothing more can happen." Increasingly, Lou feels not like a guest but a victim. Josephine again can see to the heart of Lou's anxiety: "She thinks if she eats, she may have to stay here for ever," like Proserpina in Hades, or like Lizzie, the weak sister whose resistance to the seductions of the supernatural is so terribly inadequate in Christina Rossetti's "Goblin Market."

In the end, taking Josephine out into the garden, Lou reaches a complicated point of stasis, by way of an imitation both of death and of Josephine:

> Lou lay down on the dry, cropped grass . . . shut her eyes and lay stretched, as rigid as Josephine . . . . Then slowly she relaxed. There is a moment when silence, no longer resisted, rushes into the mind. She let go, inch by inch, of life, that since she was a child she had been clutching so desperately—her obsessions about this and that, her obsession about keeping Edward. How anxiously she had run from place to place, wanting to keep everything inside her own power. I should have stayed still: I shall stay still now, she thought. What I want must come to me: I shall not go after it. People who stay still generate power . . . . I feel life myself now. No wonder I've been tired, only half getting what I don't really want. Now I want nothing; I just want a white circle . . . an ecstacy of indifference. She knew she was looking at nothing—then knew nothing . . .

That is, it seems, what it means—or what it costs—to stay still: a view into the heart of things, a view of the nothing that is so fundamentally and frighteningly there.

The very stability that houses seem to offer leads to a life, like that of Mme. Fisher and her daughter in *The House in Paris,* which is likewise stable, even permanent, and yet lonely and very nearly dead. To live in any enclosed place, any house-and-garden called "home," may involve the abandonment, as it has for Josephine's mother and as it would for Lou, of all "outside attachments—hopes, claims, curiosities, desires, little touches of greed." How appealingly that suggests relief—no more drive to know or to understand, no more of the search for the answer to dark secrets which lie near the heart of almost every one of Bowen's plots; no more desire (and thus none of the disorderly compulsion which accompanies love); no more of the obligations of kinship or duty which so clutter life with tasks to be done and actions to be expected.

It is no more and no less than the abandonment, if not of human existence itself, at least of those things which define and provoke it into being. Even the loveliest of Bowen's houses have this element of "disconnection" from life. Danielstown seems to suffer "a peculiar doom of exclusion" (*The Last September,* ch. 3). Mount Morris, when Stella Rodney visits it (*The Heat of the Day,* ch. 9), is a place beyond (or outside) time, utterly separate from (in far more than simply geographic terms) the London world of the actual—which is, however, also the "world of love" she and Robert Kelway inhabit. To find "home" has, for Bowen's displaced persons, an inevitable appeal, and one which carries an unmistakable resonance of moral correctness; but it has as well a contrasting, even a contradictory, fear—that to be "home" may mean to be alone, facing nothing and lacking even a sense of the character of the self.[10]

∗   ∗   ∗

10. At least, however, *The Heat of the Day* contains a vision of "home," and a sense that someone—Roderick, not Stella—can, should, and will live there. Whether life is truly possible at Montefort (*A World of Love*) is not so clear (the novel ends with several characters leaving, and with Jane Danby well outside its grounds); and neither of Bowen's last two novels involve any clear sense of "home" at all. *The Little Girls* is full of houses (many of them long gone, like St. Agatha's), but seems much more interested in outdoor caves and grottoes; Dinah's Applegate seems not a place to live in so much as a place to die in. Eva Trout does not have (and has never had) a "home"; the house she buys and furnishes, Cathay, is a sinister parody of a home; and after leaving there, she spends the last decade of her life moving from place to place. One of the elements of increasing doubt and darkness in Bowen's later fiction then, is a shifting of the balance: no longer can lives be lived and understood in the light of the countervailing (and in each case, highly complex) alternatives of "home" and "nowhere"—there is no more "home."

One can trace a similar path toward something like despair in the degree to which "rubble" replaces furniture in Bowen's last two novels. Dinah Delacroix is engaged in assembling a cave full of artifacts for some future archaeologist; her old school chum Clare has, in adulthood, become the proprietor of a chain of "Mopsie Pye" shops, which deal in high-class (and high-priced) jumble—antiques, arts-and-crafts, and the like; Clare's office is a cluttered warren (*The Little Girls,* part 3, ch. 1). Eva Trout is constantly buying "things" and arranging them around her inward emptiness; Cathay has, when she buys it, a great clutter of furniture (*Eva Trout,* part 1, ch. 7), on top of which she superimposes even more, all up-to-date (including, in 1959, a computer), but all apparently useless (part 1, ch. 10).

Bowen's predisposition to portray the world as a decaying house puts her, as Seamus Deane (*A Short History of Irish Literature,* pp. 203–6) reminds us, distinctly in the tradition of the Anglo-Irish "Big House" novel.

DESPITE its hazardous complexities, love is the invariable context, even the fundamental language of human relations in Bowen's fiction. Movement is the paradigmatic condition under which people live, the circumstance which both causes and threatens to end their encounters. Houses are the "stage" upon which encounters have their powerful effects—and at the same time the great hope, the dream or illusion or (to use words that occur with increasing frequency in her later fiction) the "hallucination," the "mirage" of repose, stability, and order. It is as if Bowen's characters must, in the end, choose between the rather airless spare room[11] of someone else's house or the front seat of a speeding vehicle; or as if their lives must be charted in terms of the alternation of the two. On the whole, vehicles are more risky—trips by lorry, car, and airplane result in catastrophe in any number of cases. If the entrapment of spare rooms is also potentially deadly, it is at least a slower death, and one involving the possibility of insight, even of escape. To see death at the limit of either alternative may be no more than a realization of the way things are— "Life, seen whole for a moment [so Lois Farquar decides in *The Last September*, ch. 24], was one act of apprehension, the apprehension of death."

But no matter how small and unprepossessing they may be, at the core of Bowen's fiction lie moments of choice: should Sydney Warren marry James Milton? Should Lois Farquar admit to her lover Gerald that she does not feel the emotional need which drives him? What is Jane Danby to do with the mysterious love letters she has found? The choices tend to breed more choices—if Dinah Delacroix chooses to seek out her old schoolmates (as she does), they in turn will have to choose whether to respond; and then all three will face the question of whether, quite literally, to dig up the past. And the choices often seem very much Hobson's: should Stella Rodney give in to the advances of the mysterious Harrison, thus protecting her lover Robert Kelway but perhaps destroying the supposed trust upon which that love is based; or should she refuse and thus risk yet another sort of dissolution of love, if Harrison's accusations against Kelway are at all true?

Stated this way, the questions show clearly Bowen's reliance upon the stuff of melodrama and of romantic comedy. But the decisions she presents

---

11. Although Bowen has an eye for drawing-rooms, other and less "public" areas of houses are even more important—back drawing-rooms, spare rooms converted into temporary bedrooms, attics remade into flats like Markie's in *To the North*. They represent the rather tentative hold which her characters have on home structures; and conversely, the effort of the human to "mold" the structural in contrast to the more usual flow of formative power, which works from place to (and on) person.

to her characters allow the possibility of formulating and acting upon intentions. Thus despite the power of external forces, Bowen persists in wondering to what degree notions of will, of ambition, of aspiration are at all relevant and viable, in an increasingly dissolute modern world. To explore that question she makes use, at least in her novels, really only of two plots. The first tells of a young woman of real intelligence and some "ambition," too full perhaps of a sense of her own inadequacy but with an equally active intention "to do something with [herself]" (*Eva Trout,* part 1, ch. 2). The result is likely at best to be the achievement of some point of balance "midway between defiance and resignation" (*The Hotel,* ch. 15), within a world in which "nothing ever works out the way one hoped" (*The Heat of the Day,* ch. 12).

The second plot, a variation upon the first, involves an older woman now relieved (or is it debarred?) by age or circumstance from facing with the same sense of inevitability and open-endedness the question "What will you do?" That prospective question is replaced by a retrospective one, still invoking matters of intention and result: "What did you do? And why? And to what effect?" One can roughly distinguish between those novels which are prospective—*The Hotel, The Last September,* and *Eva Trout* in particular—and those which are retrospetive, most notably *The Little Girls.* But the richest of Bowen's novels combine the two—in the lives of the widowed Cecilia and the "angelic" Emmeline (*To the North*), in the conflict between Portia Quayne and her half-sister-in-law Anna (*The Death of the Heart*), in the various parallels and imitations which link Stella Rodney with Louie (*The Heat of the Day*) and Jane Danby with her mother Lilia (*A World of Love*). Each plot invokes ghosts: the remembered figures of the past and the fearful ghosts of the future. What Bowen says (in a typically inverted sentence) of the Irish house in *A World of Love* (ch. 8)— "not memories was it but expectations which haunted Montefort"— could be said of many another place, and many another life, in her fiction.

The ghosts of expectation may, in the end, be worse than those of memory, because more prevalent and less recognizable. One can try to recover the precise details of the past—although the lesson of *The Little Girls* seems to be that such "digging" is extremely hazardous. But one can never with any accuracy determine the lineaments and character of the Something which is about to happen, although in a Bowen novel, like a Frank O'Connor story, one can say with some certainty that it will not quite match anyone's expectations. It is possible that the whole impulse to expect is the problem:

For people who live on expectations, to face up to their realization is something of an ordeal. Expectations are the most perilous form of dream, and when dreams do realize themselves it is in the waking world: the difference is subtly but often painfully felt.

(*The Death of the Heart,* part 2, ch. 5)

But expectation is also precisely what determines intention, what gives shape and character and force to it; the future as much as the past defines the present, which is why the "futurelessness" of life in wartime London in *The Heat of the Day* or in more recent times of living under the shadow of "the last bang" (*The Little Girls*) is so intolerable.

Karen Michaelis, in the first (and, as it happens, the last) weeks of her affair with Max Ebhart, reaches a moment of apparent, if fluid, equilibrium:

She found she had come to hope everything of change. Her expectation that other Mays would be different gave this May, like a tree
in front of a cloud, a fragility, or made it the past now. In her parents'
world, change looked like catastrophe, a thing to put a good face on:
change meant nothing but loss . . . . You lived to govern the future,
bending events your way. If change did break in, you bowed and
accepted it. In such a world, . . . her mind had always been very clear,
with few dreads, though she saw enough to be thankful to be so safe.

(*The House in Paris,* part 2, ch. 7)

Such "hope" drives her to think of "her home, their [hers and Max's] new house" and to begin looking for furniture. It is of course a false hope, if one is to judge it by the standard of realization; she and Max will never share more than a hotel room. But it contains an accurate sense of the power and even the shape of the future, since it includes a child who is remarkably like the son they will have, and whom in fact we have already met in the novel.

To speak of intention without invoking ideas of expectation seems, after all, impossible. But in Bowen's fiction the two elements are commonly at war. Each demands a different kind of response: intention breeds action, expectation breeds watching and waiting to see which particular "some-thing" (or "nothing") happens. Only a child or a total innocent would presume that intention and expectation will or should coincide. Thus the war is especially intense, and especially paradigmatic, in the minds and lives of children and "innocents"—central characters in many of Bowen's most substantial pieces of fiction.

Children are to Bowen creatures of great willfulness, and of an especially developed sense of emotional power:

There is no limit to the terror strange children feel of each other, a terror life obscures but never ceases to justify. There is no end to the violations committed by children on children, quietly talking alone.

(*The House in Paris,* part 1, ch. 2)

Because children live in a psychological world in which "absence blots people out" (*The Death of the Heart,* part 2, ch. 2), their attachments are all the more adhesive, their effort to defend such attachments all the more desperate and even violent, their sense of betrayal all the more acute. And because their only true test of reality is visual, they are preternaturally careful and relentless watchers. They have imagination without memory. Thus their capacity for fantasy is especially great—and in the end, "Fantasy is toxic" ("Afterword," *Bowen's Court*). They are usually[12] saved from being poisoned only by their powerlessness—they combine hope (or expectation) and desire with an almost total lack of potency, except by way of words and psychic manipulations.

All this applies equally to the older "innocents"—Emmeline Summers, Portia Quayne, Louie Lewis, Jane Danby, and Eva Trout—who are the complicating centers of so many of Bowen's novels. Like children, these women evoke the desire in others to intervene; they are thus especially susceptible to the problematic ministrations of witches and other adults. They tend, like Emmeline Summers, to display, at least initially, "ignorance . . . open-mindedness . . . [and] docility" (*To the North,* ch. 9). Their ignorance does not prevent them from being careful observers; like Portia Quayne in her diary, they can record far more than they understand. They are, again like Portia, "holy anomal[ies]" (*The Death of the Heart,* part 1, ch. 7), perilously close in their actions and appearance to the "wicked" (part 1, ch. 8). They are not infrequently victims of people like Anna Quayne, into whose care Portia is given, who admits "how much innocence she herself had corrupted in other people" (*The Death of the Heart,* part 1, ch. 3).

But the innocent are not *only* victims; in fact, within the confines of the anything-but-innocent world of the usual the effects of innocence are violent. Because the innocent especially lack the ability or the desire to make human readjustments, when they act, they can become terrible figures, like Emmeline Summers, seen here through the eyes of her lover Markie:

---

12. But by no means always: Bowen's roster of children include at least one murderer ("Telling") and several who cause real and considerable pain: the awful Hermione in "The Easter Egg Party," the schoolgirls in "Daffodils," the little girl in "Coming Home."

She had . . . stepped . . . clear of the every-day, of conduct with its guarantees and necessities, into the region of the immoderate, where we are more than ourselves. Here are no guarantees. Tragedy is the precedent. Tragedy confounding life with its masterful disproportion. Here figures cast unknown shadows; passion knows no crime, only its own movement; steel and the cord go with the kiss. Innocence walks with violence; violence is innocent, cold as fate . . .

(*To the North,* ch. 23)

The link to violence, even to evil, is not always so directly drawn, so inevitable. Portia Quayne's doing "violence" to the moderate lives of Thomas and Anna seems on the whole positive—although the openness of the novel's ending leaves moot the question of who, if anyone, has been changed by prolonged proximity to innocence, whether the death of the heart is the disease which has been cured by Portia, or the fate which she has suffered. But throughout Bowen's fiction, the innocent possess a power of the sort the novelist St. Quentin[13] defines not as an anomaly but as something fundamental:

I swear that each one of us keeps, battened down inside himself, a sort of lunatic giant—impossible socially, but full-scale—and it's the knockings and batterings we sometimes hear in each other that keeps our intercourse from utter banality. Portia hears these the whole time; in fact she hears nothing else.

(*The Death of the Heart,* part 3, ch. 6)

It is the distinction of Bowen's last, and darkest, novel to have as its title character and subject just such a giant, the innocent—and indeed, in a complex way, selfless—Eva Trout, of whom it is, quite fairly, said "You leave few lives unscathed" (*Eva Trout,* part 2, ch. 3).

St. Quentin's metaphor and Eva Trout's peculiar nature point us back to perhaps the most maddeningly fluid of all landscapes in Bowen's fiction: the self. Again, children are a primary reference point; what fascinates Bowen is their often desperate work of self-definition (and thus of the creation of a world around the self). But this is not so much a distin-

---

13. He seems to be assigned the role of devil in the novel, a label prompted by the title of the third part of *The Death of the Heart.* If so, he is a genial and even sensible devil; and much of what he says about "style" and "illusion" in art have often been taken as representing Bowen's own views. And he seems to be able to see and to tell the truth—but that, in fact, is often an attribute Bowen assigns to figures who otherwise resemble the Father of Lies.

guishable chronological stage or crisis as a persistent condition, to which even adults revert under stress of circumstances. Those few adults who seem, even momentarily, to succeed in this task are aberrations, like the deaf Queenie in "Summer Night," whose handicap allows her to live comfortably within her own "sphere of silence" or the "mad" Cousin Nettie in *The Heat of the Day,* who has chosen a life of timeless self-enclosure within a carefully arranged room in an English house-turned-asylum.

To children, to those who have grown beyond childhood, even to those who may seem to have escaped the whole problem of human identity, the question young Henrietta asks in *The House in Paris* (ch. 1) remains insistent, and seems to grow all the more unanswerable: "Who am I?" A little learning may help deflect the question's point somewhat—to move it at least from the psychic to the intellectual sphere: "That I'm I is just a romantic fallacy" (*The Death of the Heart,* part 2, ch. 5). But that is small consolation indeed. "How inconceivable oneself is" Eva Trout's former teacher Iseult says (*Eva Trout,* part 1, ch. 8)—not just unimaginable, unknowable, but impossible to generate, to give birth to.

The perilous feeling of nonexistence is present in Bowen's novels from the beginning, from the second chapter of *The Hotel,* where Sydney Warren translates the apparent indifference of her friend Mrs. Kerr into something far worse:

> If she did not exist for Mrs. Kerr as a tennis-player, in this most ordinary, popular of her aspects, had she reason to feel that she existed at all? . . . The possibility of not being kept in mind seemed to Sydney [at] that moment, a kind of extinction.

It is the obverse of the child's fear that his edge of visibility is, for others, the edge of existence itself; here *to be seen* is for Sydney the necessary defining act. But as we are told a little later, "one's own visibility is impossible to calculate" (*The Hotel,* ch. 6); indeed it is a measurement of the self which the individual—despite the prevalence of mirrors and other reflecting surfaces throughout Bowen's work—can never adequately undertake for her/himself.

This does not of course prevent individuals from trying, and especially from seeking out others, thus placing themselves within a world of social interactions. When someone else sees them, names them, describes them, recognizes them, even accuses them—then they can be sure (momentarily) that they exist. But even that reassurance becomes increasingly unavailable in Bowen's later novels, where the possibility that the individual does *not* in fact exist in any truly particular way surfaces again and again; as Stella puts it in *The Death of the Heart,* "everybody's horribly alike" (ch. 7), a sentiment that Dinah Delacroix echoes at the very beginning of *The Little Girls* (part 1, ch. 3).

Indeed, the whole of *The Little Girls* seems to address a question which Dinah raises at the outset: "What really expresses people?" That is, in its way, Eva Trout's puzzle as well; she desires at the very least to find some way to imitate life, and so she tries to acquire those elements which seem usually to define it: a house, a child, a husband. On the surface—where Dinah despairingly suspects the only true variety, the only individuation, exists—Eva succeeds: she buys and furnishes a grand house, adopts a child, cajoles a young man into a charade-marriage. But all that does nothing to correct the radical emptiness deeper down.

Even before Bowen reaches that bleak end-point, she offers many an instance of the resistance which both human nature and the world as a whole offer to the mind that would recognize itself. To begin with, she and so many of her characters are displaced, in terms of family and culture; as outsiders they can never easily, and perhaps never fully, know the fundamental language of word and gesture which prevails within any defined and defining social world. If, as is particularly the case in *A World of Love,* the ghosts of the past are also the ghosts of the future, and both are abroad upon the world of the present, even placement in time will not help one understand clearly and fully.

Bowen's devices of style and form increasingly replicate this resistance. Her sentences, in their length and frequent indefiniteness, resist the reader, her use and violations of the standard rules of such popular genres as the mystery story and the spy-novel provoke a desire to know and then deny the reader the final clue, the courtroom scene or confrontation in which all is told at last. Her novels rarely "end" and when, as in *To the North* and *Eva Trout,* they do, it is likely to be with an improbable lurch into sheer melodrama. Even in terms of plot, "something" is still "about to happen." If these are occasional annoyances to the reader, they are at least congruent with the fundamental nature of life as Bowen intends to describe it.

But if opaque, her novels are never shapeless. In fact they are full of architectural arrangements, of patterns of defining parallels and echoes, of "pairings" at the metaphorical level which are much more persistent than the romantic or marital pairings which make up the plot. It may be that we are to find an element of hope in this, a rounding by the entirety of the novel into some wholeness which is long denied to any individual character. Thus, to take only one example, the whole of *The Last September* defines a completed process; the three parts are entitled "The Arrival of . . ."; "The Visit of . . ."; "The Departure of . . ." But in the case of individuals the process is much less clear; and so the titles each invoke a different human part of the social world of Danielstown: "The Arrival *of Mr. and Mrs. Montmorency*"; "The Visit *of Miss Norton*"; "The Departure *of Gerald.*" All three parties, of course, visit; all three arrive or have already arrived when the novel begins; all depart (necessarily, since on the novel's final page Danielstown is burned to the ground). But in no individual case does the transit of three stages result in the sense of completion which the architecture of the novel seems to suggest may be the pattern of the social organism of Danielstown as a whole.

Bowen's plots almost invariably betray a predilection for mathematical patterns, for proliferations of twos and threes, of symmetries in uneasy proximity to asymmetries. This may be yet another reflection of Bowen's indebtedness to a tradition of elaborately artificial comedy of manners. But the element of pattern is of fundamental importance to Bowen. The symmetries and balances within the world of a particular novel are just as evident and just as prevalent as the asymmetries, isolations, and disruptions in the lives of individual characters, major and minor. If there is a hope to be found, a counterweight that can resist, if not quite balance (and certainly not override), the darkness that is both outside and within the self, it is to be found in *pattern*, which provides the possibility of meaning, if not always of comfort.

The peculiar horror of Stella Rodney's life as we see it in *The Heat of the Day*, for instance, is crystallized in her perception of a loss even greater than the loss of her lover. Speaking to Harrison, the "third" whose entry into her pairing with Robert Kelway has proven so disastrous, she insists:

> Were you, then, somehow, love's necessary missing part? You brought that into us, if you killed him. But now, you and I are no longer two of three. From between us some pin has been drawn out: we're apart. We're not where we were—look, not even any more in the same room. The pattern's been swept away, so where's the meaning?
>
> (*The Heat of the Day*, ch. 16)

Stella's outcry combines a new knowledge of the pattern which *had* existed with a terrible sense that her understanding will not provide an orientation for the present or the future. She couches her point in terms of love, of a mathematics of two and three, and implicitly in terms of a jigsaw puzzle. Patterns, and especially the sort of patterns which can be represented by puzzles, often take on this peculiar ambiguity, this sense of a gain in understanding leading not so much to a final "meaning" as to an emotional loss. And all too often whatever pattern exists is invisible to those whose lives fall within it. Or, more painfully still, the pattern may be apparent only in the lives of others. Still, as with travel and love, no experience of its difficulty, its pain, its ineffectuality (in practical terms) will suppress this desire for a defining order. As Lois Farquar puts it, "I like to be in a pattern . . . I like to be related; to have to be what I am. Just to *be* is so intransitive, so lonely" (*The Last September*, ch. 12). That desire seems universal in Bowen's people and, as her career proceeds, moves from a liking into something much less gentle: "The strongest compulsions we feel throughout life are no more than compulsions to repeat a pattern: the pattern is not of our own device" (*The Death of the Heart,* part 2, ch. 4).

The discovery and even the repetition of pattern depends upon memory, or at least upon the availability of a past. It may result from conscious study and observation—as it does for Bowen herself, who finds in the history of her family and house a pattern of which they were unconscious but which can, in her articulation of it, survive both the devastation of wartime London and ultimately the physical destruction of the house itself ("Afterword," *Bowen's Court*). Her Dinah Delacroix, an amateur archaeologist, proceeds in a similar way. But pattern may simply show itself in an unconscious, unexplained devotion to places which, for instance, marks the Naylors of Danielstown in *The Last September*. Their lives rest less upon any historical awareness than on the lively persistence of social and sociable habits, a sense of home and order that can accommodate the unexpected. For Sir Richard Naylor, "visitors took form gradually in his household, coming out of a haze of humor, and seemed but lightly, pleasantly superimposed on the vital pattern till a departure tore great shreds from the season's texture" (*The Last September,* ch. 16).

Within such lives there is an effective "dependence upon the usual" (*Friends and Relations,* part 3, ch. 6) rooted in and expressed by houses, and the things they contain; thus do places and things preserve, record, instantiate a past and the habitual order which derives from that past, which is again what makes them so centrally important, so centrally *orienting* in Bowen's fiction. To be "homeless"—that is, to be without a house—is thus a dissociation from time itself. That is different from the beneficent timelessness that Stella Rodney sees at Mount Morris, which includes and defeats time, rather than simply avoiding it altogether. Instead of a futureless (and pastless) day-by-day, timelessness of the good sort provides a fusion of past, present, and future, and thus accepts (and overrules) time on its own terms.

But Lois Farquar wants a pattern of relationship, not just of place; and the patterns that dominate Bowen's fiction are social. They rest upon complex but definable relationships of family—the uses and limitations of which are peculiarly the subject of the novel *Friends and Relations*. Even the most displaced of her orphans still have ties of cousinship upon which to rely. Family relations can of course be quite horrible; but at least they are *there* as a body of defining terms. Yet as both *Friends and Relations* and *The House in Paris* powerfully show, the world of love can only with great difficulty be mapped in terms of family; the pattern, itself a product of desire, even compulsion, is too often radically at odds with desire, the lunatic giant which makes men and women lovers.

There is a still larger pattern, that of "society" itself, whether it is seen in polite hotels, seaside resorts, country weekends, or city houses. Even in the lost world of wartime London, a pattern is visible—typically, Stella can see it only by way of her son: "She could perceive, too, that Roderick was ready to entertain a high, if abstract, idea of society . . . Yes, what he liked about people was the order in which they could be arranged" (*The Heat of the Day*, ch. 3). Such visions do not, however, produce any permanent reassurance. Roderick's "idealization of pattern," however appealing, at the same time "alarm[s]" Stella, in part because it seems so unlikely to withstand an adult view of things, which necessarily will cause him to be "confronted by people . . . patternlessly doing what they liked."

The ideal pattern must be social because it must accommodate human lives, must encompass and provide a language of gesture and manners by which the evanescent self may be "expressed" and seen, and must include the order of houses and families as well as the disorders of love. One might also add that, to Bowen, it must be social because she is, at bottom, an unabashed snob, as the frequency and judgmental force with which the word "vulgar" enters into her fiction will readily show. But she is not *only* a snob; nor does her sense of the ideal pattern of society prevent her from seeing the absurdity which marks actual society, and which she is at pains to include in her fiction, sometimes comically, sometimes with a more somber purpose.

The saving social pattern must be abstract precisely because the actual so often contradicts it; any concrete portrayal of social encounter is much more likely to display patternlessness and individual compulsion. Society in its virtuous form, then, is precisely analogous to art; both are illusions—"life-illusions" in fact—and both are necessary:

> Not for nothing do we invest so much of ourselves in other people's lives—or even in momentary pictures of people we do not know. It cuts both ways: the happy group inside the lighted window, the figure in the long grass in the orchard seen from the train stay and support

us in our dark hours. Illusions are art, for the feeling person, and it
is by art that we live, if we do.

(The Death of the Heart, part 1, ch. 7)

It is just such "momentary [or at least, in terms of the actual course of a
human life, quite brief] pictures of people we do not know" that constitute
the stuff of Bowen's own novels, full of groups behind lighted windows
and solitary figures in orchards and gardens. These "pictures" do their
work of orientation in exactly the way in which Roderick's "patterned"
life works for Stella: they do not make a map but provide a reassurance
of the real world.

Although several novelists appear in Bowen's fiction, and several important diarists besides,[14] the writer, the maker of patterned verbal fictions,
is at most only one instance of a larger group of world inventors, which
may encompass all "feeling persons" and certainly includes especially the
child and the innocent, both especially prone to invent worlds not so much
by action as by consciousness, as when young Leopold constructs a meeting with his mother:

[It] could take place only in Heaven—call it Heaven; on the plane
of potential not merely likely behavior. Or call it art, with truth and
imagination informing every word. Only there—in heaven or art, in
that nowhere on that plane—could Karen have told Leopold what
had really been.

(The House in Paris, part 2, ch. 1)

Such work of the imagination is to Bowen essential, and is most importantly demonstrated by way of images of pictorial representation. For
all their talk, Bowen's characters rely much more on looking; observation
is always more rewarding and more informative than any listening could
be, especially in the social world of euphemism and guarded language in
which Bowen sets her stories. If art is the final hope, the final reassurance,
the final making or discovery of pattern, it seems to derive less from the

14. Indeed, the explicit "novelists" in Bowen's fiction are not an especially admirable lot.
They range from the rather enervated Laurence in *The Last September* and the docile Clifford
Perry-Dunton in "A Love Story: 1939," both of whom are at most proto-writers; to the
unreliable Eddie in *The Death of the Heart,* with one novel under his belt; to the very
ambiguous St. Quentin (*The Death of the Heart*), his near-relations Mr. Lennicott in the
early story "The Parrot," and the parodistically Jamesian Maximilian Bewdon in "No. 16,"
none of whom seem to approach anything like a heavenly state.

ability to tell stories[15] than from the talent—if that is the word for it—
which Dinah Delacroix has, "to picture everything in advance. It's by
picturing things that one lives" (*The Little Girls,* part 1, ch. 4).

Dina's own story suggests, however, that the life-illusion really is unavailable. Dinah proves incapable of accurately picturing things in advance,
and pictures enter into that novel, and *Eva Trout* as well, only to suggest
their irrelevance to things as they now are. Eva wanders in the National
Portrait Gallery (part 2, ch. 3)—which is a place of pattern, but only in
the worst way: it is a "labyrinth" where she finds no reassurance but mere
"Images. 'Nothing but a pack of cards'?—not quite, but nearly enough
that to defeat Eva." And Dinah and her friends repeatedly encounter a
drawing of the Old High Street of the seaside town where their school
is, which at first stands up well to the test of the actual (*The Little Girls,*
part 2, ch. 4) but which becomes only a reminder of the utter falsity of
the present (part 3, ch. 2). Against this despairing realization Bowen can
propose only the perverse importance of *bad* art. Discussing how and why
pictures lie, Clare asks whether the painting of the High Street "would
be a worse lie if it were a better picture?" To which comes the answer:

> Oh, yes . . . Because this poor chap has at least only been trying to
> portray what he thought he saw . . . and, as we see, beyond getting
> the details correct, he didn't see much, and what he did see he didn't
> see right. But if he'd been a bit better then he'd have waded in and
> started portraying or trying to portray what he thought he felt; and
> as we know, what anyone thinks they [sic] feel is sheer fabrication.

Although art is still a life-illusion, there is a sinister weight on the
distance between life and illusion, the inadequacy of thought and perhaps
even of feeling and its articulation. The same note of unreliability is
sounded in terms of fiction, not painting, in *Eva Trout,* which bristles with
references, direct and indirect, to writers (Dickens, James, Lawrence,
Proust, Flaubert, Ibsen, Zola, Browning) and to a variety of narrative
forms (fairy tale, opera, film, romance), no one of which, nor all put
together, can help clarify either the novel's point or its structural disarray.
But the life-illusion has, all along, been a slender reed. As illusion, it is
perilously close to fantasy and hallucination of the sort to which Robert
Kelway falls victim in *The Heat of the Day.* In that sense, even the despair

15. Although this is, again, in part the power—or the duty—of many of her witches,
good and bad. They know and tell what happened, as Matchett does in *The Death of the
Heart* and as Mme. Fisher does in *The House in Paris;* and they do so over the objection of
other "adults," who seem either unwilling to face the truth or convinced that the young and
the innocent must be protected from the knowledge which the story of the past contains.

which juxtaposition of illusion against reality generates in *The Little Girls* can have a powerful virtue: it can be a corrective in the blending of truth and imagination, of the actual and the ideal, which appears more positively (although not, in any immediate sense, more reassuringly) in Leopold's act of creation.

WE CAN easily enough, given the world of Bowen's fiction, understand Stella Rodney's asking "why does one do anything?" (*The Heat of the Day,* ch. 17). The persistence of human action, even in the face of repeated evidence of futility, is a kind of heroism, perhaps the only commonly available sort to Bowen's characters. Any belief in order is, in the world she describes, at its best an illusion, at its worst a toxic fantasy or a crippling hallucination. The challenge which Portia Quayne issues to her guardians, and which other innocent and displaced souls invariably present to the world, is to do "the right thing" (*The Death of the Heart,* part 3, ch. 6). That in turn, according to the wise Major Brutt, resolves into "not a question of doing the best you can do, . . . [but] a question of doing the only thing possible" (part 3, ch. 5). In either case the demand is for action, but action must follow an exploration of consciousness—for how else may "rightness" or even "possibility" be defined, and then applied to actual human relations, actual and demanding and passionate human obligations?

Bowen can portray that exploration of consciousness, and the actions it may lead to, only within certain recognizable limits of time, place, and social class. The repetitiousness, in large things and small, of Bowen's fiction may in the end be a sign of the limitation of her imagination; it is fair to say that she simply cannot convincingly imagine a world without furnished drawing rooms.[16] Certainly her most deeply felt image of the foreseeable end of the world is the abandonment, dismantling, bombing, or burning down of just such a structure. But one can at least argue that

---

16. Bowen's infrequent ventures into the minds and voices of the lower classes have their defenders. Matchett in *The Death of the Heart* strikes Hermione Lee as "daringly unnatur-alistic" (*Bowen: An Estimation,* p. 115)—although the novel itself prefers to call Matchett "natural." The factory girl Louie in *The Heat of the Day* seems to Edwin Kenney to be the only figure in that novel who is "saved" (*Elizabeth Bowen,* p. 75). There are a very few smaller instances—the voice who speaks the monologue "Oh, Madam—"; the two Dublin women whose conversation makes up another wartime story, "Unwelcome Idea"; the long-suffering Mrs. Cadman whose dying sister suffers from "A Queer Heart"; the murdered cook, a lively ghost, in "The Cheery Soul." Of the vulgar middle classes there are far more examples; but they are, or at least pretend to be, more truly "housed" and thus more like unconscious (but on Bowen's part, altogether intentional) parodies of the "society" which, for all its faults and pettiness, represents perhaps the only possible repository of saving pattern.

by focusing so persistently on the moneyed upper-middle-class, Bowen—like Austen and James, whose names must inevitably arise in any consideration of Bowen's accomplishment—chooses a social context in which issues of intention and power, of the nature and limits of the individual mind and will, can be approached directly and centrally. If the word "innocence" is to have any application other than the purely ironic, it can do so, in Bowen's terms, only in the social haven of genteel life.

And so her attention, like that of Henry James, turns especially to children and unmarried women without independent wealth; people whose "power" is, within the confines of a relatively privileged and thus empowered class, doubtful and limited. That precariousness, in turn, makes all the more direct and painful the conflict in Bowen's work between aspiration and expectation, on the one hand, and the relentless forces of dissolution, on the other. Bowen's indebtedness to a long tradition of novels of manners (usually, but not always comic novels) is quite evident; but so too is her effort to put that tradition to the tests of artistic use and of moral assessment at a time when manners—and more to the point, the entire system of moral values, social order, and human relationships from which manners derive—seems to be either utterly gone or utterly futile. One might say that her work is, from beginning to end, an effort to write the modern *tragedy* of manners. The task may often be self-defeating; but the body of her fiction—from the opening page of a story called "Breakfast," where a character announces "I die daily," to the final paragraphs of *Eva Trout,* where a child is prevented only by the reflex of a bystander from falling over a dead body—has, at its heart, an unwavering vision of mortality, and of the complex ways in which it may at almost the very same instant result from and assuage the pain of human love.

4

SEAN O'FAOLAIN

The Cave of Loneliness

IN HIS perceptive and genial chapter on Elizabeth Bowen in *The Vanishing Hero,* Sean O'Faolain describes her as "a romantic up against the despotism of reality" and quickly adds, "so are many other Irish writers." He himself must surely be counted among them. During the busy first decade of his writing career, the struggle between romantic aspiration and despotically real disappointment is fought within the context of revolution and a Civil War which ended in the establishment of what O'Faolain and others had dreamed of, the Ireland of De Valera. In retrospect the Civil War seemed, to O'Faolain, to enact the utter defeat of the idealism which had attracted him to the Republican side and the triumph—to use a bitterly ironic word for it—of a "modern Ireland [characterized by] sectarianism, puritanism, middle-class vulgarity, canting pietism, [and] narrow orthodoxies" (*The Irish,* "The Rebels"). How, and whether, to live in that world are the questions which haunt him; and the appeal of exile is great indeed. But perhaps because "dis-bloody-well-illusionment" (he uses the phrase both in "No Country for Old Men" and in "Before the Daystar") seems so all-encompassing and inescapable, the path of exile proves to be no answer at all.

After World War II the time and events of the Irish Civil War largely disappear from O'Faolain's fiction, as do the political rebels who populate the earlier stories, novels, and biographies, but not because O'Faolain had somehow solved the complex problem that had for so long concerned him. The "revolution" would occupy a central and still puzzling place in his autobiography, *Vive Moi!,* and in a novel which was never finished, a portion of which constitutes the story "No Country for Old Men." Nor did he abandon his effort to define in fictional terms the moral and cultural state of Ireland. But it is at least fair to say that this diagnosis becomes less predominant in his work. Later, it is the larger questions at issue beneath the political and historical surface in his earlier writing that move to the center of his fiction: how the self is defined and maintained, how the calculus of individual nature and circumstance is played out in human lives, how the forces of imagination and realistic observation, memory, faith, and passion operate under the usual circumstances of human life. In his effort to explore these questions O'Faolain continued to find in Ireland an especially complex and rich testing-ground, a country where, he argues, "no man's life is simple" and where "to 'make do' demands a more supple and a more human technique of living than elsewhere" (*An Irish Journey,* part 2).

In the opening pages of "Midsummer Night Madness," at the very beginning of the first of O'Faolain's collections of stories, a young Cork-onian called by the author's own given name, John, experiences a moment of great and continuing significance in O'Faolain's fiction:

> For a second I looked back into the city, down through the smoke at the clustered chimney-pots and roofs on whose purples and greens and blues the summer night was falling as gently as dust, falling too on the thousand tiny beacons winking and blinking beneath me to their starry counterparts above. It was just the curfew hour and the last few laggard couples went hurrying past me, their love-making ended abruptly for the night, lest the Tans in their roaring Lancia patrol-cars should find them conspicuous on the empty white streets of the city. Then I turned to the open fields and drew in a long draught of their sweetness, their May-month sweetness, as only a man could who had been cooped up for months past under one of those tiny roofs, seeing the life of men and women only through a peep-hole in a window-blind, seeing these green fields only in the far distance from an attic skylight. Mounting my bicycle I left the last gas-lamp behind, and the pavement end, and rode on happily into the open country.
>
> Yet, though the countryside was very sweet to me after all those months among the backyards, worried and watchful lest I should run into a chance patrol or raiding party, I kept listening, not to the chorus of birds, not to the little wind in the bushes by the way, but nervously to every distant, tiny sound . . .[1]

1. Young John's angle of view, which O'Faolain repeats within a few pages, recurs again and again, especially in his early stories and his first three novels. In *Vive Moi!* (ch. 7) O'Faolain identifies the autobiographic roots of young John's vision—it is what can be seen from the spot where young Sean walked out with the girl he would, years later, marry, a walk which takes him toward "the hillock outside Inchageelah, always afterward to be my mark of arrival in the true West."

Although O'Faolain did in time learn to restrain his tendency to indulge in rather extended and even florid scene-painting, he never lost his taste for vistas—one of the clearest traces of that Romanticism (in this case, rather of the Wordsworthian variety) which he is often willing to acknowledge in himself.[2] But Johnny's Janus-view back and forward is much more than a stylistic tic, or even an obsessively persistent bit of memory. It is in fact a topographical enactment of a conflict of loyalties and intentions which is at the heart of all of O'Faolain's fiction; and Johnny's position—apparently ready to leave (and with good reason) but in fact still irremediably attached to the place he has left—is a characteristic one for O'Faolain's protagonists.

In this instance, behind and below (the hint of hellishness is not accidental) lies Cork, for O'Faolain as for Frank O'Connor the most representative (one might even say symptomatic) place in Ireland. Ahead and above lies the open country (and, if it is west, the truly, unequivocally, never-Anglicized Ireland where O'Faolain as a young man went to learn Gaelic). That way lies an apparent escape from an attic room, the sort of enclosure abounding in Cork, a "tight little city" (*Bird Alone,* part 3, ch. 5; *Come Back to Erin,* part 2, ch. 2) full of "lean, long suffocating *clausuras* of seclusion, smugness, and security . . . [of] mental suffocation and total resistance to all new ideas" (*Vive Moi!,* ch. 8).

Viewed from within the attic the city had shouted an unequivocal message: the necessity of escape, of permanent exile: "Never come back!" (*An Irish Journey,* part 2). But at the precise point where exile begins, the city's iconic message seems to change. The roofs which had "cooped" John and blocked his view out toward the countryside take on a seductive beauty.

---

2. In his preface to *The Finest Stories of Sean O'Faolain,* O'Faolain tries to write off the romanticism that was the particular, and predictable, mark of his early writing. In *Vive Moi!* (ch. 12) he says almost apologetically, "I think I have always been a romantic with a hopeless longing for classical order." As with many of the dichotomies he sets up, O'Faolain is unwilling wholeheartedly to accept one pole, searching instead for a possible balance or synthesis. Thus he resists "sentimentality" and "sentimentalism"—concepts which, like "ambition," always carry a heavy negative charge in his writing. Thus too he admires, in the chapter on Maupassant in *The Short Story,* that writer's "realism . . . cleansed of all romantic impurities." But in that chapter his account of the conflict of romanticism and realism is centered around his utter rejection of naturalism; Zola is the great villain of the piece, and Zola's method, far from being "realistic," is precisely, to O'Faolain, "what romanticism becomes." Whether romanticism and realism—in O'Faolain's terms—can satisfactorily come together in one work remains in doubt. In *Vive Moi!* (ch. 14) he accuses "anyone who wants realism plus romance" of "doublethink," and accounts both *A Nest of Simple Folk* and *Bird Alone* as to some degree failures deriving from the effort to bring the two elements together. But "doublethink" may not be an utterly damnable trait, especially to a writer who is so fascinated by doubleness and the dialectic conflict of radically opposing views.

The city which had seemed a place of death now appears to achieve some sort of healing union with nature, in which night can fall gently and calmly. Cork for a moment seems full of light and color and even—in the shape of the laggard couples—of human passion. We might easily forget the smoke, the dust, the emptiness. Fortunately perhaps, John knows those things too well; and can see too well the particular historical circumstance which intensifies the city's usual refusal to countenance any liveliness—the curfew, enforced by the mechanical, inhuman Tans.

When only a few pages later he takes a second look, John is struck by "how near and how far I was to the roofs and chimneys I had left." The mix of attachment and distance is a sign of the conflict of emotions O'Faolain always feels when he looks at the city, "one of those towns you love and hate" (*An Irish Journey*, part 2). What draws him most forcefully perhaps is the power of memory and experience; O'Faolain, like the young John, *knows* Cork as he does no other place, and as he never will the countryside toward which he turns his hopeful steps. That "free" country will prove to be hardly edenic; or rather, like any true Eden, it contains temptation and entrapments. In "Midsummer Night Madness," as throughout the collection to which that story gives its name, part of the danger is circumstantial: Black-and-Tan patrols or various factions of warring Irishmen. But the central difficulty cannot be assigned wholly to political conflict, as O'Faolain's characters learn soon enough when they are at large in an Ireland that has, officially at least, ceased to be at war with itself or with England.

The very openness of the country, so seductively appealing from the claustral attic window, threatens to engulf the individual. It can become, as it does in the later story "Love's Young Dream," a place of terrible isolation, a literal and metaphorical waste land:

> I lay down under the shelter of a furze clump . . . Once I thought I heard the coughing of a sheep. Then I realized that I was hearing only the wind rattling through some withered thistles near my feet. The wind, the darkness, the stars, the lights [of distant cottage windows], the size of the plain [of the Curragh] dwindled and isolated me. My isolation turned all those human and sky-borne lights into my guides and companions . . . I remember shouting out in my excitement, without knowing what I meant. "The lights! The lights!"—as if I wanted some pyrotechnic convulsion in nature to occur, some flashing voice to speak. Only the wind whispered. Only the dried thistles coughed.

In the city, the passional human organism must do battle with the suffocating power of moralistic provincialism and political warfare. On the plain, the individual is threatened by utter diminution and the death of all contact, human or divine. Worst of all, the voyage out of the attic may become a voyage into the wilderness of the self.[3] As the young husband in "Discord" says of his life, "There's that fear always over me—being isolated—getting away from life—getting wrapped into myself. Everyone living in the country has that feeling sometimes. It's a bit terrifying."

Young John, pausing between memory and new experience, between enclosure and—he hopes—the open field of opportunity which is the future, escaping from a city where love must hide, is a prototype of the young men (and, less often, young women) who are at the center of O'Faolain's early fiction. Perhaps because the struggle to free Ireland has not yet turned upon itself, John begins his adventure in the countryside with his youthful optimism still intact: "There was enough romance left in the revolution for me to be excited." But romance diminishes sharply as John meets the despotism of reality in a decaying Big House still occupied by its owner, an Anglo-Irish "old devil" named Henn, an aging sensualist with an appropriate fondness for Mozart's *Don Giovanni*.

Henn is both the prisoner and the host of a rebel commandant, Stevey Long, and the master, perhaps the lover, of a pregnant serving-girl, Gypsy Gammle. It immediately becomes difficult for John to keep his bearings, since his revolutionary principles are sound and his appreciation of women predictably combines adolescent longing and respectable Catholic chivalry. Long, who ought to be a hero (although John's mission is to urge him to end an unexplained period of inactivity), proves to be a troubling figure (although not yet quite so cold hearted as he will be a few stories later,

3. It is also of course a journey back in time, into the prototypical history of O'Faolain's own family before its "drift from the land" (*The Irish*, "The New Peasantry"). To retrace those steps to the country south of Limerick where O'Faolain's mother's family lived, or the plains of the Curragh where the young O'Faolain visited his father's family is to encounter an Ireland in which nothing happens, and nothing has or will change. Despite his sympathy with "all rebels, exiles, outcasts and sinners" announced in the story "Before the Daystar" and elsewhere, and for all his active involvement throughout his life in the effort to reshape Ireland, O'Faolain retains a note of what, in an English context, might be called Toryism: "No one regrets more than the artist the passing of [the] old, hierarchical form of society" (*An Irish Journey*, part 1; see also *King of the Beggars*, part 5, ch. 8). In Ireland, where rebellion is customarily, perhaps inevitably, retrospective, the conflict between this frame of mind and a commitment to radical, even revolutionary change, is perhaps less paradoxical than it seems, although it leaves O'Faolain saddened by the replacement of his old dream of "the new Ireland as a rich flowering of the old Ireland, with all its simple ways, pieties, values, traditions" by the "ambitions" of a newer generation, "younger men, proud to be called hardheaded men, indifferent to or even despising those traditional ways, now want a modernized country, prosperity, industrialization, economic success" (*Vive Moi!*, ch. 8).

in "The Death of Stevey Long"); he refuses to acknowledge the unborn child he has fathered and connives, indeed coerces, a marriage between Henn and Gypsy. Henn ought to be easy to despise; indeed, he has been nearly a legendary villain to John: "as children we thought [him] more terrifying than any of the ogres in the fairy-books." But Johnny cannot dismiss Henn's claim to have spent a life working to improve the lot of the Irish. "I tried to change them," Henn insists, the first of a long line of characters in O'Faolain's work to lament or condemn the unwillingness of the Irish to change productively. John learns to examine, even to revise, his idealized sense of how things ought to be; he finds, to his surprise, that "this Hall and estate and countryside had an unpleasant, real life of its own."

The story exemplifies a dynamic of enclosure, escape, and re-enclosure that is fundamental to all of O'Faolain's early fiction.[4] John flees his Cork attic, confronts the beauty (and the danger) of the "free" country, and then is once again "housed." Old Henn's Red House shares with the attic a sense of constriction and the death of hope, especially for Henn and Gypsy, both of whom are prisoners, the one actual, the other virtual. But the Red House is not only a prison; it is also the scene of intense human passion and sexuality. This might be thought to work against the danger of suffocation and compression, but in the perversely upside-down world of this story it serves too often only to intensify those damning elements. So John flees again, returning to his "back-yard bedroom in Cork."

Each of the individual stories within the collection *Midsummer Night Madness* offers a similarly complex "housing" of the warring principles of constraint and of passion. The collection as a whole begins, as we have seen, with the first moments of Johnny's "escape." It ends, in "The Patriot," when one Bernard, a young Irregular, learns a painful lesson about the death of revolutionary idealism in an isolated hotel which has been commandeered by the indolent, incompetent rebel leadership. He then returns to another hotel, where he can turn away from that bankrupt patriotism

4. This dynamic can serve as an important point of distinction between O'Faolain's fiction and that of O'Connor, with which it shares many elements of mood and intention, especially the persistent concern with the defeat of the aspiring individual at the hands of provincial society. O'Connor's fictional world is rigorously interior; the central action, no matter how frequently it may include characters who look longingly out to a larger world, invariably occurs within an enclosed space: a family parlor, an isolated cottage, a church or confessional, even (in "In the Train") a railway carriage. There is nothing in O'Connor comparable, in frequency or importance, to the contrast of interior and exterior to be seen in this story or in "Fugue," and so often elsewhere; nor does O'Connor devote anything like O'Faolain's energy or attention to the exterior vista as a *locus* of conflict and a point of fascination.

and toward his new wife, Norah: "He drew the blind down slowly . . . and slowly he turned to her where she smiled to him in the dark."

Bernard's gesture seems to be a quiet reversal of the defeat that commonly occurs in the previous stories. But the note of promise is at best a faint one amid the disillusionments which the other stories record. Nowhere in *Midsummer Night Madness*—or, for that matter, in *A Purse of Coppers* or *A Nest of Simple Folk* or *Bird Alone* or *Come Back to Erin*—does passion clearly find time or room to breathe. Nor will the exterior world offer relief; it proves, even in contrast to the horrors of enclosure, to be little more than a field of transition. John's earlier sense of opportunity must be set against the hard truth which a dark woman in "Fugue" states directly, pointing our attention once again back to Cork:

> You would soon tire of these mountains! The city, though, that's where I'd like to live. There's company there, and sport and educated people, and a chance to live whatever life you choose! . . . This farm is bare and high. The land is poor. And this townland has a Northern aspect . . . . It's a cruel country to have to live in.

IF WE were inclined to find something a bit hopeful in the closing moments of "The Patriot," we would soon be corrected by *A Purse of Coppers*. That book mimics the topographic "shape" of O'Faolain's first collection of stories. It begins, in the story "A Broken World," with yet another protagonist in transit and away from Cork, in this case on a train and, ominously, headed toward Dublin. It ends with enclosure, of a much darker sort than the darkness hiding Bernard and Norah. The final story, "There's a Birdy in a Cage," is a tale in which two lovers are separated; one (who appears in the story only by way of memory) is "free—yet"; the other, Helena Black, within whose consciousness the narrative ultimately settles, is left with a vision of irrevocable isolation:

> Quite clearly, and with absolute honesty and accuracy, she saw her life stretched out before her; and she faced it with courage, for there were many dreams that allured her by the way, and many hopeless possibilities that delayed her . . . . She was caught as, sooner or later, all human beings are caught in that coil of things from which there is no escape.

Like many another enclosed O'Faolain character—like young John, while he was in his attic—Helena looks out a window; but in what is, in its quiet way, the absolute low point of despair in O'Faolain's fiction, she does not even achieve a view of the outside, nor of any life beyond the limits of her cage. She can see only the window itself, "the moisture on the window-panes."

And indeed the whole of *A Purse of Coppers* lays out O'Faolain's most claustral and bleak view of Ireland and of life. Those who can see clearly are left broken and alone, either to be ignored or ridiculed. Those whose ambition has not yet altogether leaked out must flee—to America, of course. But once there, they are likely to find in the brave new world only disappointment and a nostalgic pull back to Ireland. Others, like the ex-rebel Sally Dunn in "A Meeting," can still recall the grand aspirations of the Revolution, its brave, innocent vision of "a rich flowering of the old Ireland, with all its simple ways, pieties, values, traditions"; they endure— in large part as a result of that memory—lives of melancholy and inarticulate confusion:

> I don't know. We are going to have a factory now in the disused barracks. The slum-people have taken over all the living-quarters. And they're turning it into another slum. I don't know. Honest to God, I don't know! I wonder ought we have factories like that spreading all over Ireland? We might end up with cities like Manchester or Glasgow? And look at all these vulgar people making money out of it all. It's hard to tell . . . You know, it's . . .

The land is in the power of provincial moralizers and censorious villagers and embittered clerics. The population at large is given to an absurd pseudo-Gaelicism whose one test for the irrelevance of any bit of modernity is the imagined past: "Our forefathers had no buses, and they were happy. If I were the President I'd pass a law forbidding the use of all motor-vehicles" ("Sullivan's Trousers"). The Ireland of *A Purse of Coppers* is, as the first story in the collection argues at great length, "A Broken World."

The problem is not contradictions. As O'Faolain will later formulate it in a story called "The Human Thing," there is something inevitable about them: "The truth about every place is the sum of everybody's contradictions." It is fair to say that O'Faolain with his "double-sided nature" (*Vive Moi!*, ch. 12) sees in human character and indeed in the very nature of things an array of opposites—imagination and fact, dream and reality, romanticism and realism, idealism and practicality, faith and skepticism, intelligence and sensibility. But in the Ireland of the 1930s what seems fatally visible is the total absence of any meeting-point, the failure of any element of unification. As the narrator at the end of "A Broken World" wonders, looking out over a snowy and shrouded landscape remarkably like the one Gabriel sees in the closing moments of Joyce's "The Dead,"[5] "What image of life . . . would fire and fuse us all [?]"

And that is what is most tragic about the defeat of revolutionary idealism. For all its faults, and in spite of its decay into brutal squabbling, the revolutionary idea of Ireland had seemed to O'Faolain to be just such a fusing image. Remembering, in *Vive Moi!* (ch. 9), "an autumn day of sun and shower" when he took part in a muster of the Irish Volunteers, O'Faolain speaks of "that moment [when] life became one with the emotion of Ireland":

> In that moment I am sure every one of us ceased to be single or individual and became part of one another, in union, almost like coupling lovers. It was a supreme experience to know that you may not only admire your fellow men, or respect them, or even like them, but that you can love them so much that they have no faults, no weaknesses, so that you will never distrust them even for a second, and will forgive them every slightest minor fault or flaw as they will yours. This extraordinarily heart-lifting revelation, this gaiety, this liberation of the spirit, was to stay with us all through the exciting years to come. If any of the youths and young men of those days should chance to read these lines today I am sure that he will make no wonder of them. He will acknowledge that I am describing something very simple that happened to us all when we were not bald or gray, paunching, tired or skeptical, when in our generous youth we lived and were ready to die for one of the most wild, beautiful and inexhaustible faiths possible to man—faith in one's fellows.

The very passion and ideality of this faith, and the degree to which it is ultimately based on individuals, may help explain the rapidity and inevitability of its decay. It also explains why in the stories of *Midsummer Night Madness* the disillusioning force is the unreliability and complexity of people, not the pressure of events.

However long the "exciting years" lasted, they were long over by 1937. Absent any new faith to take the place of the old, those forces which had once been fused work out their individual courses—which is to say, they each decay into a characteristic extreme. Idealism, for example, turns to a kind of self-absorbed and self-induced madness. In *Vive Moi!* (ch. 10) O'Faolain remembers Eileen Gould saying to him (and for him, an ac-

---

5. O'Faolain insists, in his preface to *The Finest Stories of Sean O'Faolain,* that if the story as a whole is "my . . . reply to Joyce's wonderful story," he "certainly did not consciously mean any such thing."

cusation levelled by an attractive woman is always close to the mark): "You are all abstract fanatics. You are suffering, if you are suffering, not out of love for your fellow men but out of love for your own ruthless selves," an assessment to which O'Faolain can only agree: "We were all idealists, self-crazed by abstractions, lost in the labyrinths of the dreams to which we had retreated from this pragmatical pig of a world."

So too passionate emotion becomes sentimentalism. The endurance and stability that remain admirable in the life of the peasantry, and which help explain the sheer survival of anything Irish under years of foreign rule, become mere obstinacy, a reactionary refusal to face the new facts of a post-industrial world. Religion, no longer balancing intelligence and sensibility (*Vive Moi!*, ch. 1) becomes a rigid and asexual moralism. In *An Irish Journey* (part 1), O'Faolain speaks of "the confused, ambiguous, mingled nature of this modern Ireland"; but it would be more accurate to say that O'Faolain—at least the O'Faolain of the 1930s—charges his country with an utter failure to "mingle." Even memory, in his view unquestionably the most powerful and necessary force in the human mind and thus too in human behavior, cannot avoid a decline into the nostalgic despair of Sally Dunn.

EXILE figures so prominently in O'Faolain's first three novels that it seemed to Benedict Kiely in 1948 that exile was the key to O'Faolain's fictional world (*Modern Irish Literature: An Introduction*, p. 52). The theme of exile is an enlargement of the desire for escape which, in *Midsummer Night Madness*, propelled so many out of Cork and into the torn landscape of the Ireland of the 1920s. The central characters in the three novels, Leo Foxe-Donnel, Frankie Hannafey, and Corney Crone, are all rebels born at the wrong time, and thus compelled to live out most of their lives after the moment of unity that O'Faolain the Irish Volunteer could feel, in the dead and deadening Ireland just after Parnell or during De Valera's dreary Eden. The path of their exile, whether or not it takes them outside of Ireland itself, must in any case lead farther than just to the edge of town. But the near-circle of enclosure, escape, and re-enclosure defines their lives as well.

The greater part of *A Nest of Simple Folk* tells Leo's story. Born simply Leo Donnel, a farmer's son, he "rises" through the machinations of his mother, who had married beneath herself, to be the heir to her family's Big House, Foxehall. As a mark of recovered gentility, Leo adds his mother's surname, Foxe, to his father's. Gentility is entirely the purpose of the move; his mother imagines him a gentleman, and perhaps a doctor or veterinarian as well. But Leo prefers a life of dissipation which ends only when a chance encounter with the Fenian James Stephens converts Leo to the cause of Ireland. His life thereafter is—in the eyes of his family at least—a long fall, marked by stretches of imprisonment and an involvement in Michael Davitt's Land League. He moves from house to house, each one smaller than the previous one; from Foxhall to a shopkeeper's cottage in Rathkeale to another in Limerick and finally to Cork, each move in part prompted by the failure of an act of revolutionary agitation, followed in its turn by a brief period of life on the run (much like that of the young man in "Fugue") and then by his capture and imprisonment. From Cork he makes one last journey of escape and action, to Dublin at Easter 1916; there (if the genealogy which precedes the novel is any evidence) to meet his death.

By then the focus of the novel has shifted from Leo himself to his nephew Denis Hussey, whose boyhood as the son of a constable in the Royal Irish Constabulary closely imitates O'Faolain's. The novel ends with Denis apparently poised to take on the life of the rebel, and thus to break free from Cork and its provincial sub-species of "Cawstle Cawtholics"— "the seduced Irish who turned their eyes—not unnaturally, Heaven knows, in so impoverished an island—on Dublin Castle and British rule as the only means and center of preferment" (*King of the Beggars*, part 4, ch. 2). But the last word of the novel is "fear," and for Denis the issue remains in doubt. He—like O'Faolain and his readers—must somehow understand the example of Leo, whose life has been both a ruinous decline and a noble self-sacrifice, whose revolutionary passion has been both a self-delusive curse and a stubborn inspiration.

The difficulty of "reading" Leo, and of Denis's youthful (he is only eighteen) effort to find in Cork some guide to his own life, is played out in the concluding scenes of the novel (part 3, ch. 4) by a characteristically restless movement in and out. Denis leaves his house, which is so suffo-catingly full of the devotion to respectability that has prompted his family to defeat his hopes of going to university and instead, after he has three times failed the Civil Service examination, to make him take a bank-clerkship, "the refuge of all dullards." Outside, at the edge of the city, he sees his uncle setting out on an obviously subversive errand; but he does not follow, and instead immediately returns home—there to argue bitterly with his father. The next morning—Easter Monday, 1916—he goes with his mother on an outing, from which he once more returns home, to hear the news of the Dublin rising. From the family kitchen he looks out a window, at the empty streets of Cork and in his imagination at Leo at the barricades in Dublin; is thrown out of his home by his angry father, who detects in Denis signs of unforgivable rebel sympathies; flees for refuge to yet another house, his uncle's; and in the very last words of the novel, looks one more time out the window at a scene which ambiguously combines peace and omen:

> Through the lobby window Shandon raising its black finger against the last ray of day, and far away a faint, faint crackling of rifle fire.
>   And then came its still fainter echo over the pale city, under its pale sky, listening and holding its breath in a silence of fear.

It is easy to presume—especially now that we can look through the deciphering lens of *Vive Moi!*—that young Denis is only a few steps, and a few years, away from the John of "Midsummer Night Madness" or the John/Sean who would ultimately become IRA Director of Publicity. The enclosure, then, is hardly final; but neither is the look out the window a brave and enticing prospect.

Frankie Hannafey's story, told in *Come Back to Erin*,[6] is an all-too-probable sequel to Denis's dawning revolutionary ardor, although the particulars of his complex genealogy in no way resemble Denis Hussey's, save for a long familial connection with Cork and with Rathkeale in the countryside between Cork City and Limerick. Denis is a rebel in the making; Frankie, whose devotion to the cause of a new Ireland has, like Leo Foxe-Donnel's in the bleak years at the close of the nineteenth century, apparently survived into a hopeless time, is the rebel at last forced to abandon his faith. Avoiding the larger chronological sweep of *A Nest of Simple Folk*, O'Faolain here observes Frankie over the space of only a few months, from spring to autumn 1936. His time of exile and return begins in the attic of his family's house in Cork, where he is hiding, wanted by the Gardai on suspicion of having taken part in an assassination. His family helps him to flee, first to his aunt's house in Rathkeale, then to America. At the novel's end he has returned to Cork, to a life not of rebellion but

---

6. If we take O'Faolain's novels in order of publication, the next is *Bird Alone*; but—as I will try to make clear a bit further on—that novel represents not so much a successor to *A Nest of Simple Folk* but a divergence toward what would in about a decade become the new terrain of O'Faolain's fiction, in which politics and its particular varieties of rebellion are much less important. It is worth noting here, however, that whatever its shifts of emphasis, *Bird Alone* does repeat the topographic cycle we have been defining; Corney Crone, now some sixty years old, sits down in yet another Cork attic to write the story of what prompts his radical exile from Cork (and indeed from humanity) in the same room from which he had years before fled. The plot moves from inside to outside, as the sequence of titles given to the three parts of the novel suggests: from cave to jungle to desert. The last act in the plot is Corney's "final" departure from Cork. But the frame completes the circle, bringing him (for reasons that are never made clear) back "home" once again.

of apparent respectability (as a "Warble-Fly Inspector"!). We see him last (*Come Back to Erin,* part 3, ch. 7) in the family parlor, overhearing a conversation about a trip to Paris that will never happen, evading his thoughts, and not even looking out the window. Placing the arc of Frankie's decisive summer after the longer movement of Leo Foxe-Donnel toward a "rising" makes for a larger, and even more desperate circle; for the parlor in which Frankie sits bears a striking similarity to the house in which we leave Denis or that where we first met the young Leo Foxe-Donnel:

> In that . . . house nothing happened from morning to night, and nothing happened from day to day, and . . . even the years seemed to fall asleep . . . Over all that rich land there is and always has been a kind of sultry sloth, dead and overpowering and drugging to all the energies of the spirit. . . . History has reverberated only in the distance, and even then but rarely and too far away to be heard. . . .
>
> (*A Nest of Simple Folk,* part 1, ch. 1)

The grand and readily apparent question which both *A Nest of Simple Folk* and *Come Back to Erin* take up at length concerns the sources and motives, and the cost, of a rebellion whose necessity is clear but whose results seem cruelly ambiguous. The whole of Irish culture, as it appears in the two books, mingles stability (which, looked at with a harder eye, resembles nothing so much as utter stagnation) with a drive for change. It emerges both in the desire of the rural peasantry to rise into landed gentility or the urban bourgeoisie, and in the more eccentric, but to O'Faolain far more admirable and compelling, lives of the handful of political and economic revolutionaries. The two forms which the principle of change takes—ambition and rebellion—are however in large measure at war; the primary rebellion is neither against the economic deprivation of the country, nor against the English colonial venture which provokes and sustains it, but precisely against the desire to rise to middle class respectability. O'Faolain rebels, in other words, against the very elements that have come into unquestioned power after the English enemy had been overcome.

The conflict is in part generational. Leo Foxe-Donnel rejects his mother's hope that he can become a gentleman. Denis Hussey refuses, in the end, to be his father's son. Frankie Hannafey has no time for his stepfather's supposed respectability, a hearty and self-congratulatory provincial commercialism. Corney Crone in *Bird Alone* abandons the world of his parents, who are (like O'Faolain's own mother) "miserable with piety" (*Bird Alone,* part 2, ch. 2; *Vive Moi!,* ch. 3). The rare alliances of spirit which these rebels, old and young, achieve tend to skip a generation. Corney much prefers the company of his grandfather; Denis Hussey likes Leo Foxe-Donnel's grandfather.

But the true rebels must learn to accept the antagonism, even the enmity of all their relations, especially of their brothers. Leo's brother James, imprisoned by the outcome of their mother's hunger for land, has no time for fraternal affection, or for rebellion either; his reaction to Leo's arrest and imprisonment is to forget his brother entirely (*A Nest of Simple Folk*, part 1, ch. 4). Frankie's brothers—the "compressed" postal clerk Michael and the wealthy and fatally nostalgic emigré St. John—are willing to help him escape the Gardai. But the news that they are about to visit his temporary hideout in Kilfinnane provokes in Frankie an anger that blossoms first into a bitter argument and then into an irrational and absurd outburst of violence, the shooting of one of his aunt's beloved ducks.

The rebel, it seems, must live out in a secular and political world the hard saying of Jesus: "If any man come to me, and hate not his father, and mother, and wife, and children, and brethren, and sisters, yea, and his own life, he cannot be my disciple" (Luke 14:26).[7] That isolation from the family is an important sign of the independence that is crucial to the rebel, who must, like Daniel O'Connell, at heart be a "solitary" (*King of the Beggars,* part 1, ch. 1). The family is inevitably an enemy since it is the locus of the prevailing Irish temper, peculiarly compounded of pragmatic materialism, sentimentality, and resignation. But it might be fairer to describe the rebel as not so much isolated *from* the family as isolated *within* the family, since both Leo and Frankie spend much of their lives in close contact with the home and relations with whom they find themselves continually at odds. Perhaps as a measure of the extent of the Irish diaspora, even O'Faolain's exiles inevitably seem to encounter relatives—Corney's cousin Mel Crone in England; Frankie's American siblings and half-siblings, the priest Leonard and the businessman St. John.

Particularly in *A Nest of Simple Folk,* affection, both familial and romantic, is a sinister force; yet Leo in a sense never leaves the family that would manipulate and betray him. His mother, like the mother of the Biblical Jacob, schemes even at her husband's deathbed on behalf of her favorite son, consigning the other son to a life of solitary labor. Leo's lover Julie

---

7. The same idea comes up in O'Faolain's biographical studies—most clearly pehaps in the case of Constance Markiewicz, whose isolation from her family O'Faolain records in considerable and rather disapproving detail. Hugh O'Neill's revolt against England is in part a rebellion against his childhood home; O'Neill lived from the age of nine to the age of seventeen in England, in London and at Sidney's Penshurst.

betrays him to the English; yet once released from prison, he marries her nevertheless, and he is not above sharing a house with the Husseys. In a world so marked by connivance, ambition, and betrayal, the rebel's isolation seems both inescapable and admirable; he is the great and necessary nay-sayer.[8] Neither Leo nor Frankie, nor Denis as yet, is fully a solitary; perhaps in part because, as the example of Corney Crone will show, the price is great indeed, amounting to the severing of all human ties.

But the rebel's iconoclasm and independence are subject to a decay of idealism into fanaticism and abstraction which O'Faolain describes in *Vive Moi!* When, in *The Irish*, O'Faolain characterizes "The Rebels," he can admire their—or at least Wolfe Tone's—effort to find balance and synthesis, to add "the logic of the Northern Scot to the passions of the Southern Irish," to combine "a controlled Anglo-Irish intelligence and a passionate sense of injustice among the native Irish," to prefer "laughter and humanity" to the catalog of vices which, as we have already seen, are too visible in "modern Ireland."[9] But he must at last offer a harsher judgment:

> What was it that the Irish Rebel always sacrificed? The better part of his life? Far worse, far more exhausting, harder far to bear, he sacrificed the better part of his mind. . . . All these men deprived Ireland of as much as they gave to it: they choked the critical side of their minds, they were good rebels in proportion as they were bad revolutionaries, so that their passion for change and their vision of change never pierced to organic change, halted dead at the purely modal and circumstantial. It had to be that way since they devoted all their lives and all their beings to passion rather than to thought. . . . It was upon the emotional content of the Revolution that they seized and not on its intellectual content, with the result that the whole of Irish patriotic literature ever since has . . . concerned itself with matters of sentiment rather than thought . . . The countryman who has invaded the towns

8. The Mephistophelean resonance is not accidental; *Faust* (not Marlowe's or Goethe's but, in good Corkonian fashion, a version by "George W. Reynolds, M.D.") is Corney Crone's grandfather's favorite text; and Robert Younger's bargain in *And Again?* is, as he knows full well, Faustian. But the Faust at work in O'Faolain's fiction is unrepentant—if nonetheless willingly Roman Catholic.

9. Tone is, in this case, almost identical to O'Faolain's Hugh O'Neill, whose great effort is to graft an English intelligence and civilization onto the tribal and passionate Irish; and indeed the whole of *The Irish* articulates the heterodox (for a "patriotic" rebel Irishman) argument that the history of Ireland should be seen not as the stubborn resistance on the part of the pure and native to the impositions of foreign invaders, but as the developing "assimilation" of "foreign influences" (*The Irish*, "Explanation").

is now fumbling there in an ungainly fashion . . . because his intellectual leaders were so damnably unintellectual . . . The Irishman the world over is to this day a nonconformist and a rebel—it is one of his great gifts to an over-regimented world; but the rebel gave nothing to political science . . .

(*The Irish*, "The Rebels")

The distinction between rebel and revolutionary, between the nonconformist and that person who may in fact produce real and widespread change, is one that Frankie Hannafey tries to articulate as well:

Revolutions . . . are very slow processes. The terrorist never realizes that. It's not his job. You must distinguish between a terrorist and a revolutionary. The terrorist may be employed by the revolutionary. I'm not a terrorist. . . . What I want is a change in Irish life. And by God we're going to get that change! We fought for it, but we didn't get it. We've got to get it.

(*Come Back to Erin*, part 1, "2 AM")

Typically, and ominously, Frankie is shouting, and at a puzzled and ultimately uncomprehending Irish audience in the person of his brother St. John, who loves his own image of Ireland because it does *not* change. Neither Frankie, doctrinaire and humorless, nor Leo, whose life is broken by prison and who is, in his old age, given to connivance no more honorable or successful than his mother's, come up to the admirable Wolfe Tone (a man of "gaiety and tolerance and a great pity and a free mind and a free heart and a full life"). They typify in contrast the "lapsed-rebel, that most common and pathetic type in the history of all peoples" (*The Irish,* "The Rebels"). Pity, humanity, tolerance, gaiety: if ever they were in Frankie Hannafey, they are gone now, and have been replaced, so Josephine Hogan says, persuasively, by a new set of motives:

He's doing it for obstinacy, and for courage, and for the folly of man. For what sense is there to it if nobody hears or heeds him? It's only vanity. Half of it is vanity and nothing but vanity . . .

(*Come Back to Erin*, part 1, "10 PM")

For the rebel, real or lapsed, the risk, perhaps even the prerequisite sin, is an irreconcilable inward division, a dissociation of the emotions from the intelligence. In framing the diagnosis in such terms, O'Faolain makes an implicit defense of his own turn from rebel to writer, especially one who so often in these early works "recompos[es his] own life in novels and stories" (*Vive Moi!,* ch. 11). But he does not write out of egotism or self-involvement so much as in an effort to bring a detached and analytic mind to play upon the decisive experiences of his youth; and they—if there is any accuracy to his accounts in *Vive Moi!*—were at bottom emotionally, not intellectually, motivated. If the rebel chokes off thought to pursue passion, then the writer's necessary balance of forces seems a powerful antidote, for it is he who is driven by the "longing to blend the intellect and the imagination" to produce "the child born of the intimate sexual union of the intelligence and the sensibility."

In those terms, Frankie's life may be less of a fall from grace. Frankie's time in America brings him up against the passional force of sexual attraction which had up to that time been suppressed by his more abstract passion for political change; and during his exile he finds ample time to think and to read. Perhaps then the conclusion of *Come Back to Erin* is no more closed than that of *A Nest of Simple Folk*. Denis, who has done little other than look and contemplate, must experience the emotional power of rebellion; Frankie, too long in the grip of that power, must abandon the revolutionary's life for something that will allow him to see more clearly. His transformation from devout revolutionary to Warble-Fly Inspector may be more or less a transitional step, like O'Faolain's own interruption of his rebel career to be a textbook salesman.

Much of the price to be paid for the passion in the lives of rebels and nonconformists falls to the rebel himself, whether in a solitary life in Ireland or—perhaps worse still—in the barbarities of imprisonment in England. But the rebel is not alone in suffering the consequences of his actions; no matter how ineffective he may be in bringing about a change in the condition of Ireland generally, he inevitably has a powerful effect on those around him. Johnny Hussey will not sit still for his wife's defense of Leo Foxe-Donnel:

> No, . . . we're not hard on him. Look at all the harm he done [sic] in his lifetime. Didn't he ruin himself? Didn't he ruin his mother's work and his father's work, that bought him a house and a farm that's all gone for nothing now?
>
> (*A Nest of Simple Folk*, part 2, ch. 2)

The accusation condemns Johnny at least as much as it does Leo, by showing how deeply ingrained in him is a spirit of ambition and respectability that can only measure a man's life in terms of land and class. But it is a fact that the pain of Leo's "ruin" spreads widely among those around him, and is no less sharp for its being, often, well-deserved. Frankie, too, unsettles and even nearly destroys the lives around him; and particularly the lives of those who love him—his mistress, Bee Hannafey, and the cousin who waits for him in Ireland, Josephine Hogan.

The life of the rebel is of course not without gain; for Leo, as for his nephew Denis, the discovery of political nonconformity amounts to a major act of self-definition, a profound and probably irrevocable step away from the ambitions which their families have for them, and which—judging from *Vive Moi!* in particular—constitute perhaps the greatest threat to their spiritual and intellectual lives. Among the catalog of evils O'Faolain sees, retrospectively, in the world of his childhood, ambition has a necessary, even conclusive place: "One may be happy though poor; to be poor, frugal, parsimonious, and ambitious is quite another matter. It leads to a dull and disciplined degradation of life" (*Vive Moi!*, ch. 4). To rise in the world, on the world's terms, is potentially fatal, as both Leo and Denis learn. To have resisted that call, to have cut himself off from the barren world in which it is the ground-note, brings Leo, in his prison cell, some consolation:

> Why should he have any love for that place, or for the people of it—dead, lazy, lifeless wretches, as he called them. But he would chuckle like a madman to himself at that; remember that it was not love for them . . . that drove him to what he did. Aye! First it was his mother, forcing him to do what he had no wish for, then it was his aunts . . .
>
> (*A Nest of Simple Folk*, part 1, ch. 4)

The cell is at least the fruit of his own intentions, not one more house forced upon him by another's well-intended but suffocating ambitions. Denis Hussey has had less time to ponder, but his assertion of independence is nonetheless clear: "I go around with no one" (*A Nest of Simple Folk*, part 3, ch. 4).

The rebel may also achieve, if only for a moment, that sense of emotional oneness which O'Faolain recalls experiencing at the Volunteer muster. That satisfaction is, however, only dimly visible in the novels; it lies, we assume, in Denis Hussey's future and far in Frankie Hannafey's past, and so in both cases outside the chronological frame of either novel. The fact that it is missing gives a sinister measure of the feeling of unity itself—rare, hard to predict, impossible to see coming, and so quickly and perhaps irrecoverably gone. Leo, even in his Fenian days, retains the shards of a gentleman's education; among the most important of which is a bit of Boethius: "*Fuisse felicem et non esse, omnium est infelicissimum genus;* to have been happy at one time and then to be unhappy after, isn't that the greatest unhappiness in the whole world?" (*A Nest of Simple Folk*, part 1, ch. 4) The lines could serve well enough as the rubric under which to set down the lives of Leo, Frankie, Sally Dunn, and so many others of the central characters in O'Faolain's earlier fiction.

THIS is also true for Corney Crone, at sixty an aged solitary whose recollections constitute the substance of *Bird Alone*. Corney too is the child of a respectable family; the Crones, however, have already risen by way of a prosperous contracting business, and are poised on the verge of decline. Corney's Cork childhood rehearses, in great detail, that of Denis Hussey and John Whelan—to such an extent that O'Faolain repeated almost word-for-word Corney's account of his time at the Lancastrian School when years later he set down his recollection of his own schooling (*Bird Alone,* part 1, ch. 5; *Vive Moi!,* ch. 4). Politics form a crucial context within which Corney moves toward a point of self-definition and individuality; born in 1873, he becomes in his youth a "mad Parnellite" (*Bird Alone,* part 2, ch. 2) under the tutelage of his grandfather, in much the way that Denis learns from the Fenianism of Leo Foxe-Donnel.[10] Like Leo, although in a much smaller way, he becomes involved in a "bit of a mess" involving revolutionary activity; flees the city but is captured— betrayed (so he thinks) by his girl-friend Elsie, as Leo is by Julie Keene. Like Frankie Hannafey in his American exile, he finds himself in "that acrid sea of Despair that swims in the heart between the hills of Anger and Desire" (*Bird Alone,* part 2, ch. 8; cf. *Come Back to Erin,* part 2, ch. 4).

It is, then, the old O'Faolain story: a young man of passion and intelligence (and Corney has as much of the first, and perhaps more of the latter, than any figure in the other two novels) seeks to escape Cork and, in a larger sense, to find a way and a place to live in a "sad country" (*Bird Alone,* part 3, ch. 1) that begrudges life. Like *Come Back to Erin* especially, *Bird Alone* plays out the conflict of attachment and estrangement between this solitary figure and the land of his birth both in physical movement (out into the country; and to London and Youghal) and in contentious dialogues with those who would either seduce or educate him. Frankie's arguments with his brother Leonard (*Come Back to Erin,* part 2, ch. 2) and with Bee Hannafey (part 2, chs. 6 & 7) echo those of Corney with the

---

10. In that sense, Corney is even more like John Whelan than is Denis; for, as has often been observed, Parnellism of a kind is a central element in O'Faolain's view of life as it was in Joyce's (see, for instance, Benedict Kiely's introduction to the Oxford Press edition of *Bird Alone* [p. x]). The Crone family has an argument about Parnell (*Bird Alone,* part 2, ch. 5) that exactly corresponds, both in its setting (the dinner table) and its substance, to the one which the Dedalus family has in the first part of *Portrait of the Artist.*

mad Christy and Tom Scanlon the carpenter (*Bird Alone,* part 3, ch. 5) and with Stella Taylor, a painter whom he meets in Youghal (part 3, ch. 1).[11]

Corney's cottage in Youghal at first seems to be a refuge, but once the terrible last act of his love for Elsie is played out, becomes yet one more cage which Corney must abandon in his effort to accept, fully and knowingly and unrepentantly, the life of the "freeman among the dead" of whom the Psalmist sings in the scriptural text that Corney makes the keynote of his story (*Bird Alone,* epigraph[12] and part 3, ch. 6). Corney and Stella meet by accident, talk about painting, have tea together in Stella's cottage, where Corney can indulge in a favorite habit of staring out windows. In another and much less melancholy novel, this might be the quiet beginning of an important affair, as Stella seems to know—almost the last thing she says to Corney is "Are you in love with me?" The question is never quite answered; or rather Corney answers it in terms of angry self-denunciation. He is in any case already deeply, irrevocably, and guiltily in love with Elsie; and Stella disappears from the novel altogether.

What makes this interlude seem more than peripherally interesting is the shape and direction of their colloquy and the odd way in which Corney's encounter with Stella can be viewed as, implicitly, a meeting of Corney with himself (rather like O'Faolain's encounter with Sally Dunn, in "A Meeting"), a self that he will in the end abandon. Corney becomes—as we know from his introduction of himself at the very beginning of the novel—a man without place or country, a man outside even of time itself: "Time's wheel has stopped for me" (*Bird Alone,* part 1, ch. 1). But that exile—the most radical and thoroughgoing, in a spiritual sense, of any exile to be found in O'Faolain's fiction—is peculiarly rooted and defined by place and nationality, as the details of Corney's account of how his exile came to pass show on almost every page. This is one of O'Faolain's

11. The construction of prolonged arguments—about art, about life, about Ireland—as an arena within which his protagonists can attempt to articulate a coherent sense of purpose and meaning is a continuing element in O'Faolain's fiction; it appears full-blown as early as "Midsummer Night Madness," where John argues both with Stevey Long and with Old Henn. The "debates," which customarily do not result in the victory of one point of view, represent for O'Faolain a way to play out the conflict of forces—emotion and intelligence, detachment and affection, the dream of exile and the dream of a happy return—which is at the heart of almost all of his characters. His most self-conscious use of the device occurs in *Vive Moi!* (ch. 11), when, long years after, he tries to assess the Irish revolution and his own part in it and convenes a panel consisting of an historian, a psychologist, and Flaubert, with each of whom, serially, he engages in debate. In the end, he agrees with all of them.

12. As the epigraph informs us, it is Psalm 87 in the Vulgate and Douai Bibles; in the King James version, and those later (Protestant) versions which derive from it, the Psalm bears the number 88.

consistent arguments about exile—that it is not so much a final separation from the enclosures of home as it is a carrying of that enclosure, of the habits and memories which constitute it, into a safely foreign environment.

Stella's peculiar heritage is an actualization of this mixture of nationality and statelessness: "I'm not really English. My mother was Irish and my father was born in India. I was educated in Belgium and I have lived almost as much in Paris as in London, so there you are." Stella might more fairly be called a cosmopolite than an exile; but like an exile, she begins by defining herself in terms of what she is sure she is *not*—which is, of course, just what she most apparently *is*, in the eyes of others. She will in time mount accusations against "You Irish"—forgetting, or suppressing, the fact that she too is, if only distantly, Irish; a gesture exactly parallel to Frankie Hannafey's frequent outbursts against the sentimental, unrealistic, and unambitious Irish, oblivious of the sentimental, idealistic, and lethargic elements in his own nature.

The most striking thing about her to Corney is the way Stella uniquely carries with her into adult womanhood the "gaiety" which most young girls abandon when they leave the "cave of the self" (*Bird Alone,* part 3, ch. 1). Looking back from his old age, Corney sees his much younger self "doomed to come from his Dark Cave out into the Jungle" (part 1, ch. 5); and as a young bank-clerk, he idles away some time composing a set of quatrains which begin ". . . but keep it deep within its cave. Love is a girl that shuns the light . . ." (part 1, ch. 5). One escape from the cave is apparently the troubled, inevitable one of aging, though Stella has somehow bypassed it. Another and more important one is by way of human intercourse:

> The end and measure of utter friendship, the only release from the cave of loneliness, is with him who knows how to accept most. That discovery has meant everything to me. For as it is with men, so it is with life which we understand and love in proportion as we accept without question what it gives, without question as to whether we need it, not even questioning whether its gift seems cruel and kind. It is the supreme generosity because we do not even know who the Giver is; why He has given; or what.
>
> (part 3, ch. 3)

If that is the wisdom life has taught Corney, he has found few if any people who have acted upon it; and certainly not himself.

Stella, even after only a brief acquaintanceship, can see in the younger Corney that unremitting "Search for the Absolute" (part 3, ch. 1) which marks him, and we can still hear it in the rigor of his definition of friendship, bristling with imperatives and strictures—*utter* friendship; the *only* release; acceptance *without any question;* the *supreme* generosity. Stella sees too the underlying religious impulse, in his nature as in his speech; this despite Corney's overt refusal to accept the rituals and dogmas of the Irish church and his admiration both of his grandfather's religious iconoclasm and of the mad Christy Tinsley's atheism. "I'm not a Catholic . . . It's all over and done with as far as I'm concerned," he tells Stella; but she will have none of it: "I think . . . that you're a good little Catholic" (part 3, ch. 1)—a role and a faith that Corney will accept later, if only for the sake of argument with Christy Tinsley. The provincials of Cork also seem to recognize this in him, when they give Corney (now a "character" like the priest in "A Broken World") a new name: "the Third Person" (*Bird Alone,* part 3, ch. 5)—a holy ghost indeed.

Corney insists later that there are "only two things anyone ever talks of in Ireland—Religion and Politics" (part 3, ch. 5): a principle that is well supported in the lives portrayed in *A Nest of Simple Folk, Come Back to Erin,* and much of *Bird Alone.* Even Elsie and Corney as courting lovers seem to spend more time discussing church doctrine and Parnell than romance. Stella will not let Corney sidestep the religious question, which— young free-thinker that he imagines himself to be—he would so much like to do. But neither will she let him introduce politics:

> "Your poor grandfather!" She sighed deeply. "And your poor friend Christy Tinsley. What a life they have made for themselves."
> "But they didn't," I protested crossly. "It wasn't his doing. I mean to say, politics . . ."
> "This is a sad country."
> "It's your people who made it sad," I cried. "You English."
> "No . . ."
> (*Bird Alone,* part 3, ch. 1)

It begins to sound like the old, old argument; but in fact the terms of the argument, indeed the substance of what it is that needs to be argued *about*, have undergone an important shift. Stella will not even allow a sentence containing the word "politics" to be completed; she will not allow the final responsibility for the broken lives of Grander Crone and Christy Tinsley to be laid at any other door than their own. Her rejection of Corney's Parnellite accusation against the English is not to be couched in terms of a defense of that nation—she has already refused to accept the label of Englishwoman. Her charge is larger and deeper than politics:

> You all remind me of flies a bold boy would put under a glass, all beating against it. Even my old men down the quays [the subjects of

some of her paintings]—they talked to me like that. And, then, poor Parnell. No, no! . . . There are some prisons you can never break. You Irish don't know, and you never will know, the ones you can break and the ones you can't break. I believe you don't want to know. You remind me of Dante's people in Hell who lived "wilfully in sadness"! . . . Your mind is a core on core of prisons. It's an onion of them.

(part 3, ch. 1)

Stella sees a final, utter, and most maddening of all, nearly invisible enclosure, within walls that are, painfully, all glass, all window, allowing a view out that can only make the constriction within the more painful. The prison can still be defined nationally, culturally; but it is in the end a matter of the self, of will and knowledge.

And in Corney's case, it is a prison of human passion as well; for what seems at first to be a novel about culture and politics in post-Parnell Ireland becomes more centrally what O'Faolain says it was intended to be from the start: the tale (modeled on, of all things, *The Scarlet Letter*) of "a young man's and a young woman's passion in a community as merciless and alien to passion as Hawthorne's Salem" (*Vive Moi!*, ch. 14). One can argue, even in *A Nest of Simple Folk* and *Come Back to Erin,* that politics, however prevalent, are really no more than the context within which the drama of human passion is to be played out; and we have already seen the degree to which O'Faolain places passion and emotion at the heart of political action. O'Faolain's fiction since the publication in 1940 of *Come Back to Erin* clearly shows that politics need not be the primary context, even if the setting is Ireland. Corney's exchange with Stella hints at that. Corney's effort first to understand, and then to escape, his prison abandons even the language of politics. This abandonment is demonstrated by a peculiar absence in *Bird Alone.* The crucial moment in the lives both of Leo Foxe-Donnel and Denis Hussey, the beginning point of the revolutionary dream which defines and deforms Frankie Hannafey's life even two decades later, is the Easter Rebellion; and as we have seen, to O'Faolain himself the decade of revolution and civil war which followed it was the breaking point of Irish culture in this century. Corney—born, you will recall, in 1873; writing, at age sixty, in 1933; and in his youth proudly claiming to be a mad Parnellite and rebel—certainly lived through the events of Easter Week; but he mentions it directly not at all, and implicitly only by way of an iconoclastic apology: "Once, for a week, I was untrue to my sins" (*Bird Alone,* part 3, ch. 6).[13]

13. The reference is so oblique as to be almost invisible; and it must be admitted that to identify "week" as April 24–29, 1916, is purely supposition. In a strict sense, the "week" in

Corney's story of exile and return is thus not so much a match to that of Leo, Denis, and Frankie as it is a counterpoint. For the other three political activity, political commitment, is both the vehicle of, and the provocation to, those acts of self-definition which in turn amount to an exile from their society. For Corney an exile *from* politics is in a sense the crucial step; and it is not a sad disillusionment, an unwilling stripping away of ideals and dreams, but a conscious and willful act of defiance:

> I am become an old man and my friends are few, and that new faith I set out to find I never did find, and because I have sinned all my life long against men, that whisper of God's reproof, who made men, has been my punishment. I have denied life, by defying life, and life has denied me. I have kept my barren freedom, but only *sicut homo sine adjutorio inter mortuous liber*—a freeman among the dead.
>
> (part 3, ch. 6)

If the price the rebel too often had to pay is the sacrifice of intelligence for the sake of emotion, the price of Corney's understanding of himself and of the dead land around him has been the abandonment of nearly all of the human contacts that would give emotion a place in which to survive. He can remember, with great clarity of detail; he can analyze and judge, with a Biblical rigor and music; but he can feel no more than a bleak contentment and an aged sadness—and, too, a stubborn pride that insists he would change nothing of what he has done.

YET EVEN Corney is one of that long line of figures who experience what O'Faolain makes the theme-note of his revised biography of De Valera: "the tragedy of the idealist in a world of compromise." The shift away from an explicitly political frame of reference and away from a view of Irish culture which is directly haunted by the events of 1916–1927 is in fact no more than a shift in emphasis. The principal figures are still solitaries (although not so permanently so, perhaps); still idealists, or at least dreamers and believers; still poised at a locus of conflict between, on the one hand, the desire to change place and condition and their very nature and, on the other, a longing for home, for stability, for continuance. By reducing the prominence of a particularly Irish language of politics, O'Fao-

---

question might in fact be any of those which Corney has lived through in his forty years in the desert; and the betrayal of his own sins which Corney mentions might be any return to close human communion.

lain allows the fundamental calculus of selfhood to appear more clearly to a non-Irish reader. He will not abandon an Irish setting, however, nor turn from his effort to understand the peculiarities of that nation, those resistances to individual human aspiration which arise from a recognizably Irish mingling of religion, moralism, and—to use again his favorite concept—provinciality.

For Teresa, the young and troubled novice whose decisive trip to the shrine of St. Therese Martin et Lisieux is told in the story "Teresa" (also the title of O'Faolain's first postwar story collection[14]), the issue is neither political commitment nor geographic exile. The journey, like so many journeys in O'Faolain's fiction, is at once physical and spiritual, a testing of her vocation. She is another absolutist: "If I can't be a saint, I don't *want* to be a nun!" And the fear that lies beneath that aspiration is that, if her vocation proves false, she will be wholly at a loss: "If I find out there [at the shrine] that I have no vocation, what'll I do?" Like O'Faolain's revolutionaries, she has defined herself altogether in terms of her intense faith; the death, even the weakening of that ideal feels to her very much like the utter dissolution of her being. Sister Patrick, the good-hearted but worldly older nun who accompanies Teresa, cannot understand the younger woman's intensity; Teresa's announcement that she will join the strictest of orders, the Carmellites, leaves Sister Patrick speechless and "as restless as if she were in bodily agony."

Teresa tells Sister Patrick that she seeks "the death of Love," but it is love, human love, which prevails in the end. She flees the nunnery, and we last see her married, and what is more to a Protestant. Bringing her husband, George, to see the convent, she realizes what she has left and what she has become: "She felt that the woods enclosed a refuge from the world of which she had, irrevocably, become a part." There is no apparent reason for her to regret her decision; no sign whatever that her husband is anything but adoring, if perhaps a bit thick-witted; and yet there is regret: "Ah, George! George! You will never know what I gave up to marry you!" Her renunciation is in its way an exact reversal of her initial "intention"; she has chosen love over its death, human contact over a "saintly" life of withdrawal and devotion. Oddly, her choice seems in part to be based on a distaste for the middle ground, even among the devout; she finds the amiable Sister Patrick, whose vocation demands of her neither anguished thought nor physical pain, to be an unsatisfactory companion and a poor example of the cloistered life.

---

14. That is, to the English edition; the same collection appeared two years later (1949) in America under the title *The Man Who Invented Sin*.

Teresa will not accept the particular compromise the older woman has made between the human and the divine. Teresa—apparently an idealist to the very end—prefers the abandonment of her ideals to any such compromise, any life of (by her standards) lukewarm and sentimental faith and modest good works. But even having made the choice, she remains marked by the necessity of having to choose. Like so many of the figures we have met in O'Faolain's fiction, she cannot forego the retrospective view toward a refuge that had never really existed for her; a life of simplicity and order that she had more imagined than lived or seen.

In O'Faolain's later fiction, those whose dreams are put to the hard test of reality do not come through the conflict unscarred; but neither do they seem as broken and self-exiled as those in his earlier fiction, and especially in his first three novels and *A Purse of Coppers*. The people who suffer the greatest pain are not those who make their renunciations in favor of human love; rather, they are those whose ideal (or vocation) cannot escape the bonds of abstract duty—those who decide, or are forced to decide, to shut out the disorientation, passions, confusions of life as it is customarily lived and, like Brother Majellan in "The Man Who Invented Sin," fall back on the melancholy belief that "it's not good to take people out of their rut."

Against that self-defeated, and self-defeating, resignation, O'Faolain arrays voices and lives like that of Rose Powis, the "Rosebud" of the much later story "£1000 for Rosebud," who demands of her reluctant Irish lover Milo "Why don't you chance it . . . ? We could be very happy. We could make a go of it. . . . It's not such a big chance to take." Teresa's flight from the convent is one such chance; and that it is a flight into love and marriage makes her even more representative of the people whom O'Faolain chooses to observe. Each of his first three novels (although *A Nest of Simple Folk* only minimally) and many of his early stories, especially those in *Midsummer Night Madness*, are concerned with the possibility of human love, and with the particular obstructions which political faith and political conflict present to it. But the failed loves in those stories reach their sad end not so much because of external forces as because of individual hesitancies and obstinacies; the lovers whom John sees scurrying away from the Tans as the curfew comes to Cork are in worse danger from a force within each of them which cuts off love. Corney Crone and his beloved Elsie, for example, may be the victims of a moralistic society; but no agent of destruction or rebuke enters their cottage in Youghal. The affair comes to a sad end because the two of them have so thoroughly internalized the standards of the world which gave birth to them, as Corney sometimes realizes: "I began to see how much Elsie was really fashioned by her parents as I by mine, made part and parcel of them, almost without a will" (*Bird Alone*, part 2, ch. 2). Between Elsie's moral conservatism and Corney's emotional iconoclasm, the only meeting ground is guilt.

That the individual is formed (and indeed often deformed) by outside forces—by parents; by teachers; by political leaders; by Ireland itself, and especially by Cork; even by lovers—had long been a concern of O'Faolain, not only in his fiction but in his biographies as well. They are all in some way investigations of the degree to which even dominant public figures are shaped by the political and cultural contexts in which they live and act. In his earlier stories, it is a rare individual indeed who can triumph; who can even survive in an approximately whole and contented condition. The moments of escape are few and temporary, as we have seen; the more usual outcome is defeat and betrayal. In his later stories O'Faolain does not deny the very real possibility of defeat. But defeat is no longer the ground-note in O'Faolain; it is at least balanced, and often outweighed, by people who endure and even (in a modest way) prosper. At the center, for instance, of one of O'Faolain's richest stories, "The Silence of the Valley," we encounter an old woman presiding over the funeral of her husband, a cobbler and storyteller:[15]

> The crowd seeped in among the trees. The widow sat in the center of the chapel steps, flanked on each side by three women. She was the only one who spoke and it was plain from the way her attendants covered their faces with their hands that she was being ribald about each new arrival; the men knew it too, for as each one came forward on the sward, to meet the judgment of her dancing, wicked eyes, he skipped hastily into the undergrowth, with a wink or a grin at his neighbors.

That same powerful, clear-eyed figure reappears in many guises, not all of them so unequivocally admirable. If it would not be quite right to call them happy, they are nonetheless content, no matter how unprepossessing

---

15. The old woman and the dying old woman in "The End of the Record" are in part O'Faolain's tribute to the redoubtable "Ansty." She and her husband, "The Tailor," were the subject—indeed the victims—of one of the more disgraceful cases in the history of the Irish Censorship Board, in which both O'Faolain and his friend Frank O'Connor took an active, if ultimately ineffective part on behalf of the old couple. Some of the tales told by these two were collected and preserved by Eric Cross in *The Tailor and Ansty*.

The old widow, with her almost supernatural power to judge the quick and the dead, is a direct descendant of the old tinker woman whose stubborn survival is the substance of O'Faolain's first published story, "Lilliput"; to read the two tales alongside one another is one way to appreciate the distance which O'Faolain had traversed, in voice, style, and construction, between 1927 and 1947.

their lives may seem viewed from the outside. Many of the characters in O'Faolain's earlier fiction managed, at moments, to catch sight of such lives, but the glimpse usually served only to prove how impossible the order and satisfaction of those lives were to emulate. In the later stories the view is longer, deeper; and the lesson to be learned therefrom is less despairing.

Take, for example, "The Planets of the Years." It is yet another tale of exile, of the peculiar sort to be found in these later stories. The narrator, a young Irishwoman, is married to a dedicated scholar at work on a life of the obscure "Henri Estienne, a character about whom I knew nothing except that he was a sixteenth-century French wit whose most famous *mot* is 'If youth but knew, if age but could.' " That endeavor takes the scholar and his wife to a less-than-gracious corner of Cambridge, Massachusetts; and the scholar's dedication leaves the wife with time on her hands, much of which she spends wishing she were back in Ireland. That wish, which she is forming into a letter to her sister, is interrupted (or perhaps answered) by an unannounced visit from two strangers, the older of whom, an "ancient" woman, stays even now in the narrator's memory, but strangely transformed (as memory almost always is in O'Faolain) by imagination:

> Whenever I think back to her now I always see an old peasant woman wearing a black coif, bordered inside with a white goffered frill that enclosed a strong, apple-ruddy face netted by the finest wrinkles. I know this is quite irrational. She cannot have been dressed that way at all. I am probably remembering not her but my old grandmother Anna Long from the town of Rathkeale who came to live in our house in Limerick city when I was a child, and who was the first person I ever heard talking in Irish.

The old woman had spent thirty-five years as a maid-of-all-work in the house where the narrator now lives; she came with her middle-aged niece to see the house one more time. To her, the house is full of lively memories against the contrasting reality of the house as it now is—pleasant enough, but no longer her home. To the narrator, the old woman's memories announce, in painful detail, a terrible burden of work: breakfast trays to be carried upstairs, "baskets and baskets of washing" done by hand at a stone trough in the basement. "You must have been happy here," she says to the old woman diplomatically, only to realize how inapplicable the word is. But there is a word that will serve: "I was contented all day and every day as I never was before or since. I found my first and only home in this blessed house."

To the narrator, an exile longing for home, the old woman has one more lesson, derived from her only visit to her native Ireland; and it is a lesson which O'Faolain has offered before, with particular reference to Cork: "I did not enjoy it. It was not the way I remembered it to be. Whenever you go back to any place . . . across the planets of the years, nothing is the way it was when you were young. Never go back, girl!" Here, "back" is a matter not so much of place as of time. As the protagonist of *And Again?* puts it, in a neatly ambiguous phrase, "No present joy is ever quite the same thing as memory will later make it" (*And Again?*, part 1). To O'Faolain that is a statement of fundamental fact, not of preference; what the old woman in "The Planets of the Years" has managed to retain is the emotional force of memory combined with an awareness that life is lived not in the past but in the present, what O'Faolain is fond of calling the Now—something even Frankie Hannafey had been able, in his own melodramatic terms, to understand, although not in the end to enact: "life that makes itself out desperately and magnificently of the Now and the Nakedness" (*Come Back to Erin*, part 2, ch. 8). That Now is the substance upon which memory will inevitably work; but it must be lived, insofar as possible, outside memory's shadow.

The old woman somehow manages both to be sentimentalist and realist; to hold on to the enlivening, sustaining power of her richly colored memory of the home she once had without sacrificing her ability to compare it accurately with the inevitably changed present condition of things. The encounter with the old woman brings no simple wisdom to the narrator, no sense that this last visit has been the occasion of the old woman's "rejoicing in her last backward look," no diminution of her sense of the sadness of the old woman's life: "Somewhere there had been a lost childhood. Somewhere, at some time, in some house, there had been a vision of home." But neither does the encounter leave her, like Sally Dunn or Frankie Hannafey, embittered even by her own nostalgia. She turns again to her interrupted letter; and to her wish to return to an Ireland which is not a vision of the past but the scene of her future, the vision of home in which her sister and she and her husband and their as-yet-unborn child will live out their lives. The final image is one not of separation and exile but of return; yet another window, yet another snow-scape, but this time with a different import: "How gently the lighted snow kept touching that window-pane, melting and vanishing, and, like love, endlessly returning across the planets of the years."[16]

*   *   *

16. It is of course also yet another echo of (and a quiet but firm answer to) the final moments of "The Dead."

THE FUNDAMENTAL terms in O'Faolain's later fiction are not exile and return but love and memory; the fundamental question is no longer where to live so much as it is with whom to live, and how; the "chance" to be taken, although it still may involve questions of nationality and religion, is at heart the chance inherent in any human relationship. The point of decision must now be located more in time than in space:

> All that matters is the fear of being on the brink of some essential revelation which we fear as much as we need it. These brinks, these barriers, these *No Road* signs recur and recur. They produce our most exhausting and hateful dreams. They tell us every time that we have to be born all over again, grow, change, free ourselves yet once again. Each teetering moment is as terrible as the imaginary point of time in Eastern philosophy when a dying man, who knows that within a few seconds he will be reincarnated, clings to life in terror of his next shape or dies in the desire to know it.
>
> ("Love's Young Dream")

The older language, of enclosure and escape, of entrapment and movement, is still apparent, but now the themes of O'Faolain's last novel, *And Again?* come up. That novel begins with a moment not unlike that "imaginary point of time in Eastern philosophy" and as its title suggests, it is much concerned with recurrence. But the fundamental terms of the decisions which these "brinks and barriers" mark are now wholly inward; the conflict is between dream and those actions which will put the dream to the test.

We have seen the moment when Teresa's vision of sainthood "fails" this test—although O'Faolain, who has always rather distrusted abstract standards of purity of action, seems on the whole to call it not a failure but a step into adulthood. The dreams often die hard, and the individual cannot always bear the stress of that inevitable test. But even the most shocking revelations need not be destructive. And in any case, not to undergo the test of experience is an acquiescence to self-entrapment, as the old Cork peasants (in fact, the Whelans) who appear in "The Sugawn Chair" and "The Kitchen" prove, but never realize.[17]

Men who twist the real to fit their particular imaginative projections can only be suffered, not admired, whatever their charm and energy. This applies to the Irish Don Juan (and "a natural revolutionary . . . born in the wrong place and time") Charlie Carton ("Charlie's Greek") and to

---

17. An exception must be made for those rare beings whose life approaches the condition of sainthood, such as the Cardinal Newman who appears in O'Faolain's *Newman's Way*.

Clarence Michael Dunally, whose aspirations to a place in society Rose Powis must in the end flee ("£1000 for Rosebud"). The disillusionment which had, in its earlier, political context, seemed sadly inevitable, now appears necessary and even healthy; but it is not a case of abandoning dreams altogether. Those who find happiness are likely to do so by way of balance, even if it is momentary; a balance which, not surprisingly, is still often acted out spatially, for instance by Bertie Bolger, erstwhile bachelor and "conflator" of antiques in "An Inside Outside Complex." The story, as its title may suggest, represents either the logical extreme or a near-parody of O'Faolain's lifelong interest in the view through windows; Bertie achieves his moment of happiness, both ideal and real, looking both out and in at the same moment, by means of mirrors. Such moments of satisfactorily double vision are hard to come by; neither dream nor reality is usually so obedient to the human will.

Dreams, even though they are rooted in memory and thus (at some remove) in the real past, are to a large degree *constructed*; but they are hard indeed to maintain. Walter Hunter, for example, in "One Night in Turin," imaginatively transforms Molly O'Sullivan into a figure of romantic possibility. This task takes years, both of recalling the night which gives the story its title—a night when he watched her sing the role of Amina in Bellini's *La Sonnambula*—and of keeping just near enough to watch her transform herself into "the Countess Maria Rinaldi." Walter proves to be rather a silly man, and we soon learn how far his image of Molly/Maria is from the reality of her life. But it turns out that the night he so lovingly recalls is a genuine, if complex, moment of happiness, for both of them:

> "I don't know," he gasped. "I was so lonely! And I was so happy!"
> She threw up her chin and she laughed the strangest laugh, a laugh like a breaking wave, curling and breaking between pride and regret.
> "I was happy too. If you only knew! I often wonder was I ever quite so happy since. . . ."

His disappointment when the dream will not engender a common future for the two of them is thus to some degree healed by his remaining faith in the act of dreaming itself: "A dream? Ah, well! It wasn't such a bad dream. If only I hadn't tried to make it become real. Still, isn't this the way most of us spend our lives, waiting for some island or other to rise out of the mist, become cold and clear, and . . . so . . ." The story has given us ample time to see Walter clearly and from the outside; but O'Faolain arranges it so that Walter's hesitant credo is the final word.

To have had the dream at all is of value; another disappointed lover,

Mary Anne Gogan, learns this lesson as well, and it can bring her solace even when she returns from a romantic trip to Italy to her usual, rather grey life near Limerick ("The Time of Their Lives"). Hearing news of the marriage of the rather comical Italian count whom she had herself nearly married, she judges the affair, and the count, kindly:

> It [that is, to have accepted his proposal] would not have been honest, and it would not have worked. But nothing he had ever done had worked. Nothing ever would work. However! He'd had something. They had both had something. Something precious, brief, and almost true that, she felt proudly certain, neither of them would ever forget.

The motive power behind this machine of dream and realization is memory, from which dreams are made, by which dreams are kept—"precious, brief, and almost true"—long after the despotism of reality has done its work. The nature and operation of memory is perhaps the most predominant theme in O'Faolain's later fiction, culminating both in his own autobiography—which might more precisely and fairly be called a memoir—and in his last and warmest novel, *And Again?* It may be more accurate to call it a puzzle rather than a theme; for what O'Faolain asks again and again is: "Why do I remember X when I have forgotten Y?" (*Vive Moi!*, ch. 4). The story "A Touch of Autumn in the Air" begins with an answer: "It was, of all people, Daniel Cashen of Roscommon who first made me realize that the fragments of any experience that remain in a man's memory, like bits and scraps of a ruined temple, are preserved from time not at random but by the inmost desires of his personality." That personality, however, may be lost; Cashen, "a caricatue of the self-made, self-educated, nineteenth-century businessman," finds himself "playing archaeology with his boyhood, trying to deduce a whole self out of a few dusty shards. It was, of course, far too late." The memories at the core of many another O'Faolain story prove no less compelling, and no more easily decipherable.

And the effort to encompass, to comprehend (which is to say, to arrange) memory, to find pattern amid randomness has its perilous side. The apparent enthusiasm in the title "I Remember! I Remember!" proves to be a sign of something much darker; and the story as a whole is perhaps O'Faolain's most provocative consideration of the varieties of memory. It begins by proposing a link between memory and action: "I believe that in every decisive moment of our lives the spur to action comes from that part of the memory where desire lies dozing, awaiting the call the arms." The story centers on Sarah Cotter, and especially on "her infallible memory," which at first seems admirable, even if the narrator's appreciation of it is couched in rather peculiar terms: "If she were not so childlike, so modest, so meekly and sweetly resigned, she could be a Great Bore, as oppressively looming as the Great Bear." Her life is, in a sense, all memory; and not even quite *her* memory; crippled since the age of eleven, she "has lived for some twenty-five years in, you might almost say, the same corner of the same room of the same house" in "the little town of Ardagh"—perhaps the most utterly enclosed character in all of O'Faolain's fiction. She lives for, and by, the chance to talk with others; most especially with her sister Mary, long ago married to an American, living half the year in New York, half the year in Switzerland. Mary visits rarely. The story proves to be an explanation of her ceasing altogether to visit Sarah, and of the sense of threat which, at first, seems almost a trick of the narrator's voice: "I have met nobody who does not admire [Sarah], nobody has the least fault to find with her, apart from her invulnerable memory, which all Ardagh both enjoys and fears, and whose insistence can kill like the sirocco."

That memory is, if you will, the victim of its own accuracy; Sarah can recall every detail that is reported to her. Mary too has a rich memory; but of an altogether different sort, which retains not fact and detail but emotion: "All I have is the feeling I had at the time. Or else I can't remember at all." To Mary, Sarah's memory is a sort of vampirism—and both the persuasiveness of her voice and the narrator's decision to let the story be told not from outside but from within her mind and perceptions make it hard to believe she is not speaking for O'Faolain. Mary complains to her husband:

> It's not just that it's disconcerting to be reminded about things you've said, or discarded or forgotten years and years ago. Oh, if it was only that! She brings out these bits and scraps of things I've forgotten since I was ten, . . . grubby, pointless, silly, worn, stupid things— and she says, 'That's you.' . . . She knows more about me than I know myself. I keep on wondering what else does she know about me that I don't know. What's she going to produce next? Isn't my life my own, goddammit, to keep or to lose or to throw away if I want to? Am I me? Or am I her? I sometimes think I'm possessed by that old Chucklepuss the way some people are possessed by the devil!

Mary at first tries to defeat Sarah's memory on its own ground, "by catching [Sarah] out in an error of fact"; but that puts at risk what is richest in her own memory, and it is in any case a doomed effort. The only answer is escape; and as she leaves for the last time Sarah's little room, she draws the curtains, as if either to hide her departure or to seal her sister utterly in the little room.

And Again?, as we will see, is much concerned about the accuracy of memory, its tendency to operate not as a precise record or even as the key to character but as a fluid, emotionally charged, reconstructing principle, a force which (as Robert Younger, who has a rather florid style, puts it in that novel) can be "poured over actuality, detaching a mood from its context, so lifting it that it becomes isolated . . . Memory [idealizes] life, shedding it into literature." Sarah Cotter's memory is like the work of naturalist writers whom O'Faolain so roundly and repeatedly condemns in *The Short Story*, full of a mistaken belief in objectivity and a devotion to a precise—and to O'Faolain, unselected and thus imaginatively dead— record of what is, or what has been. Against them O'Faolain places the work of Stendhal, whom Robert Younger cites as well: "True feeling leaves no memory" (*And Again?*, part 1). What may be of equal importance to O'Faolain is the inverse: how much true feeling resides in, is fed by memory—but only of the properly imaginative sort.

MORE is at issue in "I Remember! I Remember!" than just memory. Mary's husband is, ominously, rather like a more worldly, more mobile Sarah; he too wants to know Mary utterly and in detail; his "memory is just as unerring as Sarah's; and his interest in Mary's past just as avid." The imaginative richness of Mary's recollections he dismisses as a "wonderful Irish gift for fantasy." The misunderstanding is fundamental; the marriage, seemingly happy and healthy, is growing stale; and lost amid the bits and pieces which Sarah can recall so clearly, and can understand so poorly, are the evidences of an old affair of Mary's. Her husband's apparently loving desire to know her, like Sarah's similar desire, is a wish to remake, to possess her in a devilish and corrupting sense.

For O'Faolain's characters love rather too often involves a kind of imaginative projection of the self on to and into the beloved: a kind of egotism, in other words. Corney Crone, with his usual mixture of self-accusation and pride, of self-analysis and resignation, looks at Elsie Sherlock—they are not yet lovers; hardly more than friends, in fact—and sees a strange transformation:

> Her curls under her father's old hat became the curls of all the women in the world: her waist was the waist of a statue: she was losing her identity for me already, merged into myself. But that is the misfortune

of my nature, that all things end by becoming me until, now, nothing exists that is not me.

(*Bird Alone*, part 2, ch. 6)

Corney is an extreme case. Besides, he is young, with no real knowledge of women, or even of Elsie for that matter, against which to test and alter his generalized abstraction. This is also the problem of the young narrator, very like O'Faolain save for being a Dubliner and eventually a medical student, who recalls the events of "Love's Young Dream." He too knows too little; like Mary Carton's husband, he wants

to know what there is to know; to possess life and be its master. The moment I found out nobody knows, I had exposed myself to myself. I would never do it again. The shame of it was too much to bear. Like everybody else I would pretend the rest of my life. I would compound; I would invent—poetry, religion, common sense, kindness, good cheer, the sigh, the laugh, the shrug, everything that saves us from having to admit that beauty and goodness exist here only for as long as we create and nourish them by the force of our dreams, that there is nothing outside ourselves apart from our imaginings.

Perhaps so; Corney (and of course that much earlier Irishman, Bishop Berkeley) could agree; but the flow of the rhetoric, the admirable catalog of products, can hardly defend the desperate solipsism at the heart of this epiphanic moment.[18]

Yet the predominance of imagination in love is argued elsewhere in O'Faolain; by the cynical T. J. Mooney, for instance, in "One Man, One Boat, One Girl": "Why is it in the name of all that's holy that fellows see things in girls that simply aren't there?" Mooney, who likes to think he

18. O'Faolain may well be more approving of this statement than I suggest; at the very least, the idea that all life is in some way a projection of the individual imagination bears an intriguing similarity—in substance and in manner—to the way in which O'Faolain characterizes the way we read, and the degree to which we "learn" from literature. "Literature teaches nothing. It merely confirms Life, which leads, lures, pushes, drags us mindlessly into our own hopeless heartburning longings or frustrations. Seeking about us, then, for clearer images of our longings and frustrations, we alight on Wordsworth or Chekhov and cry: 'That's marvelous! That's true! That's good! I recognize it! *It's me!*'" (*Vive Moi!*, Ch. 1). That idea derives in its turn, from a comment by Thierry Maulnier which O'Faolain quotes at length in *The Vanishing Hero* (p. 139), and which says in part, "The reader responds to work of art only in proportion as he finds in it whatever idea he has already formed of himself, of his own life."

has an objective view of human relations (in a life which avoids them altogether), offers several definitions of love:

> I have decided . . . that in what is commonly called love man creates woman after his own unlikeness. In love woman is man's image of what he is not. In love man is his own creator, midwife and grave-digger, awake, asleep, dreaming or hypnotizing. . . . Love, my dear, poor boy, is a sedative disguised as a stimulant. It's a mirror where man sees himself as a monster, and woman as a thing of untarnished beauty.

But despite Mooney, O'Faolain's women are not so willing as he assumes to be so "created." The individualistic—and, sadly, doomed—Jill Jennings in "Our Fearful Innocence" turns away from the amorous Jerry Doyle with the explanation, "You are not in love with me. You are only in love with an imaginary me. Somebody you've made up inside in your head." Her clearheadedness is echoed by Molly/Maria in "One Night in Turin" and (eventually) by Rose Powis in "£1000 for Rosebud." Indeed, a whole chorus of women's voices is raised against men's idealized abstractions, political and philosophical, optimistic or pessimistic: a line stretching from Bee Hannafey in *Come Back to Erin* down to Eileen Gould O'Faolain in *Vive Moi!* and Nana in *And Again?*

Imagination, even in a delusive form, can have its place—that seems to be the comic point of "The Woman Who Married Clark Gable" and of "Marmalade."[19] Both stories are about marriage, which is on the whole a rare and unhappy phenomenon in O'Faolain's earlier work. In his later fiction marriage becomes the fundamental testing ground of the "chance" which Rose Powis so urgently proposes; of the possibility and contour of human relations generally. Given his belief in the power of dream and memory, and in the self-creating and projective imagination, O'Faolain sees a common element in relationships which we might, for convenience, call the Pygmalion theme. It is the tendency—not usually ill-intended, but dangerous nonetheless—to want to "improve" or to convert the beloved. The closest O'Faolain himself comes to giving a mythic label to this behavior occurs in "Liberty," when Doctor Reynolds, thinking of Jack Corn-field, whom she loves and will in due course marry, asks "Am I his female

---

19. The latter story can stand intriguingly beside a whole series of tales by William Trevor, in which the willful self-delusion of characters seems to be the last refuge in a barren world—for instance, "The Property of Colette Nervi" and "Bodily Secrets," both to be found in Trevor's *The News from Ireland and Other Stories*. The juxtaposition defines sharply the contrast between the two writers, especially Trevor's icy despair and O'Faolain's fundamental amiability and warmth, even at his darkest.

Orpheus?" But as we will see, her "rescue" of Cornfield from the hell of madness and self-isolation is only one particular (albeit particularly rich and important) variant on the theme; and the beloved need not seem damned to attract the lover's transforming impulses.

In one sense, this is a later version of a theme that has been of interest to O'Faolain since the beginning, a domestic version of the desire to effect change which has long marked his characters (and for that matter himself, in his public role as revolutionary, editor, social critic). O'Faolain had observed the efforts of the revolutionaries to build a new, independent, and culturally lively Ireland, only to find they have contributed to the creation of a dreary Eden of suffocating enclosure and complacency in which, among other things, any gesture of intellectual or artistic independence was to be rigorously suppressed. In a parallel vein, ambitions of parents for their children may engender change of a kind that is radically at odds with what the parents had intended. Parental ambitions breed, or at least foster, a spirit of rebellion rather than a taste for bourgeois respectability. Likewise, Corney Crone's attempt to find or construct in Elsie Sherlock an image of his own independence of mind drives her deeper and deeper into moral doubt and dogmatic religious guilt, to the point of despair and self-destruction.

Within the marriages in O'Faolain's later fiction, the desire to remake the beloved is usually less explicit and not so clearly self-defeating or damnable. As in the case of Corney Crone, the context is often religious, as it is when the widowed Anna insists that her long-time lover Frank Keene, a lukewarm Protestant and ex-soldier, convert to Catholicism and marry her ("In the Bosom of the Country"). Frank is reluctant but in the end willing; his conversion to a faith more precise and "complicating" than she can comprehend takes its course with the help of a priest who turns out to have an interest in old war stories that matches Frank's own. Frank has a view of love whose bitter edge is reminiscent of what we heard from T. J. Mooney: "Love is like jungle warfare at night, it keys you up, you feel things you can't see. . . . Love lives in sealed bottles of regret." Frank undertakes the conversion in the familiar hope that he might understand Anna better; what he accomplishes is more or less the reverse. But the outcome is hardly bitter; they do marry, apparently happily; Frank's friendship with the priest is real and important; and the groom even achieves a kind of visionary insight: "Heaven is a gift. The heart is the center."

In that result Anna is perhaps no more than an initiator, in contrast to the redoubtable Moll Wall's more thorough, more controlled, and more self-aware remaking of Georgie Atkinson. Georgie is by birth, name, and manner "an Edwardian hangover," uncomfortable in post-World War II Ireland ("Foreign Affairs"). Moll is a realist, even a bit of a skeptic, especially about men. She is an anomaly at her job in the Department of External Affairs in the Dublin government, being solitary, female, and Jewish—and intelligent enough to be fully capable of running the place, albeit from behind the scenes. Having made her Georgie, she is in the end willing to accept him fully—if not quite willing to call it happiness:

> Happy? I remember what happened to poor Pygmalion. He worked for years on a statue of the perfect woman and found himself left with a chatterbox of a wife. I think of all the years I have devoted to my chatterbox. . . . Never mind. I am really very fond of poor old George. I always have been. And he needs me.

Moll, unlike Pygmalion, has never thought of Georgie as perfect; the union of fondness with need is not a grand passion perhaps, but neither is it an impossible basis on which to live.

The statue does not always prove susceptible to the shaper's hand. O'Faolain seems to think that Henry James understood this too, if we are to judge by O'Faolain's brief "sequel" to *The Wings of the Dove*, in which an older Morton Densher observes the Kate Croy whom—so he thinks—he played a large part in creating. A more interesting and less derivative case is that of Jack Cornfield and his female Orpheus, Dr. Reynolds ("Liberty"). Georgie Atkinson and Frank Keene are amiable and not especially bright; essentially comic characters. Jack Cornfield has at least the dimensions of something more poignant and significant. He is a journalist and was once a novelist who had, like O'Faolain himself, recomposed his own life into fiction. Something of an exile from birth (born in England but Irish and Catholic by parentage, he flees in young manhood from "insensitive and brutal England" to Dublin, only to flee once more, back to "cruel, cloddish England"); a refugee from a difficult, perhaps even a violent, marriage—he is, as the story makes explicit, a kind of Crusoe, albeit hardly as self-reliant as Defoe's. He acts out, again and again, the old O'Faolain dynamic of escape and return: England to Dublin to England to an Irish asylum, from which he escapes to London once more and—as the story begins—to which he has just returned.

Dr. Reynolds's desire to help him, indeed to restore him to life and health, is rooted in part in her own sense of need and fondness: she knows her own ugliness but also her own passion. She sees in Cornfield a project (to use an unduly mechanical word for it) that is the distant echo of O'Faolain's own lifelong hope of changing, enlivening, saving Ireland; to her Cornfield, despite his mixed heritage and unusual life, is an example of a "well-established male Irish type":

> He is simply a sound, healthy, ordinary, bad-tempered man whom we have ruined by domesticating, nationalizing, habituating, acclimatizing or, in the neologistic gobbledygook of our bombastic profession, institutionalizing so thoroughly that he is now afraid to live a normal life. . . . Self-absorbed? Self-pitying? Egocentric? Chip on the shoulder? Truculent? Timid? Incurably self-referential? All that. . . .

Save him she does, by unorthodox means: they run off together, marry, move back to the ground floor of a house near the asylum. As the "cure" proceeds he becomes less and less enclosed, more and more able to wander the streets of the village; and at last he is eager to go off beyond the mountains which encircle them; at last, too, he announces that he needs no help—leaving the doctor to confront directly the distance between intention and effect, between things as they are (and people as they are) and things as she would have them. "This was, no doubt, since it had so happened, and, after all, Saint Augustine once said that whatever is is right, exactly what was to be expected, but it was not at all what she had wanted." This is not resignation, but what O'Faolain in *Vive Moi!* (ch. 11) calls "the frank acceptance of the nature of life"; the difference being that the resignation which O'Faolain has for so long seen at work in Ireland saps ambition and postpones action of body and mind, whereas this mood allows, indeed in a wry way *encourages* more effort—not any longer to shape Jack, who is no longer a statue, but to live with him in a mood of something like real contentment. The story does not end with the doctor looking out a window, like so many earlier, defeated O'Faolain figures, but taking up the small task of setting the table to receive the meal her husband is happily cooking. Imprisonment is on her mind (by way of yet another quotation); but so is hospitality and welcome.

Dr. Reynolds has, in small, lived through the contact between idealistic aspiration and the resistances of the real. Earlier in the story, the still "insane" Jack explains his withdrawal by way of one more of the doctor's favorite epigrams: "It simply happens that I do not like this horrible world. And that is your own word. Or, you said it, quoting Bertrand Russell, 'This world,' you said he said, 'is horrible! Horrible! Horrible! Once we admit that we can enjoy the beauty of it.'"

To which the doctor replies: "His Lordship might just as well have said, 'This world is lovely! Lovely! Lovely! Once we admit that we are ready to suffer the horrors of it.'" The witty parallelism of the two versions of

Russell's assertion corresponds to the balance within either version of horror and affectionate joy. In a very rough sense one can plot the course of O'Faolain's fiction between Jack's and the doctor's citations: the early fiction exists within a world that is, if not always truly horrible, then at least grim and threatening, and yet characters find, or try to find, moments of joy; the world of the later fiction seems considerably less dark, considerably more full of human connection rooted in knowledge *and* emotion, but it is hardly a world without suffering.

THE PROTAGONIST of O'Faolain's last novel, *And Again?*, must at the very outset of his story come to some provisional decision about the balance of joy and suffering in life as it is; and must then decide whether detachment or involvement is the proper course. The whole of the novel is an extended narrative "proof" of Doctor Reynolds's redaction of Russell; it portrays a world that is lovely (and full too of complicated human loves) but nonetheless full of suffering. The prologue, entitled "A Note from Olympus," begins like a fairy tale. Robert Bernard Younger, more customarily known as Beebee or Bob, a retired journalist living alone in a quiet corner of Dublin, awakes one March morning in 1965 to find several sheets of yellow paper under his bedroom door. It is a letter from the Secretary to the Department of External Affairs of "Our Celestial Beings," headquartered on Olympus, which offers him the chance to be the subject of an "experiment of permitting some mortal to live again. Our interest is solely to decide, once for all, whether what you humans call Experience teaches you a damned thing." There are of course some restrictions, based on what the letter writer (who combines, as the preceding quotation may suggest, a certain colloquial ease with a diplomat's concern for the fine points and a lawyer's for the niceties of contracts) calls "a divine regard for consistency."

Younger has, of course, no way to test the letter writer's veractiy, and there are enough references to *Faust* scattered through the book to remind us that supernatural spokespersons may, like Mephistopheles, be accomplished and persuasive liars. This message presents a few axioms about the Nature of Things: "There *is* a pattern down there, . . . and every single life since time began [is] linked with every other life . . . . In life nothing happens twice." The restrictions are two: Younger's "memory of the details of your first sixty-five years" will be "severely limit[ed]" although he will "retain all the fruits of your experience." The second—arising from the difficulties that would accompany Younger's now being "discovered at the start of your second life gabbling in a cradle like a man of sixty-five" or alternatively "growing more and more silly until you become one hundred and thirty"—is that Younger will "live backwards for sixty-five years, growing younger, and younger [the pun is unavoidable, and of course quite intentional], until at the ripe age of zero you are whisked back into the womb of Mother Time."

The Beings will offer no help for the second round—"We shall have no further verbal communication, though you are certain to infer our presence now and again, incorrectly." New life, increasing youth, even an absence of memory: it seems an irrefusable offer. Younger already knows too well the "quiet joys of age" (he lists them, at length; the first few items give a reasonable sense of the whole: "debility, impotence, incontinence, diverticulitis, colonic cancer, stones in the gall bladder") to hesitate long. So he accepts (the Beings of course knew he would; but insist, in typically paradoxical Divine fashion, that they do not "foreordain" his choice); and immediately the fable darkens: the truck which might have run him down, had he chosen not to accept the offer, instead runs down and kills a child.

It is only the first, and in fact one of the more distant, sufferings that Younger will be compelled to observe. "It would be pleasant," he thinks, "to have no relations, no connections, no genealogies, a sea gull volplaning over the wind-tracked sea"—to be another bird alone, but a much happier one. But having been granted a reprieve from memory and genealogy, he immediately sets out to recover or reconstruct both; and in so doing not only puts together a complex family tree that amounts to a kind of parody of the genealogies behind any number of other Irish novels (Kate O'Brien's *Without My Cloak*, for instance; or *A Nest of Simple Folk*) but uncovers considerable evidence of suffering. Younger in his first life had, for instance, a wife, Christabel Lee, blinded during the Blitz; a nephew, Henry, who dies shortly after birth; a twin brother, James, who has just been killed in a plane crash as the novel opens; a rather mysterious older brother, Stephen, a rebel in 1916, then an emigré to America, never to be heard from again. And most important of all, he had—and soon has again—a lover, Ana ffrench, who endures a rather unpleasant marriage to a doctor.

In his second life Bob will have to live through the aging and death not only of Ana ffrench but of her daughter (and, again, his lover) the robust Juno Anador[20]; and then the disappointment of his love for another Christabel, as well as a long separation from his final, and truest love, his

20. She may well be Bob's daughter as well—the mystery of her paternity surfaces often in the novel—although Bob, and her daughter (and Bob's wife!) Nana both come to believe she is not. In *The Vanishing Hero* O'Faolain has hard words indeed for Faulkner; is the flirtation with incest here in part a final satiric gesture in Faulkner's direction?

wife Nana. The ghosts of the past—his dead first wife; and later, that of Ana—haunt the present. The old notes of betrayal ("Are you a natural ditcher?" Bob is asked; and later he turns the tables and demands of Nana "Don't betray me" [*And Again?*, parts 3 and 5]) and loss ("Am I to lose her utterly?" he wonders, again of Nana [part 3]) and of the pain of self-division ("Passion and Reason? Divided? Every man and woman alive a collective self?" [part 3]) are all present, with undiminished force.

And indeed one of the pleasures of the book is the way it returns again to old and persistent themes in O'Faolain's writing, with a sense of acceptance and yet of continuing reflection; and particularly the way it takes up at length the workings of memory, imagination, and love. Bob is obsessed with memory; the book is itself yet another memoir, yet another retrospect, yet another effort to make an account of past experience which is accurate and comprehensive and yet still alive and true to the fluidity both of experience and of its recollection in the individual mind. The structure of the novel encompasses a debate about memory itself, not only within Bob's mind, but between his own meditations and the commentary of Nana, who at his request annotates—indeed corrects—the manuscript and writes the final pages, taking the story down to the point at which Bob, as promised, disappears into the Womb of Time. And the book as a whole stands as an intriguing fictional commentary upon O'Faolain's actual memoir, *Vive Moi!*, which sums up his life from much the same chronological perspective as that of Bob (the autobiography is dated, on its final page, 1964, at which point O'Faolain was about a year younger than Bob is at the beginning of his narrative). The autobiography had at last made clear the degree to which O'Faolain's fiction, especially that of the first two decades of his career, had been a "recomposition" of his life.[21] It is in keeping with his life-long sense of duality and contradiction, of

21. Some interconnections had long been apparent. All of his novels, for instance, are in whole or in part set in Cork; and it takes only the most general knowledge of O'Faolain's biography to recognize Denis Hussey, the son of an R.I.C. constable named John, as a close copy of John Whelan, the son of an R.I.C. constable named Denis, or to see the parallels between the drift of the Foxe-Donnel and Hussey families toward Cork and the migrations of O'Faolain's parents. The resemblances between Denis Hussey's family and childhood, especially in part 3, ch. 2 of *A Nest of Simple Folk*, and O'Faolain's own reminiscences in the second chapter of *Vive Moi!* are extensive and quite detailed, including habits of speech, the boys' fascination with lodgers, the pattern of daily walks in Cork, and an embarrassing incident with a coat. It is not just O'Faolain's first novel that draws so heavily on his own life; Corney Crone's schooling, for instance, is as we have already noted repeated almost word-for-word when O'Faolain recalls his own days at the Lancastrian National School in Cork; and in *Come Back to Erin* (part 2, ch. 6) Bee Hannafey delivers a diatribe against the Irish that is taken directly from a letter which O'Faolain himself received from the woman to whom he gives the pseudonym Anna Marie Kauffmann (*Vive Moi!*, ch. 13).

the profit of argument, even within the self: O'Faolain, having reclaimed his life from fiction into the more "factual" form of autobiography, then set out to write a novel which rebuts the whole notion that autobiography *can* be accurate. Nana says of Bob's memoir, "Everything he has written in his manuscript is a warning against the futility of trying to write a wholly truthful autobiography" (*And Again?*, part 4). That of course leaves ample room for inaccuracy of precisely the sort Mary Carton defended: the autobiographer (like his near-twin, the story-teller) is the most common, and the most necessary, of liars.

The construction of *And Again?* allows O'Faolain an extended exploration of a point of view that is both objective and subjective. In his earlier and shorter fiction this is often worked out by the use of a narrating voice which can, however, enter into the minds of characters (as, for example, in "I Remember! I Remember!"), or by the use of a kind of shifting narrative consciousness in which various characters take over the narrative focus (as in "There's a Birdy in the Cage" or "The Silence of the Valley").[22] Bob's account of his earlier life is rooted of course in what he has "learned" from experience; but as to detail, there is nearly as much distance between his understanding of what has happened and ours of what happens in his second life. The novel manages as well to find some point of mediation between the romantic and the realistic—between, if you will, Balzac and Hawthorne. Setting the novel in the future (from 1965 to 2030) relieves O'Faolain of the burden of including, in scrupulous detail, historical facts of the sort which slow his earlier novels, especially *A Nest of Simple Folk*, and it allows him to focus more directly on what Hawthorne insisted was the province of the romancer, "the truth of the human heart." But since the future is in fact much like the present (no space travel, no nuclear apocalypse; a London, a Dublin, a Boston, a Texas, a New York which are all recognizably as we know them) he does not have to abandon altogether his interest in observing the way we live now. The initial premise of the novel, and its bewildering repetition of names (three Robert Youngers, and three James Youngers; two Christabels; three women who bear the name Anna or some "anagram" thereof) suggests some vast Nabokovian artifice; but the effect page by page is anything but artificial.

Very near the end of the novel Bob offers an articulation of a powerful and complex idea of human love, couched in terms—again!—of a narrow aperture and a wide landscape:

22. In the chapter "On Construction" in *The Short Story*, O'Faolain defines what he calls "the camera-angle," and in so doing provides a very useful description of his own way of organizing longer stories.

You know what happens if you take a card and stick a pin through it and then hold that pinhole close to the eye. It can see not alone a landscape, wide as far lakes, tall as far mountains, real but also more than real: an ideal framed by desire, memory, imagination.

(part 5)

Through such an aperture, Bob claims, he can see not only the present but the past; not only his adult love for Nana but "the key to my beginnings"; and a way to "kick aside all abstract ideas, all general drifts and concepts and clamber back into one's primal, animal human self." From that vantage point he attains what amounts to a kind of faith—one which, however, depends on duality and even human argument:

> I have held and I hold that we are not only divided in our minds but honeycombed, and you have however rightly insisted that each of us is nevertheless accountable to some immutable indivisibility. I know now for certain to what and to whom that points. To some inner principle in me since my mothering childhood, and to my life's love, which means to you.

We—and the body of O'Faolain's fiction—began with a young man poised between escape and return, uncomfortably pulled both by retrospect and prospect, by self-involvement and the perception (as yet external to his own experience) of the power of human connection through love. We can fairly end with Bob Younger similarly poised, but much more contentedly, looking within and without, at the past and at the present, at life in its resistant detail and in its generalizable truth.

5

FRANK O'CONNOR

A Certain Mournful Pride

WERE one to compile a concordance to the work of Frank O'Connor, it would be wise to set aside the largest of spaces for the entries under the word "loneliness." The sad isolation of the individual is, of course, a condition easily enough observed in the work of his Irish contemporaries. Yet O'Connor's version is unmistakable. As James Matthews has shown, this distinctiveness largely results from a powerful and characteristic use of voice. The world O'Connor chooses to observe is much like the one at the heart of Kate O'Brien's and Sean O'Faolain's fiction: the life of the petty bourgeois (usually not far removed, genealogically, from peasant origins) in a provincial Irish city, sometimes explicitly identified as O'Connor's native Cork, and in any case highly reminiscent of the Cork he describes in *An Only Child* and *My Father's Son*. In this world domestic responsibilities, habits, and troubled consciences exert a determining force. Oddly enough, for all O'Connor's insistence upon isolation, human contact in his world is inevitable and frequent, at least at a superficial level. That sociability allows for the possibility that loneliness can be escaped; but at the considerable cost of the morally censorious attention of "the town" to even the smallest details of an individual life.

Early in his study of the short story, Frank O'Connor observes of Guy de Maupassant that he writes "the same story again and again." It is not a condemnation; in his repetitiousness, O'Connor argues, Maupassant is "like every other writer, either when he has got tired and begun repeating himself or when he is at the top of his power and can only repeat himself" (*The Lonely Voice*, "Country Matters"). There is a similar formulaic repetition in the latter half of O'Connor's *Collected Stories;* to come, for instance, after some five hundred pages of that volume, to the opening of "The Impossible Marriage" is to experience a sense of returning to a familiar place:

It wasn't till he was nearly thirty that Jim Grahame realized the trick that life had played on him. Up to that time he had lived very much like any other young man, with no notion that he was being imposed upon. His father had died ten years before. Jim, an accountant in a provision store, had continued to accept his father's responsibilities, and his mother, a lively, sweet-natured little woman, had kept house for him in the way that only mothers can. They lived in the house into which she had married: a big, roomy, awkward house on the edge of the country where the rent they paid was barely enough to keep the building in repair. Jim had never been very shy with girls, but none of them he had met seemed to him to be half the woman his mother was, and, unknown to himself, he was turning into a typical comfortable old bachelor who might or might not at the age of forty-five decide to establish a family of his own. His mother spoiled him, of course, and, in the way of only children, he had a troubled conscience because of the way he took advantage of it. But spoiling is a burden that the majority of men can carry a great deal of without undue hardship.

The story is a useful starting point in part because it combines two of what O'Connor himself might have called his obsessions: the complex ties of love, jealousy, and duty which "marry" parent (especially mother) and child (usually son); and the slow, reticent, and—to the eye of an outsider—seemingly passionless dance of Irish courtship.

The narrative voice too is unmistakable; easy, rather wry, conversational, although the narrator here forgoes both the first person and the array of names (Larry Delaney, Michael Murphy, Jackie Dooley, Denis Halligan, Jerry Moynihan: the list is quite long) from behind which O'Connor frequently observes the world. That voice, even when it speaks "autobiographically," is always at a little distance from the events of the tale itself—near enough to see, and to be drawn sympathetically into the moment of contact and conflict which is the heart of the tale; far enough to know, or at least to predict, the outcome and to try to judge both character and action. The teller is himself a "reader," not of fiction but of events and of the general truths which they may be said to illustrate.[1] The voice—like

---

1. O'Connor, in one of his last efforts to come to grips with the maddening ghost of Joyce, argues that the "new" or Joycean style causes the loss of the union of reader and writer and of their shared view of the "object" of the story. Joyce, he says, makes the reader at best a "third party, present only by courtesy" (*A Short History of Irish Literature,* ch. 17). O'Connor's stories almost invariably underscore that union by pretending to be things overheard and then passed on; and indeed a reading of James Matthews' biography of O'Connor makes it clear just how often O'Connor *did* overhear, or had the germ of a story

O'Connor's own, when he writes criticism or history or cultural analysis—has a fondness for categories and (not always defensible) generalizations of the sort with which this particular paragraph closes.

Even offered to us by such an engaging narrator, the "life" he observes seems narrow and not a little sad. The settled, even claustrophobic environment in which Jimmy Grahame has spent so many years cries out for some sort of change, some intrusion of imagination or romance, some element of unpredictability to shock even the teller of the tale, fond as he is of types and of generic labels like "mother" and "bachelor." And when, in the next paragraph, one of the nameless "girls" whom Jimmy knows suddenly merits a name—Eileen Clery—we can predict that the particular force which is perhaps to enlighten and certainly to complicate his life is a love which can compete with his devotion to his mother; somewhere ahead perhaps lies a marriage to supplant the cozy but "impossible" marriage of mother and son in their shabby house near the edge of town. Eileen is herself an only child with a mother to look after. Indeed, in the Ireland O'Connor explores, almost anyone "could have listed a score of families where a young man or woman walked out for years before he or she was in a position to marry, too often only to find themselves too old or tired for it." That in part explains how "the fear of loneliness" drives mothers and sons, friends and brothers, lovers and priests into impossible but necessary relations. The very impossibility of their union is, in the first instance, what seems to bring Jimmy and Eileen together. More often than not, the unlikeliness of any stable relationship, paradoxically, engenders relationships of the most compelling sort in O'Connor's Ireland.

The emotional direction of the story is toward, but not quite ever to, a condition of escape. But it is important as well to understand the appeal of Jimmy's early life, the solace which even a restricted and enclosed "home" offers; otherwise it is hard to understand why O'Connor's people so stubbornly resist change, why they cling to a place and shape of life which even they themselves see as imprisoning; why, in short, they do not do as so many Irish have done and simply leave. Jimmy's bachelor life is "comfortable" in more than an ironic sense. It is, first of all, the place

---

told to him. See, among other instances, Matthews' account of the genesis of "Guests of the Nation" (*Voices,* pp. 71–72) and "The Sentry" (*Voices,* p. 196). Sean O'Faolain's "How to Tell a Short Story" gives some idea of how O'Connor, as a young writer at least, went about collecting tales.

The full course of O'Connor's encounter with Joyce can be found in the chapter "Work in Progress" and in the opening pages of the chapter "A Clean Well-Lighted Place" in *The Lonely Voice;* in the last chapter of *The Mirror in the Roadway;* and in the whole of chapter 17 of *A Short History of Irish Literature.*

he knows, the one place in which the duties, the conditions, even the turns of speech are familiar. O'Connor's Irish provincials never travel well, whether they head for Dublin or England or America. Nor do "foreigners" fare well in Ireland, as the sad case of "The American Wife" and the misadventures of an American cousin in "Ghosts" make clear. Any geographic (and of course cultural) movement seems to have an inevitably disorienting effect.

A house at the edge of the country, like the Blarney Lane "home" O'Connor recalls in the first few pages of *An Only Child;* a steady job, preferably one which can be called a profession, in a land where poverty, both urban and rural, is a continuing fact; a father long dead (and thus no longer a competitor) and easy to replace; a doting mother whose affection does not need to be won or guarded from the incursions of siblings—all these represent a kind of ideal to O'Connor's people. At the very least, the advantage of such a life is that the pangs of conscience are modest and easily comprehensible, and duties are clear-cut and thus more readily accepted and fulfilled. Once broken, however, that world will be next to impossible to recreate, as Jimmy and Eileen indeed learn.

From this starting point, the story proceeds through an almost fugal development of the ideas of union and impossibility. Jimmy and Eileen, for all their sense of filial duty, cannot resist the force of attraction, which is, the teller informs us, not a matter of "tanned chests and voluptuous contours" but of the power of "human loneliness." Working against this attraction is a counter-force of guilt, itself rooted in the lovers' empathetic understanding of the "fear of loneliness and old age" which inevitably governs their mothers' lives. At first, the two play the game of courtship by the accepted rules, walking out together but doing no more out of respect for maternal jealousies. Then Jimmy proposes his "impossible" idea: that they "get married and go on the way we're going," each still living at home, meeting for brief and occasional moments of mock connubiality. Each for his/her own reasons, the two do marry on just those terms, arousing in the town a sense of scandal and confirming the two mothers' sense that their children are hopelessly selfish. The various "duties" imposed by the marriage (the word *duty* rings with particular frequency through the last few pages of the story) seem momentarily in balance; but the balance cannot endure the inevitable death of Mrs. Grahame, followed all too soon by Jimmy's own death. The assorted "marriages" come full circle: a story which begins with Jimmy in the care of his mother ends with the widowed Eileen caring for her mother, living only to fulfill that duty: "Once Mammy goes, there'll be nothing to keep me." It is a grim destiny indeed for two modest people who wanted only "something, however little it might be, of the pleasure of marriage while they were still young enough to enjoy it."

Yet the story ends with Eileen's claim to "relatives and even neighbors" that "in spite of everything she had been intensely happy, happy in some way they could not understand." Her insistence compels belief, if not understanding. O'Connor's belief that happiness occurs even in guises and places in which it seems impossible, and that the actions and responses of the human animal will resist the closest observation, are important guidelines to his fiction. The story ends with the narrative voice combining incomprehension with affection grounded in empathetic understanding, a mixture which should serve as a reminder of the limited degree to which we can trust the knowing teller instead of—or in explanation of—his tale.

WHATEVER the dimensions of the particular struggle between loneliness and communion, between conscience and happiness, in an O'Connor story the arena will almost invariably be domestic and familial, the primary setting a modestly furnished interior. It is no coincidence that in the second chapter of *The Mirror in the Roadway* O'Connor claimed Jane Austen as one of his favorite novelists. In this typically eccentric study of the novel, he begins (in a chapter called "Preliminary") with the assertion that "to have grown up in an Irish provincial town in the first quarter of the twentieth century was to have known the nineteenth-century novel as a contemporary art form." And a few pages later he observes that "except for the moral passion which is literature's main contribution to the arts, a Dutch interior might be chosen as the ideal of the nineteenth-century novelist." Elsewhere O'Connor insists that the novel and the short story are distinct, but the last, rather gloomy chapters of *The Mirror in the Roadway* suggest that in his view the short story must take up the unfinished—indeed abandoned—work of the nineteenth-century novel: the realistic observation of things as they are, the moral assessment of the state of the individual, the understanding and judgment of the domestic life.[2]

2. O'Connor's definition of the nineteenth-century novel and his differentiation between that form and the short story, rest upon the further notion that the novel "concentrate[s] on the study of society and the place of the individual within it" (*Mirror in the Roadway*, ch. 1) and that "without the concept of a normal society the novel is impossible" (*Lonely Voice*, "Introduction"). But, as he puts it in the essay-review "And It's a Lonely Personal Art" (*New York Times Book Review*, April 12, 1953, p. 1), "the thing which makes the Irish novel impossible is that the subject of a novel is almost invariably the relation of the individual to society, and Ireland does not have a society which can absorb the individual." That is why, says O'Connor (for the moment putting aside *Ulysses*, not to mention the work of the writers discussed in my own first four chapters), Ireland has "failed to produce a single

The centrality of the family in O'Connor's fiction is frequently visible in his titles: of stories such as "The Luceys," "The Mad Lomasneys," "The Corkerys," "The Grip of the Gerahty's"[3]; of collections such as *Domestic Relations;* and of course of his autobiography, *An Only Child.* In fact we might say there are two families, or sorts of families, in O'Connor. The one can be fairly represented the "mad" Lomasneys in the story which bears their name:

> Harry Lomasney, the builder, was a small man who wore gray tweed suits and soft collars several sizes too big for him . . . . He was nick-named "Hasty Harry." "Great God!" he fumed when his wife was having her first baby. "Nine months over a little job like that! I'd do it in three weeks if I could only get started." His wife was tall and matronly and very pious, but her piety never got much in her way. A woman who survived Hasty would have survived anything. Their eldest daughter, Kitty, was loud-voiced and gay and had been expelled from school for writing indecent letters to a boy. She had copied the letters out of a French novel but she failed to tell the nuns that. Nellie was placider and took more after her mother . . . . Rita was the exception among the girls . . . . There was something in her they didn't understand, something tongue-tied, twisted, and unhappy.

These families, large and contentious (sometimes fatally so), center on the marriage of not-altogether congenial opposites (one partner, usually the wife, sensible but reticent; the other loud, opinionated, and quick-tempered). Able somehow to accept and contain behavior by their young which flies in the face of the rules of the censorious place in which they live, the family members often bear the label of wildness or eccentricity either with good humor or with an utter obliviousness, and maintain despite this a solid bourgeois position. These family groups exert a powerful fascination over those who look on, perhaps primarily because what-

---

novelist" but has "produced four or five storytellers who [seem] to me to be first-rate" (*Lonely Voice,* "Introduction"). The reader is left to puzzle out how to square this lack of a society with the profoundly important social forces—the pressures and habits of a provincial Irish city—present in most of O'Connor's stories. Certainly, in broad terms, "the study of society and the place of the individual within it" is a suggestively accurate label for much of O'Connor's short fiction. But it may be that the predominance of the family over other "social" groupings and standards such as class and occupation is in fact a reflection of the weakness, in O'Connor's view, of those larger social categorizations. Indeed it seems logical that the lack of a society to escape *into* makes the family all the more inescapable.

3. The last of these is omitted from *Collected Stories* but is included in *The Cornet Player Who Betrayed Ireland,* with the notation that it is "the story [O'Connor] was working on when he died." Along with "The Little Mother" and "The Cheat" it forms a trilogy, or suite, of tales with shared characters, especially the Twomey family and the "atheist" Dick Gordon.

ever the internal stresses and conflicts they contain, they are, like the Corkerys in the story named after them, "rarely dull and never predict-able"—no small compliment in the complacently provincial world of Cork.

But what generates the story, usually, is the contact between these noisy eccentrics and the more isolated children of another sort of O'Connor family, central to his autobiographies and to a series of stories, most of them written after 1945 and many featuring O'Connor's alter ego, Larry Delaney. In these families it is the singular and very nearly obsessive force of the relations between mother and child that is determining; if there is a father at all, he is likely to be either a shadow or a sharp but occasional annoyance. From that vantage point, the more populated, noisy, and energetic world of the Twomeys, Corkerys, and Dalys is often mystifying at first; but observed more carefully, over time and usually with the added inducement of romantic attachment, that world seems to offer the pos-sibility of freedom of movement and independence of mind, perhaps even a respite (certainly not an escape: escape is unthinkable) from the terrible duties of winning and keeping a mother's love.

Maurice Wohlgelernter has outlined the degree to which the family as it appears throughout O'Connor's work might be seen as paradigmatically "Irish" (*O'Connor: An Introduction,* pp. 65–108). This may be so, but from a larger perspective O'Connor's familial relations and gestures define the inertial condition toward which all human relations tend, for good or ill. Certainly the family acts as a magnet for the "orphans" (usually illegitimate children) and foster children in such stories as "The Pretender," "Babes in the Woods," and "A Set of Variations on a Borrowed Theme." This last story in particular explores the degree to which an invented or "foster" family can function as if it were real, and how the complex roles of mother and son can be undertaken as "trades" to be learned and perfected, rather than conditions to be experienced. In a world so defined by family relations as O'Connor's Ireland, to be altogether outside the family is to be pro-foundly unstable, as the "terrible" story of O'Connor's mother's life dem-onstrates (*An Only Child,* ch. 3). Such exclusion is in fact very nearly a metaphor for hell, as O'Connor puts it: "For me, there has always been in imagination a stage beyond death—a stage where one says, 'I have no home now.' "

The family as an arrangement of habitual roles and gestures of rela-tionship is powerfully present even in stories which are not explicitly domestic at all. Consider, for example, the best-known of O'Connor's stories about the Troubles, "Guests of the Nation."[4] Overtly, the story

---

4. I have used the text as given in *Collected Stories,* although O'Connor revised the story heavily several times. Indeed, O'Connor seems never to have felt quite comfortable with any

has no Dutch interior. Its characters are a band of IRA "soldiers" and their British captives living in a world of all-night card games and rich argument. But viewed by way of the Dalys, the noisy talk around the card table begins to look more like an argumentative family dinner. The two prisoners, Belcher and 'Awkins, look like many a pair of O'Connor brothers (or, alternatively, like husband and wife): one tall and quiet, the other short and loud.

But an O'Connor family cannot exist without a mother, real or created. Here there is, in the near background, the old woman in whose house the whole menage is staying. To the Irishmen, she is "a great warrant to scold, and crotchety" (if we can judge from O'Connor's other accounts of the "great improvisation" which was Irish political conflict in the early 1920s, the men are enjoying their first "escape" from their true home). But the adaptable prisoners (of whom the narrator, a "town" man who is a little out of his element, remarks, "I never seen in my short experience two men that took to the country as they did") make this temporary shelter into a home. Belcher, the quiet Englishman, immediately adopts the role of the good son, winning the affection of the crotchety old woman by being imperturbably helpful, "ever . . . at her heels carrying a bucket, or basket, or load of turf, as the case might be." The louder 'Awkins is the inevitable rebellious free-thinker who dares to challenge even the mother, but "I am glad to say that in her he met his match," the pride of a son and of an Irishman coming together in the narrator's voice.

The stability of this artificial family is brief, however; and, strikingly, the threat to its continuance, the "duty" which will lead the Irishmen to execute their "guests," is itself couched in terms of family. Warned that the Englishmen will be shot in retaliation if rebel prisoners are executed, the narrator tries to put aside his doubts: "in those days disunion between brothers seemed to me an awful crime. I knew better after"—knew, we might say, more clearly who his true brothers were. Led out, as he thinks, to be shifted to a new "prison," but in fact to be shot, the noisy Englishman

---

of the stories in his first book, called *Guests of the Nation* and comprising the bulk of his stories dealing directly with the Troubles and Civil War. On the grounds that a collection of his "best" stories should include nothing that is "less than perfect," he excluded all of the stories in *Guests* from *The Stories of Frank O'Connor*. It may be, however, that his exclusion was motivated as well by his effort, at about the same time, to reuse much of his own experience in the Troubles and the Civil War, both in stories such as "Freedom" and "The Martyr" and in part 4 of *An Only Child*, which repeats some of the events, and much of the atmosphere, of the more autobiographical stories in *Guests of the Nation*. The editor of *Collected Stories* takes a middle course—following O'Connor's lead in omitting most of the stories to be found in *Guests*, but including both the title story and "The Late Henry Conran"—one of the few stories in *Guests* not at all concerned with civil war.

grumbles, "Just as a man mikes a 'ome of a bleedin' place, some bastard at Headquarters thinks you're too cushy and shunts you off." The reticent Belcher is, for all his helpfulness, a little less responsive to the attraction of the domestic order, having been abandoned by a wife; but even he admits, in almost his final words, "I likes the feelin' of a 'ome."

The fundamental battle in the story is between the web of human affection which makes of this crowded country cottage a home, and the political and military duty which demands violent action against humankind. The narrator, for all his adeptness as a storyteller a man awkward with words and more than a little resistant to complex ideas, is left profoundly unsettled: "I was somehow very small and very lonely. And anything that ever happened me [*sic*] after I never felt the same about again." Insofar as it undercuts the absolute force of abstract duty, this moral uncertainty is a bitter gain; but against the gain is set the figure of the old woman, demanding an explanation which none of the executioners can offer. We last see her praying over her lost sons. The narrator has, in a sense, suffered that most painful, if inevitable, of condemnations: a mother's disappointment.

The whole of O'Connor's first book of stories, also entitled *Guests of the Nation*, explores the exhilaration of escaping from home and the comfort of returning there—less a place than a complex of contentious family relations. Home represents even in these earliest stories a stage from which an escape into independence can be undertaken, however hazardous and temporary it may prove to be. The possibility, indeed the necessity of such escape is underscored by the accident of historical circumstances (the various rebel bands provide a proximate and acceptable place to escape *to*). But home is at the same time a body of language and organizing principles which defines and thus limits escape; and O'Connor's characters more often than not choose to return from the seductions of the city or of America to the home which they have in a sense never truly left, armed if they are lucky with a clearer sense of its dangers. In his later stories, those dangers are less melodramatically presented than in *Guests of the Nation*; but the fear that the price of stability and human connection might be a fearful entrapment remains.

IF HOME and family are a fundamental language that expresses the possibilities of human choice and happiness, the crucial "words" are three lines of relationship. The first is that between mother and son, a "connection" which can easily appear, as it does to the robust young Irish-American "outsider" who will in the end become "The American Wife," to be "an attachment . . . that [is] neither natural nor healthy." The relationship rests upon a ceaseless expenditure, by the son particularly, of "concentration" (to borrow a word from the story "The Man of the House") in order to understand, to accept, and to perform responsibilities, and upon the shame and disappointment which the usual failure of that effort engender. This attachment is explored directly in "My Oedipus Complex," where the nostalgic irony of the narrative voice emphasizes all the more the conflicts and shocks which separate the son from the mother, and make allies even of those apparent natural enemies, son and father. The second fundamental bond, between brothers, is one of antithesis, to apply a notion which is at the heart of O'Connor's remarks on Turgenev (*Lonely Voice*, "Hamlet and Quixote"). It is often paralleled by those "passionate relationships that spring up in small towns where society narrows itself down to a handful of erratic and explosive friendships" ("The American Wife").

And then there is the union of husband and wife, for which "antithesis" may well be too mild and too simple a word. As O'Connor's narrator remarks in "My First Protestant," "All marriages are mixed marriages." His sympathies are generally with the women, at least after the marriage, when she is likely to provide whatever stability and good sense is to be found in the house, in contrast to the husband, who like so many O'Connor adult men is likely to be little more than "mean and common and a drunkard" ("My First Protestant"), or at least a creature of stubborn habits and disappointed aspirations. There are happy exceptions, of which "The Impossible Marriage" is one, in which "the mixture is all right." But a more characteristically mixed and lonely romantic relationship is that described in "The Frying-Pan":

> Father Fogarty's only real friends in Kilmulpeter were the Whittons. Whitton was the teacher there. He had been to the seminary and college with Fogarty, and, like him, intended to be a priest, but when the time came for him to take the vow of celibacy, he had contracted scruples of conscience and married the principal one. Fogarty, who had known her too, had to admit that she wasn't without justification, and now, in this lonely place where chance had thrown them together again, she formed the real center of what little social life he had.

That "little social life" is a terribly weak antidote to the voracious loneliness of Fogarty's life; and before long it occurs to him that "he was . . . trying desperately to stuff the yawning holes in his own big, empty heart." It is not a great surprise to the reader to find him, a few pages later, alone with

Una Whitton, realizing that "in the simplest way in the world he had been brought to admit to a married woman that he loved her and she to imply that she felt the same about him, without a word being said on either side." What brings him to this is not so much sexual passion as a craving for domesticity; he finds himself seduced, at least spiritually, by the thought of children and the fact that Una's house is "gay and spotless."

What is more unexpected is the nature of Tom Whitton's jealousy. As Una explains to Fogarty, "He's jealous of you because you're a priest . . . . You have all the things he wants . . . . Respect and responsibility and freedom from the worries of a family, I suppose." It dawns on Fogarty at last that Whitton is "really a lonely, frustrated man who felt he was forever excluded from the only things which interested him." The same could easily be said of Fogarty himself, and indeed of the vast majority of those who appear in, and tell, O'Connor's stories.

That each man's exclusion derives from his own decision, his own sense of vocation, acted upon or abandoned for cause, makes the frustration no easier to bear. The "marriage" of these three, with Una at that uncomfortable, highly visible, and yet oddly powerless center where O'Connor's women so often find themselves, is a bleak one. As Fogarty comes to believe, "the three of them, Tom, Una, and himself, would die as they had lived, their desires unsatisfied." But the relationship is also passionate and necessary; Fogarty and Una's one kiss, however awkward, expresses as well "an agony of passion, and it was as if their loneliness enveloped them like a cloud." Thus again loneliness is both the sign of separation and the force which strives, however briefly, to overcome that separation; it is both the mark of the failure of human connection and the shared element upon which love and friendship are to be built. Even more than that, it is the fundamental human fact, the necessary subject of any true story and the condition which the telling of a story endeavors to overcome. "The short story," O'Connor wrote in his *New York Times* essay-review "And It's a Lonely Personal Art," "is a lonely personal art; the lyric cry in the face of human destiny." And (speaking of Kipling, whom he finds to be the unique exception), "all . . . great storytellers speak to us with a lonely human voice, almost as though we were strangers and they were apologizing for their intrusion" (*Lonely Voice*, "You and Who Else?").

IT MAY seem paradoxical that such loneliness occurs within a community, but in fact communities make loneliness all the worse, deepening it into "a new and disturbing feeling of alienation" ("My First Protestant"). But given the nature of the towns in which O'Connor characteristically sets his stories, loneliness takes on a new and more virtuous cast as a sign of individuality and resistance. This is the case of the atheist Dick Gordon, whose story ("The Cheat") builds to the argument that "a man's loneliness is his strength," with the bitter qualification that "only a wife can really destroy him because only she can understand his loneliness." O'Connor's world is full of places where any intelligent man will likely (as Father Fogarty predicts about Tom Whitton) "grow stupid and wild for lack of educated society" or, like Tom Lucey, "as is the way of men of character in provincial towns" will "more and more . . . become a collection of mannerisms, a caricature of himself" ("The Luceys"). Like families, small towns may look lively and appealing enough from the outside, as does Cork to Joe Saunders in "The Weeping Children," but he is soon reminded by a more knowing voice: "This may seem a big city to you, but it's not big enough for those who have to live in it."

Cork is the bitter standard by which Irish communities are measured, a city full of a "warm, dim, odorous, feckless, evasive . . . quality, and the last drop of enterprise oozed away" (*Irish Miles,* ch. 14). Whatever their precise name or location or size, such towns share a strict standard of respectability, a heavy dose of moral censoriousness and sexual repression, an abundance of talk and an absence of significant action. The energies of the schoolteachers, doctors, lesser clergy, lawyers, and builders who populate O'Connor's stories are, most often, invested in harsh rivalries over petty rewards. In "A Great Man," for example, the doctors of the town of Dooras are "at one another's throats, fighting for every five-bob fee that could be picked up." It is not quite accurate to say that such communities *engender* loneliness and frustration. O'Connor will not easily grant his characters that excuse, as we may observe in the case of Fogarty and Whitton, both of whom are where they are in large part by their own choice. Still the town has its power, and O'Connor's characters are ready to place the blame for their own condition on the town's shoulders:

> Now I know what you're thinking. You're thinking how nice 'twould be to live in a little town. You could have a king's life in a house like this, with a fine garden and a car so that you could slip up to town whenever you felt in need of company. Living in Dublin, next door to the mail boat and writing things for the American papers, you imagine you could live here and write whatever you liked . . . . All I mean is you wouldn't stay it for long. This town broke better men. It broke me and, believe me, I'm no chicken.
>
> ("Public Opinion")

The complaint is not entirely self-delusive; the towns and provincial cities of Ireland, as O'Connor portrays them, are ready even to condemn children for the imagined sins of their fathers, as is the case in "A Set of Variations on a Borrowed Theme." "Full of cliques and factions" ("My First Protestant"), they are places in which no quarrel is small. "I suppose living more or less in public as we do we are either cured or killed by it, and the same communal sense that will make a man be battered into a reconciliation he doesn't feel gives added importance to whatever quarrel he thinks must not be composed"—that is the bitter moral of "The Luceys."

But even on the score of internecine contentiousness such towns are not quite predictable, as the parish priest Father Crowley learns at some cost in "Peasants," when he attempts to take a strict moral line with regard to the theft of "the funds of the Carricknabreena Hurling, Football and Temperance Association." What obstructs Crowley is the town's precise sense of foreignness, and its willingness at all costs to protect its own from the hands and judgment of foreigners. Crowley is rebuked by one of his parishioners: "I won't sit here and listen to insinuations about my native place from any foreigner." A few sentences later we learn that the "foreigner" Crowley's "own country" is all of "fifteen long miles away." The defining unit of "foreignness" is in fact narrower even than that; it stretches no further than the limits of an individual family, that unit by which any individual is inescapably defined.

The desire to escape such towns needs little explaining; the means of escape, however, are few indeed, and rooted more in imaginative hope than in experiential fact. Tom Whitton's dream of freedom is not unrepresentative. He imagines a priestly vocation which, as Fogarty knows but can never tell him, bears little resemblance to the actual life of the clergy and would in any case do little to resolve the struggle within Tom, "a man at war with his animal nature, longing for some high, solitary existence of the intellect and imagination" ("The Frying-Pan"). It is a bitter lesson, parallel to that of Nan Ryan ("The Ugly Duckling"), a woman in whom her longtime but unsuccessful suitor, Mick Courtney, sees "depths of sensuality," but who in the end enters a convent. There an older Mick visits her and formulates this "true" idea:

> It was something that happened . . . in different ways. Because of some inadequacy in themselves—poverty or physical weakness in men, poverty or ugliness in women—those with the gift of creation built for themselves a rich interior world; and when the inadequacy disappeared and the real world was spread before them with all its

wealth and beauty, they could not give their whole heart to it. Uncertain of their choice, they wavered between goals—were lonely in crowds, dissatisfied amid noise and laughter, unhappy even with those they loved best. The interior world called them back, and for some it was a case of having to return there or die.

This is O'Connor's ironic version of the temptation of Christ in the wilderness. The way of the imagination, however productive as the motive for storytelling, is invariably doomed by the hard facts of the matter. If loneliness is an inevitable part of the human condition, so too is disillusionment, a part of "the pattern of human life as we have all experienced it—nostalgia and disillusionment and a fresh nostalgia sharpened by experience," which is, he argues, the "narrative line" of the short story itself (*Lonely Voice*, "Introduction").

O'Connor's stories are full of dreamers, or as he often calls them, "romantics." They create an imagined alternative to the actual life within and around them, and their climactic moment of realization and disillusionment is frequently the focal center of the story. The dream, no matter how short-lived, has considerable power. In the story "A Romantic" (in *More Stories by Frank O'Connor*) O'Connor argues that "eventually, to the romantic, reality itself becomes romance, but not until he has let it slip from his hands. That is the romantic's tragedy." In "The American Wife" it is the title character's "glorification of Irishmen" that moves her to marry Tom Barry. That marriage of high hopes collapses when she realizes that Tom and his cronies "belong to a country whose youth was always escaping from it, out beyond the harbor, and that was middle-aged in all its attitudes and institutions." In "The Corkerys" May McMahon, having joined a cloistered order of nuns, tries to solace herself with the imitation of "more heroic times," an effort she cannot sustain in the face of the obvious: that she is "alone in a world of bad actors and actresses."

For some of O'Connor's characters, many of them women, it seems that sex is an answer, a way to escape the frustration of the moralistic town while avoiding as well the sense of failure and dissatisfaction engendered by the life of the imagination. Rita, the most compelling of "The Mad Lomasneys," has an "affair" with a seminarian (which may, for all we and her family can tell, be wholly imagined); but it proves to be no more than a temporary stop on the way to an unsatisfying marriage to a stuffy lawyer she has known most of her life. An unnamed young girl, in "News for the Church," exasperated with the way "people make such a mystery of [sex]," sleeps with her sister's former suitor, but nothing much happens.

The commonsensical (if comic) conclusion she draws from the experience ("It's all over and done with now. It's something I used to dream about, and it was grand, but you can't do a thing like that a second time.") is too weak to withstand the ministrations of Father Cassidy, to whom she has come for what she thinks will be an easy confession.

There is no mistaking O'Connor's contempt for the sexual repressiveness of Irish society; it is a point he makes at great length in his longest story, "The Holy Door," in *The Common Chord*. But he finds little reason to believe in any Lawrentian redemptive power in sex. Una McDermott, in "The Sorcerer's Apprentice," "an intensely pious girl" who nevertheless has an eye for "facts" which do not easily correspond to the "exceedingly orthodox" standards of the town and of her "serious and rather pompous" suitor, Jimmy Foley, takes up with Denis O'Brien, who preaches a notably unorthodox doctrine: "You talk far too much about sex. That's because you should be enjoying it instead." But when she and Denis act upon that wisdom, she finds herself "alarmed and disillusioned," even if, surprisingly, with "no more sense of guilt than if they had been married." She ends up with a terrible sense of failure, stranded somewhere between Denis (separated but of course not divorced from his wife and thus safely insulated from marriage to Una) and Jimmy, still mired in "his smugness and his celibacy." If Una's goal is change, she is indeed a failure; "I'm not in the least changed," she tells Jimmy. But she has at least found a way to make a final choice, to abandon Jimmy in favor of an uncertain future with Denis. The result is a bitter if overdue loss of innocence: "All the time she had thought she was learning the business of love, but now she knew every man and woman is a trade in himself, and he [Denis] was the only trade she knew."

Far from being a cure-all, sex in O'Connor's world is likely to be so bound up with self-delusion and self-defense that instead of promoting an escape from habit and loneliness, it becomes a verifying symptom of them. The point is most clearly made in "Don Juan's Temptation" in the case of Gussie Johnson:

Despising youth and its illusions, he could scarcely ever think of his own youth without self-pity. He had been lonely enough; sometimes he felt no one had ever been so lonely. He had woken up from a nice, well-ordered, intelligible world to find eternity stretching all round him and no one, priest or scientist, who could explain it to him. And with that awakening had gone the longing for companionship and love which he had not known how to satisfy, and often he had walked for hours, looking up at the stars and thinking that if only he could meet an understanding girl it would all explain itself naturally.

Gussie, the Irish Don Juan, meets the aptly named Helen, a woman whose resistance to his seductive offers seems to him to be no more than "ordinary schoolgirl romanticism." But in the end he feels he can understand her all too well, as someone who wanted "something bigger in life that would last beyond death . . . . Perhaps people couldn't do without illusions." Tempted to replace sex with love, to seek communication rather than mere intercourse, Gussie is "saved" by sex, when Helen is "converted" to the idea that she should sleep with him. It is, in a way, Una McDermott's story viewed from the other side.

If neither imagination nor sex (which is, of course, often inextricably tied to imagination) can release the individual from the grip of the town and its moral and intellectual restrictions, moving away is no more effective. The rather morose Ned McCarthy, in "Fish for Friday," rejects as "simpleminded" the "notion that life was merely a matter of topography." O'Connor's characters do sometimes leave, but they are likely to find themselves in the position of the schoolteacher Ned Keating in "Uprooted":

> Spring had only come and already he was tired to death; tired of the city [Dublin, not Cork], tired of his job. He had come up from the country intending to do wonders, but he was as far as ever from that . . . . The city was what he had always wanted. And now the city had failed him.

Ned's brother Tom, who has undertaken his own escape into the priesthood, has reached that point where: "It's the loneliness of my job that kills you." The two brothers' return home to a country farm brings Ned into contact with a kind of passion he does not seem able to find in Dublin; but it brings little ease to either brother, although Ned stands by the decision he had made to leave for the city. What he realizes is that "the trouble is always in ourselves. If we were contented in ourselves the other things wouldn't matter." For Ned, as in the paradigmatic case of Stephen Dedalus and his creator, geographic exile, however eagerly sought and elaborately defended, does not necessarily imply imaginative exile. Indeed, as *Ulysses* had proved, a physical departure may be the most effective way to stay perpetually at home, intellectually and psychically.[5]

5. In O'Connor's reminiscences, the most chilling example of the price of exile is not Joyce but Æ. *My Father's Son*, ch. 13, recounts the bitter story of Æ's departure from Dublin and

If "home" cannot be escaped, then may it not be reformed? O'Connor, especially outside of his fiction, had a taste for didacticism, even sermonizing. Especially in the 1940s and after, he frequently took the opportunity to point out to the Irish exactly what sort of change was necessary, writing one book proposing the need for "civilization" in Ireland *(Irish Miles)* and another angrily berating a state of affairs in which "the [Irish] literature of the past is simply ignored; the literature of our own time is either ignored or banned by law" *(A Short History of Irish Literature)*. And one can certainly suspect that O'Connor's relentless depiction of an Ireland which is "more than ever sectarian, utilitarian (the two nearly always go together), vulgar and provincial"[6] has, as at least part of its intention, the moral regeneration which Joyce offered as a justification for *Dubliners*.

Yet it seems a faint hope indeed. Like Una McDermott, O'Connor's characters rarely see marked change, in themselves or in others. And indeed O'Connor has a considerable distrust of "improvers," as he makes clear at the beginning of one of his finest stories, "Song Without Words": "Even if there were only two men left in the world and both of them saints they wouldn't be happy. One of them would be bound to try and improve the other. That is the nature of things." Among the more complex of O'Connor's considerations of the possibility, or impossibility, of change, both personal and social, is the story "The Lady of the Sagas," which tells of Deirdre Costello, who has come as a schoolteacher to a town that is "no great shakes today," which she soon comes to believe "isn't a town at all. It's a camp of highway robbers." But, bearing the name of a legendary doomed lover,[7] "she naturally thought of herself in terms of the sagas and imagined Connacht raided and Ulster burned for her." Her imagination leads her from dissatisfaction to action, and the object of her work is Tommy Dodd, "almost obtrusively pious," a man with "a fine but blunted intelligence," whom she endeavors to teach about life and love. Uncovering what she believes is the dark secret in Tommy's past—a girl he "lived with" in Dublin—rouses her anger at his stuffy hypocrisy and her worry that the revelation may destroy Tommy's career as a solicitor "in a town like ours, [where] every remark starts a long and successful career as a

---

from Ireland, a departure prompted by the suppression of his newspaper and amounting to a kind of suicide.

6. Thus he describes it in "The Future of Irish Literature," an essay which appeared in *Horizon*, 5:25 (January 1942), pp. 55–63.

7. Deirdre, the daughter of Felimy, the storyteller in the entourage of King Conor, is born in secrecy after a prophecy that she will cause much blood to be spilled in Ulster. She falls in love with Naisi, a match that has a tragic and bloody outcome, including the death of Naisi through the treachery of Conor, whom Deirdre rebukes in a famous love lament. One version of the story is Synge's play "Deirdre of the Sorrows."

public event." But the final blow to her work as a reformer and to the possibility of an "heroic" marriage to Tommy, who does at long last propose, is the revelation that the scandal is no more than a yarn, "a queer sort of joke," a revelation that leaves Deirdre wailing "Oh, God, for the age of the sagas!" Deirdre's failure may be a sign that there is something unreformable about the complacent bourgeois Ireland of Tommy Dodd. Or it may only be that she needs a new standard, rooted less in an imagined heroic age and more in hard-headed practicality, and a new patience, which can accept the long and difficult process by which (if at all) obstinate humankind may be brought round to true good sense. What she needs to reform then is not Tommy or Ireland but herself.

YET EFFECTIVE modification of the self seems to O'Connor highly improbable. His characters live at the troublesome point where will emerges from the cloud of habit, only to confront responsibility. Habit—often indistinguiushable from obsession, to borrow another of his favorite words—makes few compromises, as "The Long Road to Ummera" demonstrates. There, a stubborn old countrywoman (derived from O'Connor's grandmother, Julia O'Donovan) longs to be buried in her native village, not in Cork where she has lived much of her life. Her "good son" finds this obsession nearly incomprehensible. But having diplomatically promised to accede to her wishes, he realizes that her obsession has been transformed into his duty, and one which must be carried out, even at the price of appearing nearly mad to his neighbors and cronies.

Similarly, Nan Ryan, who is "The Ugly Duckling," demonstrates early on that she is "exceedingly obstinate in a way that did not suit either her age or her sex, and it made her seem curiously angular, almost masculine." Her old friend Mick Courtney is himself "a creature of habit who controlled circumstances by simplifying them down to a routine." This tells us why habit may be so appealing to him and to others: it is, even at its worst, a way "to understand things, if only so that he could forget about them and go on with his own thoughts." When the circumstances of Nan's life do change (she turns from ugly child into beautiful woman), the two obstinacies collide. Hers drives her to seek a new world, one in which she can avoid "just getting stuck in the mud, not caring for anything," a condition she sees all around her. His resists her desire to marry and move to Dublin from Cork, the city "he really knew"; he finds unthinkable the "idea of having to exchange it for a place of no associations at all." Driven apart (he alone, she in a convent), they end with at least one consolation, or so Mick imagines: "however the city might change, that old love affair went on unbroken in a world where disgust or despair would never touch it, and would continue to do so till both of them were dead." "The Mad Lomasneys" tells another version of the same tale: Rita Lomasney's habitual willfulness and Ned Lowry's equally customary patient acceptance can never quite find a point of synchrony.

It may be that the most to be hoped for is the replacement of one set of habits by another; thus Sheila Hennessy in "Expectation of Life" imagines "how good a marriage could be, with the inhibitions of a lifetime breaking down and new and more complicated ones taking their place." It is not clear, however, that this is any more than yet another impossible dream. If there is a force which can break, or at least constrain, habit, it is responsibility, not conscious intention. In *An Only Child* (ch. 19), O'Connor concludes with his mother's urging "freedom" upon him, but adds a crucial gloss on the meaning of the word: "To her, of course, 'freedom' did not mean freedom to do what one pleased—that never crossed her mind—but freedom to do what one thought 'right,' whatever the consequences"—a message which, O'Connor says, is "the very voice of Antigone." In his autobiographies O'Connor condemns his own father and his fictional fathers for ignoring this wisdom in favor of a more personal freedom of action. But it is possible that the acceptance of the duty to do what is right amounts in the end to a confirmation of habit; thus Ned McCarthy, in "Fish for Friday," sadly acknowledges that he has "descended . . . by the quiet path of duty" into the life of "a steady man, a sucker for responsibilities," from which life one can do no more than gloomily observe "the illusion of regeneration . . . the illusion of freedom."

The complex intersection of habit and duty may provide a clue to what is otherwise, in the array of O'Connor stories dealing with courtship and marriage, an important riddle. It is clear enough that people in O'Connor's world rarely undergo any substantive change in character. But the young (and of course not-so-young) men whom O'Connor watches going courting are not the bold and prideful men who obstruct so many of the marriages he sees; they are, in fact, more likely to resemble the son or the mother than the father in the autobiographical stories: slow to understand, devoted, long-suffering, rather isolated, and not a little melancholy. And the women they woo are less like the sensible and dutiful Eileen Clery, and more like the iconoclastic Rita, "maddest" of the Lomasneys. Those who are wooed in O'Connor stories have imagination, passion, energy, and no small share of obstinacy; those who have been won, or at least those whom we see married and mothering, are creatures of patience and sober good sense.

O'Connor is not of course obligated to trace the path between the two, although *Dutch Interior* tries to do so, with limited success. The apparent decay of his young men into older and painfully disgruntled fathers is not hard to understand as the product of disillusionment within the barren context of Irish society. The virtues of the admirable mothers who recur in his fiction (of whom his own mother, described at length in *An Only Child*, is the acknowledged model) may also be a response to the force of the nightmare of reality and the acceptance within the manifold duties of motherhood. In at least two cases, however, O'Connor does explicitly approach the issue. The stories[8] of Joan Twomey and Susie Dwyer directly explore the conflicts within the self between the individualistic search for happiness and the responsibilities, moral and social, which operate with special force upon women. And they complicate considerably O'Connor's lifelong obsession with mothers, suggesting that the necessary virtues of that role may rather too readily be made the devices of manipulation.

In "The Little Mother," the Twomeys, "a family that lived up Gardiner's Hill in Cork," represent a significant variation on the standard larger O'Connor family; the father—almost inevitably "a small builder"—in this case seems the more stable, if "unbusinesslike," parent; it is the mother who is the disappointed romantic. The three girls ("as wild as they make them") are, at first, relatively undistinguishable except by age; but Joan, "the eldest, who had a broad, humorous face, an excitable manner, and a great flow of gab," proves to be the center of the story. On her mother's unexpected death, she is visited by her father with the hard news: "You'll have to be a mother to [the other two girls] now, Joan girl . . . . They have no one else," which prompts her to take up the job with a will:

> That night, as she knelt by her bed, she made a solemn vow to be everything to her father and sisters that her mother had been. She

8. "The Little Mother" and "A Sense of Responsibility" were both, according to James Matthews, written in 1952 (*Voices*, pp. 274–75 and 279) and are placed side-by-side in *Collected Stories*. They were similarly placed by O'Connor himself, in *More Stories by Frank O'Connor*, where they appear on either side of the much earlier story "The Mad Lomasneys." In both cases, the two stories are followed by the unpleasant "Counsel for Oedipus," which amounts to a diatribe-by-narrative proving that in "a case between wife and husband . . . no matter what happens the man hasn't a chance," one of the few places within the *Collected Stories* where the difficult (not to say downright cruel) side of O'Connor, amply documented in *Voices*, shows through. It is also one of O'Connor's darkest expositions of the dangerous side of the "saintly" role of Mother. The wife in "Counsel for Oedipus," whose "piety" proves to be monstrously powerful, suffers at the hands of her drunken and "unfaithful" husband, and is at one point locked out on a cold night; it is a surprisingly misogynistic inversion of an incident from O'Connor's own childhood (*An Only Child*, ch. 2).

The autobiographical resonances of all three stories are complicated by the fact of their having been written during or just after the time when O'Connor had brought his own mother from Cork to Dublin, to live within his unusually complicated household.

had no illusions about its being an easy task, and it filled her with a certain mournful pride. It was as though within a few hours her whole nature had changed; as though she no longer had a father and sisters, only a husband and children: as though, in fact, her girlhood had suddenly become very far away.

The "change," however, is less a modification of her nature than a change in role and circumstance, of her position within the inescapable context of family relationships. It is important to understand that the change arises in part from a vow of her own, not just from a responsibility presented to her by her father. As events soon prove, she will not simply take over the position of the ineffectual Mrs. Twomey, who confronted by the misdemeanors of one daughter or other would "fly into a wild rage . . . and threaten to tell their father, and then remember an identical occasion in her own girlhood and laugh at her own naughtiness and her dead mother's fury till, the immediate occasion of her emotion forgotten, she went about the house singing sentimental songs."

Joan brings to her new duty a rather different character, fueled by an almost apostolic sense that "God in His infinite wisdom had . . . been compelled to remove her mother to bring her to a proper sense of responsibility," a sense which, as the narrator immediately adds (his humorous irony does not altogether remove the ominous note) is "a common stage in the development of spiritual pride." Joan's way seems, to herself and to those who look on, to be a radical change in her very nature. Joan herself can feel the change: "The excitement in her blood when dusk fell on the fields and trees behind the little terrace house and the gas lamp was lit at the street corner was no longer the same. It was always qualified by her new sense of responsibility." "Qualified" is an intriguingly noncommittal word; it might be more precise to define what is happening to Joan as a new emphasis, imposed by circumstance and pride, on what had all along been part of her nature:

It was true that Joan had always had a touch of Reverend Mother about her; had been serious and bossy and attempted to make up in knowingness for the affection which had been diverted to her younger sisters. But this had only been swank. In all essential matters she had remained part of the juvenile conspiracy . . . . [But] now that she had deserted to the enemy, she was worse than any parent because she knew all their tricks.

The application of the language of espionage and warfare to the workings of what had at first seemed no more than a usually unpredictable family emphasizes the way in which Joan has recast the powers of remembered childhood—part of her mother's response to the juvenile conspiracy—into a rigorous ideal of controlling motherhood.

Joan's mothering becomes almost unbearable to those who suffer its ministrations: her free-thinking suitor, Dick Gordon, whom she turns away because new responsibilities make marriage inconceivable, but also because, from the vantage point of respectable motherhood, his atheistic notions no longer seem suitable; her father, whose small "gifts" to the other two daughters Joan increasingly sees as the immoral equivalent of marital infidelity; and of course the sisters, one of whom begins to develop a relationship with Joan's former admirer. Joan interrupts this, "intensely aware of the purity of her own motives," which however appear, from the outside, to be rooted in nothing more noble than jealousy. Dick Gordon—himself, predictably, "a creature of habit"—insists that it is all "rotten pride and vanity."

But to Joan the question is not one of vanity but of the stern renunciation of her old wildness in favor of a dream of normality, the attraction of which derives in part from a growing realization of just how rare it is:

> There were few pleasures more satisfying than those of normality. To walk out of an evening from your normal happy home with a normal respectable young man [not Dick now, but the "pale, pious, harassed young" civil servant Chris Dwyer, "devoted to the care of his mother"] and realize that the head of his department, though a Sanskrit scholar, lives in a home where the dirt and confusion created by eight children make life intolerable, and that the second assistant, though a man of genius, is also a dipsomaniac, makes you feel that if cleanliness isn't next to godliness, respectability certainly is.

In the end, the dream will drive Joan from her imitation of motherhood within the Twomey household into marriage to Chris and biological motherhood, in the "idyllic" privacy and much greater quiet of "a little bungalow in the hills behind Dublin." It seems a sad diminution of the "excitable" young girl who first appears in the story; the spirit of provincial Ireland has won out over excitement in the blood.

But this isn't the end of the story. The respectable stability which is Joan's dream and her destiny is anything but easy to obtain: "that was one of the drawbacks of respectability—the odds were so high." And it turns out that all her suffocating "mothering" proves both necessary and productive of happiness. One sister drifts into a hopeless affair with a silly married man, whom Joan must scare off; the other is made pregnant by an unprepossessing student in Dublin, who lives in terror of his own mother. The sister whose married lover proves to be a coward must admit she's better off without him. The marriage which Joan arranges for the other sister proves surprisingly successful; the young man turns out to be "an extraordinarily acute businessman" and a more than satisfactory husband. The little bungalow which Joan finds for herself is indeed a haven from at least some of the premature responsibilities upon which her life has been so focused; the unreliable father/husband has been replaced by the dutiful Chris Dwyer, and the baby in the crib has at the very least some years to go before he demonstrates whether he's a wild Twomey or a respectable Dwyer.

Kitty, one of Joan's sisters, insists at the story's end that Joan's life is a study in hypocrisy; an interpretation of the events which parallels the narrator's use of the word *pride* and Dick Gordon's accusation of vanity. The reader, who has less personal stake in the matter than either of those two, is more able to see the humor in the yarn, but may nevertheless share some of Kitty's and Dick's annoyance and moral outrage. The difficult and ambiguous calculus of habit, circumstance, will, and duty has exacted a considerable toll on all with whom the "little mother" comes in contact, not least upon herself. But if the true measure is to be heard in the "voice of Antigone," the voice which preaches the primacy of doing not what pleases but what one feels is right, then Joan cannot be condemned wholly. In a world of sexual complications, dipsomania, and disorder, she has chosen and indeed created a domestic order that gives every sign of lasting, and one which readily accommodates Joan's once again "vivacious way." Her sister's annoyance is only intensified by Joan's apparent happiness. And as is the case when one reaches the punch line of many of O'Connor's narrative jokes, the interaction between skepticism and happiness seems to be much of the point.

SUSIE Dwyer, the middle daughter of yet another "large, loud-voiced family" ("A Sense of Responsibility") experiences the impact of responsibility in rather a different way, but with a similarly mixed result. Again mothering lies near the heart of the problem; but in this case Susie is the victim. Not of her mother at first: Mrs. Dwyer is not especially difficult, perhaps because she has a hard enough time putting up with her husband, "whose huffy shyness had never permitted him to get anywhere in life," and whose disappointments he inflicts, loudly, upon his wife. Susie's real adversary is Mrs. Cantillon, ultimately her mother-in-law, "a tall, mournful, pious woman with the remains of considerable good looks," who "naturally" adores the one of her sons who is "a thundering blackguard" and despises the other, Jack, "a slow, quiet, conscientious chap" who—by agreement among the Dwyer girls—is to be Susie's husband.

Jack, however, will have to be won, although Mrs. Dwyer soon begins to doubt whether he's worth winning: "He hasn't enough manliness to make anyone a good husband." Jack's prevailing characteristic, his defining habit, if you will, is signalled by the story's title. He takes on the support of the widow and child of his blackguard brother, for instance, an act which offends the Dwyers' sense of "respectability" as being well beyond the acceptable bounds of "decent grief." And then Jack turns to another work of grief, the mourning of his friend Pat Farren, which rapidly becomes, as Susie can see, "a sort of fixation with him . . . . It was morbid."

Susie will not be warned off, either by her mother's advice or by the evidence of her own observations. She too, in her own way, is willing to go beyond all respectable limits: "She was gentle and a nagger; alarmed at the idea that Jack did not appreciate her, she was more concerned with making him change his mind than maintaining her dignity." She sees it as her "duty" to break Jack's fixation on his friend, and goes to the extreme of claiming that "Pat and myself were—living together." Jack, however, dismisses her confession as a lie, to Susie's "stupefaction" and anger. But the rupture is temporary; by now "Jack had become a habit with her." The first movement of the story ends with their marriage, which, while it seems "smooth" (perversely, "almost too smooth for Susie's comfort"), breeds "thorough, good, old-fashioned scene[s]" provoked by Susie's still bitter memory of the "sacrifice" she had made in revealing her "affair" with Pat to him so many years before.

The marriage is an odd but apparently successful balance of rituals of placidity and violence; even the outbreaks of emotion seem to have an element of habit about them. O'Connor calls it "their married happiness," and the word "happiness" carries its usual complex weight of accuracy and irony. Susie has what she wanted, or at least what she worked very hard to get. But soon "the worst happened"; Mrs. Cantillon moves in with Susie, Jack, and their two children, despite the sensible warning that "she'll make a wreck of your house." The conflict of obligations—which Susie had understood much earlier when she tried to correct Jack's apparent preference for the dead over the living—is laid out for Jack by Mrs. Dwyer, who reminds him what he owes to Susie. But Jack refuses to choose among his responsibilities: "There are certain things you have no choice about." And suddenly even the sensible efforts of Mrs. Dwyer are recast into prideful impositions: "[Mrs. Dwyer] realized with irritation that this intolerably weak man, this sucker who was allowing himself to be imposed on by his mischievous and selfish mother, had some source of strength that made him immune from being imposed upon by a woman of character like herself."

The dark course of manipulation is worked out within the Cantillon house and, as predicted, "Mrs. Cantillon made a hell of the home all right," but with the surprising side effect that "as the home grew more wretched, Susie came to depend more and more on her mother-in-law." This condition of dependency persists even after Mrs. Cantillon's death, when Mrs. Dwyer moves in and Susie, like all the Dwyer girls, "instantly reverted to a dependent position." Now Mrs. Dwyer, her old doubts about Jack's manliness apparently forgotten, becomes his ally against his wife. In this new triangle Susie says: "I mightn't last long between the pair of ye." The story offers one last quiet surprise when Jack, after Mrs. Dwyer's death, can at last admit (but only to himself) that he "had always hated his own mother."

What Joan Twomey and Susie Dwyer each experience is the hard price of the interaction of their own stubborn habits and the burdens of responsibility. Susie and Jack share a sense of duty—Susie to "change" Jack, to rescue him from morbid fixation; Jack to care for both his widowed and homeless mothers, no matter how hateful or disruptive the task. Duty is the foundation of their marriage, and its destruction as well. It is not enough to say that responsibility and habit are customarily at odds; "a sense of responsibility" is itself a prevailing habit, and the actual responsibilities upon which that habit must operate prove, usually, to be multiple and conflicting. The most sensible of O'Connor's priests, Father Fogarty, painfully discovers this in "An Act of Charity," where he is called upon to deal with the suicide of a young curate. The risk of scandal is obviously great, and the parish priest, Father Maginnis, "a professional to his fingertips," takes the matter in hand. Fogarty sees the importance of keeping the exact nature of the curate's death a secret: "That one of God's anointed should come to such a state of despair was something the Church could not admit." But his responsibility to the Church is complicated by "the sleeping rebel" within him, the man of principles for whom a lie is no more acceptable than a scandal; a rebel who finds an ally in the doctor who is asked to provide a false death certificate. Nor do Fogarty's obligations end there: he feels perhaps more than his share of guilt for the young man's death, and especially for his failure to see in the curate the lonely despair that could lead to suicide. That guilt emphasizes Fogarty's sense of responsibility to the dead man, upon whose memory the scandal of suicide would cast a dark shadow indeed. At least the various duties which Fogarty feels mostly lead in the same direction, toward his active participation in the cover-up which is, and not altogether ironically, "an act of charity." But the more personal effect of the conflict is that it deepens Fogarty's sense of "what lonely lives we lead," since he cannot even find a way to speak openly about the "whole significance" of his act.

THE EFFORT "to do what seems right," and thus somehow to satisfy habit, volition, and the complex web of responsibility all at once, is a frequent, and in its broad outlines rather bleak, formula in O'Connor's fiction. The outcome is not always unsatisfactory, as in the relatively early story "There Is a Lone House,"[9] where for once "the shyness of lonely souls" produces a clearly happy result, the marriage of a young wanderer and a reclusive woman. What in any case lends to the best of O'Connor's stories their peculiar force is not the presence of a formula, but the variations he plays on it. O'Connor has a certain fondness for beginning his stories with a moral generalization, as for example in "Song Without Words" and "Counsel for Oedipus"; but the richness of the former tale and the stridency of the latter are due to the degree to which the narrative accommodates and yet resists the moral provided by the narrator or by any of the characters. The lives O'Connor portrays, with remarkable economy, are usually more complex than the generalizations about them formulated by the characters themselves or the storyteller who remembers them. That is a predominant source of O'Connor's humor; but it is at the same time a wholly serious realization of the limits of any judgment, even of any narrative or moral formula.

What persists, even in a world of nightmarish realities, incorrigible fixations, and draining obligations, is first of all human passion, and the amount of human contact it engenders. If the case of Father Fogarty proves anything, it is that despite loneliness, even within loneliness, there is lasting communion; thus although his life is, to his own eye, painfully and irreparably lonely, his funeral (in "The Mass Island") is crowded with those who love him. Even simple obstinacy has its value, especially when it is harnessed, as it is in Dick Gordon in "The Cheat," to a resistance to the prevailing religiosity and materialism, or to humane service to others, in defiance even of the shaming power of small towns, as in the case of the redoubtable doctor Jim Fitzgerald, whose "pernickity sense of responsibility" is seen in "A Great Man."

Again and again, O'Connor allows his characters to *choose*. He knows

9. Matthews dates the story in the winter of 1932–33 (*Voices*, pp. 103–4), although the story did not appear in book form until *The Cornet Player Who Betrayed Ireland*. All of the stories taken from *Cornet Player* appear near the end of *Collected Stories* but date from earlier in O'Connor's career, between 1933 and 1950.

well enough what complex and usually misunderstood motives may underlie and constrain those choices; and what is to be chosen from often amounts to an array of disappointments. But neither the barrenness of the provincial Irish world nor the obsessive unconscious buried within the individual mind can deprive his characters of their individuality and their intention to act upon that individuality—not necessarily of course to do what immediately pleases them, but certainly to do what they feel, deeply, is right. O'Connor's preference for the individual over any abstract notion of morality, of duty, of the nature of reality which that individual can be made to illustrate, is what fires his anger at Joyce, in whom he thought he saw an increasing interest in the grand scheme at the price of the diminution of the humanity of the figures who populate it.

It will help us to judge O'Connor's people more fairly if we remind ourselves that he is in fact a comic writer, and often a very funny one indeed—something that can only be proven by reading him with the awareness that comedy need not compel a happy ending. And too we should allow him to redefine *happiness*, a word he often interjects into an unlikely context, as if following T. S. Eliot's advice that language must be dislocated and thus refreshed. O'Connor will not let us assume that happiness is at all likely, or that it is the necessary measure of human action; as his narrator asks at the end of "Unapproved Route," reflecting upon yet another unlikely union:

> As for unhappiness, nothing I have heard suggests that Rosalind is unhappy with Jim Hourigan. It is a grave mistake to believe that that sort of thing leads to unhappiness. Frankie's conduct [which has just before been described as a misplaced form of "magnanimity"] certainly does, but is that not because to people like him happiness is merely an incidental, something added which, taken away, leaves them no poorer than before?

The stylistic tactics of this passage deserve careful attention. Characteristically, "happiness" can only be defined in terms of human lives and human actions, and as well by an application of negatives: "happiness" is a less significant standard than is "not being unhappy." The narrative voice has a truth to offer, but he will not free it from qualification. This near-dismissal of happiness applies *only* to "people like Frankie," but the story has made it clear that Frankie is markedly unusual. And it is couched in no more definite form than that of a question, a hypothesis if you will—this despite O'Connor's readiness to propose declarative assertions of an almost proverbial shape and force.

How remarkable that happiness is even this tentatively possible, given

O'Connor's insistence on isolation as the prime fact of human existence. And in spite of his belief in "the basic human incapacity to communicate" (*The Lonely Voice,* "The Slave's Son") and his perception of the deforming effects of the actual small-town "communities" in provincial Ireland, happiness in part results from the entrance of the individual into a group. "The feeling of belonging to a group, and of the best kind—well balanced, humane, and necessary" is experienced, briefly, even by the lonely Father Fogarty in "An Act of Charity," as well as by Dermott O'Malley in "A Great Man," who observes how "everybody was madly curious about everybody else." Such passionate desire to know and to understand others lies behind and within all of O'Connor's stories, as the only effective resistance to the nihilistic inactivity that might otherwise arise in a world of incurably lonely souls.

But despite the frequency with which his characters explicitly seek it, or explicitly bewail its absence, the pursuit of "happiness" is not their most basic quest. In his commentary on Chekhov O'Connor raises, and in a characteristically heterodox way inverts, a traditional Catholic moral standard (*The Lonely Voice,* "The Slave's Son"):

> We are not damned for our mortal sins, which so often require courage and dignity, but by our venial sins, which we can more easily conceal from ourselves and commit a hundred times a day till we become as enslaved to them as we could be to alcohol or drugs. Because of them and our facile toleration of them we create a false personality for ourselves—a personality predicated on mortal sins we have refrained from committing, ignoring altogether our real personality which is created about the small, unrecognized sins of selfishness, bad temper, untruthfulness, and disloyalty.

This is why Joan Twomey suffers, for all her virtue and despite the accuracy of her eye for the sins of others; and why Father Fogarty, even when he appears to abandon the strict road of truthfulness, gains through the power of his own self-awareness. The test of "damnation" becomes as much a matter of self-consciousness and self-analysis—even at the risk of self-pity—as it is of behavior and action. The "false personality" is not quite a hypocritical mask, although it can come perilously close; it is more a habitual refusal to look into the darkness of the true self and to see clearly the sins which are at the heart of it. Given a view of the "real" that is "created about . . . selfishness, bad temper, untruthfulness, and disloyalty," the whole idea of happiness seems very nearly a siren song of self-delusion.

*   *   *

THE LURE of the false personality is all the greater for people whose roles carry especially high public expectations of virtue. O'Connor insists that "the short story has never had a hero. What is has instead is a submerged population group" (*The Lonely Voice*, "Introduction")—a phase which he readily admits is ungraceful, but which certainly fits quite aptly the provincial Irish who populate his stories. What is striking, however, is how often he focuses on those who, at least within their own "submerged" context, are particularly visible: women and especially mothers, for example (this in a society in which "mother" is the almost inevitable image for the country as a whole[10]); and "good" children, for whom the price of clumsiness is terrible emotional isolation; and of course priests.

O'Connor long ago acquired a reputation for anticlericalism, notably (if rather politely) formulated by Benedict Kiely: "O'Connor's teeth are almost always on edge at the sight of a black coat. His approach to the priesthood is . . . instinctively irreverent."[11] He is indeed wary of those priests who take up their public role zealously and uncritically. Sometimes the effect is comic, as in the case of the "foreigner" Father Crowley in "Peasants." But often O'Connor's treatment of such men is more pointed, most notably in the cases of Father Ring (in "The Cheapjack," "The Masculine Principle," and "The Holy Door"), whose greed is made even worse by its energetic application to the "good" (mostly material) of the Church; and of the ambitious Canon Lanigan, who complicates the life of the affable Bishop of Moyle in "The Miracle" and "The Old Faith."

"News for the Church" is O'Connor's clearest attempt to study how a sense of the requirements of the priestly vocation may too easily override

10. Two rich elaborations of the image, and of its impact, are Conor Cruise O'Brien's essay "Introducing Ireland" in *Conor Cruise O'Brien Introduces Ireland*, edited by Owen Dudley Edwards (New York: McGraw-Hill, 1969), pp. 13–20, and Edna O'Brien's book *Mother Ireland*.

11. Benedict Kiely, *Modern Irish Fiction: A Critique*, p. 144. Kiely's view of O'Connor is, in general, guarded; but in this case it must be added that his remark antedates a significant number of O'Connor's stories about priests, especially those centering on Father Fogarty ("The Frying Pan," "The Wreath," "The Teacher's Mass," "Requiem," "The Old Faith," "An Act of Charity," and "The Mass Island"), most of which appeared in the 1950s. Fogarty is not the only priest toward whom O'Connor feels something much richer and more sympathetic than irreverence; the same combination of humanity and self-doubt is reflected in Father Devine (in "Shepherds," "The Wreath," and "The Old Faith"), Tom Keating (in "Uprooted"), and Father Hogan (in "The Cheat"). Maurice Wohlgelernter's extended consideration of the precise nature of O'Connor's alienation from Irish Catholicism does a solid job of identifying the good and the bad in O'Connor's priests (*Frank O'Connor: An Introduction*, pp. 41–63). James Matthews describes the writer's friendship with Father Tim Traynor, from whom much of Fogarty's character is drawn, and who was the source of several priest stories (*Voices*, pp. 89–92). O'Connor's own description of Traynor and his direct expression of distaste for "priest-ridden Ireland" are in *My Father's Son*, ch. 15.

humanity and common sense. There the "notoriously easy-going" Father Cassidy seems at first a "kind" man, in spite of "a mind . . . full of obscure abstract hatreds." But that kindness cannot survive his encounter with the nameless country girl who confesses to him a sexual encounter. Suddenly Father Cassidy lets his "fighting blood" emerge, moved by an interesting mixture of inward pride and concern about his reputation:

> He saw now how he had been taken in. This little trollop, wandering about town in a daze of bliss, had to tell someone her secret, and he, a good-natured old fool of sixty, had allowed her to use him as a confidant. A philosopher of sixty letting Eve, aged nineteen, tell him all about the apple! He could never live it down.

Armed with a "knowledge" of sex that is entirely without any basis in his own experience, he proceeds to exert a subtle, brutalizing force of words; and having reduced the girl to "a tiny, limp, dejected figure," Cassidy's apparent warm heartedness returns with a bitterly ironic force, of which he is, however, wholly unaware: "he suddenly began to chuckle, a fat good-natured chuckle."

Acting from motives that are both priestly and human and which his society would all-too-readily endorse, Cassidy has made the fatal error of letting the sins of pride and ill-temper (the cornerstone of his real personality) emerge unchallenged and unrestrained. He has judged as the priest at the price of the human warmth with which he had at first dealt with the girl, and worse yet he has preferred the abstract to the particular, the human, and the experiential. "Theory might have its drawbacks but there were times when it was better than practice," he argues to himself; but his "theory" of sexual behavior wholly distorts his view of the human being before him, who is neither promiscuous nor blissful. Cassidy's delight in what he has done, his certainty about what is sinful and what is to be done about it, are thus symptoms of a profound ignorance, both of himself and of others.

That certainty—which Joan Twomey shares—makes the self-doubt which besets Father Fogarty and his spiritual brothers, Father Devine and Father Tom Keating, seem considerably more admirable; if they risk the mortal sin of despair, they avoid the venial sin of self-delusion. Placed within the church hierarchy,[12] they can see at first hand the results of moral

---

12. But, it is important to notice, usually not very high up—usually only curates; if they have a parish of their own, it is likely to be obscure and isolated. Meanwhile Father Ring prospers, and Canon Lanigan in due time attains the bishopric he craves. O'Connor's willingness to grant to individual priests a profound and virtuous humanity does not, then, temper his dislike of the institutional church and its long alliance with the De Valera government, a frequent target in *Irish Miles*.

rigidity which ignores both human nature and immediate circumstance. As priests they cannot always avoid participating in the too-often misguided "work" of the Church, such as, for example, Father Devine's "rescue" mission in "The Shepherds." Nor can they always avoid narrow moralism, as when Father Fogarty refuses to say a mass for the soul of an old woman's dog ("Requiem") or when he experiences great annoyance at the tiresomely pedantic old schoolteacher who insists on serving as acolyte at mass ("The Teacher's Mass"). But what saves Fogarty in both those cases is that his initial reaction cannot prevent the breaking through of his compassion. The acuity of his eye for the facts of human behavior and the sensitivity of his ear to the truth of human speech are the instruments of his self-correction. In the end Fogarty can see clearly the eccentric old woman with the dead dog. Her "eyes . . . seemed to contain all the loneliness in the world," and her rebuke ("They *have* souls . . . . Anything that can love has a soul.") cracks Fogarty's theologically sound conviction. And "the passion of will" of the old teacher, which is compounded of "obstinacy" and yet of "something else, which [Fogarty] valued more" and for which "faith was one name" although not, Fogarty thinks, the best or most accurate one, arouses in Fogarty "a compassion that almost revolted him" but which is in fact the surest sign of "Fogarty's profound humanity."

Such humanity is a considerable complication; the burden of doubt and self-doubt which Fogarty must bear is the hard price of resisting the public purity of Father Ring and Father Cassidy. It is especially burdensome to a priest who must live always in the public eye to be measured against the strict and abstract standard of the town, which leaves no room for doubt or for a complex moral vision, and which therefore, and most painfully of all, forbids those small acts of honest speech which are the only real interruptions of the loneliness of human life. As Tom Keating laments in "Uprooted," "Even to talk about it would be a relief but there's no one you can talk to. People come to you with their troubles but there's no one you can go to with your own."

It is clear that on both moral and practical grounds happiness, however seductive, is mostly an illusion. If it exists at all, it is rare and evanescent; but—maddeningly, at times—it *does* occur, and O'Connor's characters may experience it in unlikely ways in the most mundane and unlikely places, as does Joe Saunders in "The Weeping Children":

There were times when he saw everything with a sort of double vision, as though he were not only doing whatever he was doing—like pushing the pram around the estate, or creeping into the back room at night to see that the baby was covered—but watching himself do it, as though he were someone in a film or a book, and the conjunction of the two visions gave the thing itself an intense stereoscopic quality. He was sure this must be what people meant when they talked of happiness.

That kind of double vision is what the best of O'Connor's stories provoke in the reader, for whom the characters and actions presented are at once immediately recognizable and yet explicitly located at a remove in place and time. An ability to look carefully and passionately both at the self and at the lives which surround it is the distinguishing mark of the characters around whom O'Connor builds his stories, and in fact underlies the whole task of storytelling.

Whatever their origin, and whether they pretend to be overheard, remembered, or imagined, O'Connor's stories are seen, in great detail, from a precise vantage point that is at once close enough to bring attachment (whether compassionate or angry) and understanding (however tentative) to the narrating consciousness, yet far enough away to allow, even to demand, judgment and a sense of protective separation. This is, even in the darkest stories, a stay against the utter despair which O'Connor's view of human entrapment might otherwise engender. The narrator is in and of the world he describes; but never wholly contained and, more importantly, never silenced by it. That place, precisely balanced between familiarity and sharpening estrangement, is where Ned Keating finds himself, back home for a visit and (as it turns out) a final farewell, in "Uprooted": "Something timeless, patriarchal, and restful about [the house] made Ned notice everything. It was as though he had never seen his mother's house before." From such a place one may not only see with unusual clarity, but speak with a freedom and directness that would be unthinkable within the home and the home town.

O'Connor does not follow Joyce and other modernists in making the artist the moral and intellectual center, and the predominant subject, of the art work. It is the act of telling stories, rather than the intellectual power of the storyteller himself, which is fundamental in O'Connor's world. Far from being the especial preserve of the artistic elite, storytelling is very nearly an habitual response. O'Connor is quick to claim for that habit a long and honorable pedigree, and at the same time a unique centrality in the modern world:

In its earlier phases storytelling, like poetry and drama, was a public art, though unimportant beside them because of its lack of a rigorous technique. But the short story . . . is a modern art form; that is to say, it represents, better than poetry or drama, our own attitude toward life. Almost from its beginnings the short story, like the novel, abandoned the devices of a public art in which the storyteller assumed the mass assent of an audience to his wildest improvisations . . . . It began, and continues to function, as a private art intended to satisfy the standards of the individual, solitary, critical reader.

(*The Lonely Voice,* "Introduction")

Whatever its limitations as an accurate history of storytelling, O'Connor's point is significant in that it asserts the importance of representative accuracy in attitude as well as in fact. And his intention is to make a direct communication from teller to reader, each solitary (or, we might say, lonely), but brought for the time being into human contact.

The point is developed in two stories[13] that focus directly on stories and storytellers. "The Grand Vizier's Daughters" is yet another of O'Connor's explorations of the painful complexities of domestic relations; "The Story Teller" recounts the death of a *seanachie,* or traditional Irish teller of tales, a practitioner of that "public" art of storytelling to which O'Connor contrasts the modern, "private" art-form.[14] In each case the storyteller is an ambiguous figure, especially by the world's ordinary standards. "My uncle" in "The Grand Vizier's Daughters" is "the world's worst town clerk" and a loud and heavy-drinking man, given to maudlin and overly theatrical pronouncements. At times a terror, especially to his younger daughter, Josie, he is somehow also admirable: "I worshipped him and he never saw it, the old idiot," as the narrator/nephew puts it. The dying *seanachie* in "The Story Teller" is "a famous and popular man," surrounded on his deathbed by moralizing women who insist that his stories were "all lies, and . . . God punishes people for telling lies." The admiration of his sons is tempered by a sense of opportunities missed (" 'Tis a pity he didn't do more with himself—a clever man.") and by a mixed attitude toward the

13. The placement of the two stories at opposite ends of *Collected Stories* obscures the fact that the two were written at about the same time, although "The Story Teller" appeared in book form only after O'Connor's death.

14. O'Connor's indebtedness to such storytellers is laid out in Daniel J. Casey, "The *Seanachie*'s Voice in Three Stories by Frank O'Connor," in *Anglo-Irish Studies III* (New York: Humanities Press, 1977), pp. 96–107. O'Connor presents a longer and—in intention, at least—more scholarly account of early Irish storytelling in *A Short History of Irish Literature,* ch. 3 and Appendix. The story of one such storyteller, Tim Buckley, whom both O'Connor and Sean O'Faolain knew well, and whose condemnation by the Irish Censorship Board is among the most infamous acts of that misguided body, is told briefly in *Voices,* pp. 192–193, and at greater (and angrier) length in *Irish Miles,* ch. 17, and in *My Father's Son,* ch. 15.

force of the stories he told: "You wouldn't miss a day in a bog or a night in a boat with him. Often he'd keep you that way you wouldn't know [sic] you were hungry . . . . And there were times we were hungry."

"My uncle" is not that accomplished a storyteller. Like O'Connor himself, he pretends merely to be passing something on ("Damn it, who was it told me or did I read it somewhere?") but his tale of the Grand Vizier needs constant prompting from the audience, his two daughters and his nephew. The story is at first an exercise in avoidance—a way of *not* answering his sarcastic older daughter, who asks for the story of the "skite" from which he has just returned. The work of storytelling is however stronger than any such evasive intention; what begins as a mixture of reprocessed fairy tale, improvisation, and comic double-talk, surprisingly darkens when "my uncle" tells of the Grand Vizier's daughters, and in so doing acknowledges the disappointment of his hopes, his painful sense that he is "a drunken, blasphemous old man" and no better than an embarrassment to his own children. Monica, the sarcastic daughter, insists she is not ashamed; but "my uncle" insists upon the "truth" to which the story has, however unintentionally, led him:

> With eyes that seemed to see nothing, my uncle rose and moved towards the door like a man in a trance. For a moment I forgot that he was only an adorable, cranky, unreliable old gasbag of a man who had just been out boozing with Owney Mac in Riordan's disreputable pub on the quays. He looked like a king: a Richard or a Lear. He filled the room, the town, the very night with his presence. Suddenly he drew himself erect, head in air, and his voice rang like thunder through the house.
>
> "God help us," he said bitterly, "she was ashamed of her father."

That truth may only be partial, and even melodramatically self-serving; but what is unquestionable is the power of storytelling to compel the revelation and judgment of the self.

The story ends after the yarn itself is finished; ends, in other words, with the response of the audience to the teller. "My uncle's" younger daughter Josie is driven to near-hysteria. The expressive power of the story her father has told breaks through the comfortable rituals by which the family keeps the uncomfortable truths of their lives safely at a distance. In other words, it has captured, for all the silliness of the yarn itself, the sound of "the lonely human voice" and at the same time exacted a terrible price in confirming the isolation, indeed the abandonment, of the daughter.

The effect is similarly mixed for Afric, the child whose view of the night of her grandfather's death is the substance of "The Story Teller." She refuses to abandon her belief in her grandfather's stories, and she is still young enough to grant them literal truth, full as they are of fairies and other improbabilities. To the very end (and despite the ominous fact that her grandfather, before death takes him, has fallen silent) she awaits "with a sort of fascinated terror" the literal enactment of his folk-tales of magical death. The result is, inevitably, disappointment—a shattering of hope and belief by the force of experience: "There was no farewell, no clatter of silver oars or rowlocks as magic took her childhood away. Nothing, nothing at all. With a strange choking in her throat she went slowly back to the house. She thought that maybe she knew now why her grandfather had been so sad."

Both these stories grant to the act of storytelling a power that is in large part uncontrollable and certainly not restricted either by the will of the teller or by the shapeliness of the tale. That power resides in the way that stories form a passionate bridge between people, a sharp (and by no means especially comforting) point of contact which, however ambiguously and briefly, defeats the usual isolation of individuals and inevitably *teaches* something, however little we may be able to formulate it. Of all the forms of human communion available to the lonely souls in O'Connor's world, storytelling is the most common and by far the most reliable.

IT IS fair to say that one misses little of what is most important in O'Connor by passing over his two novels. *The Saint and Mary Kate* has attracted the admiration of James Matthews and of Maurice Wohlgelernter for its detailed picture of the slums of Cork where O'Connor grew up, and it includes at least one marvelous extended scene, at night in an abandoned house. But it has as well more than its share of stage-Irish moralizing. Nor can O'Connor ever quite convince the reader that the doomed relationship between the two title characters, Phil Dinan with his "curious methodical piety" and Mary Kate McCormick, a passionate and disillusioned dreamer, is more than a narrative device. O'Connor made better and richer use of his material later, in "The Mad Lomasneys," "A Set of Variations on a Borrowed Tune," and "The Sorcerer's Apprentice," for instance.

Dutch Interior has found few admirers and is, it must be admitted, a grim book to read: a prolonged study of the inevitable suffocation of youth by Cork, a set of bitter variations on the ultimately impossible idea of "escape." Formally, it has some interest as an experiment in the building of a novel out of nearly separable sketches and stories, but in the end we weary of "how much life remained the same" despite the passage of some twenty-five years. O'Connor endeavors to play off this awareness against the "obstinate secret life of the soul," but when worked out in nearly three hundred pages, it is too easily reducible to simple repetition. And O'Connor cannot quite decide what maintains this dreadful inertia—whether the external forces of family and culture, or some inner nihilism.

But the effort to come to grips, at some length, with Cork and with its impact, both formative and deformative, remained alive to O'Connor and prompted the only one of his longer works with anything like the power and accomplishment of his stories: *An Only Child*.[15] Indeed, a substantial part of that book's appeal lies in the extended application of the supple narrative voice which O'Connor had, by the 1950s, perfected in his stories. And despite the geniality and sentiment which the narrator is willing to display, it is full of antithesis and conflict. The tale is remembered and told, rather than seen and written as are O'Connor's two novels.

> As a matter of historical fact I know that I was born in 1903 when we were living in Douglas Street, Cork, over a small sweet-and-tobacco shop kept by a middle-aged lady called Wall, but my memories have nothing to do with living in Douglas Street. My memories begin in Blarney Street, which we called Blarney Lane because it follows the track of an old lane from Cork to Blarney.

These first sentences quietly introduce a central issue: the play of memory and imagination on the "facts" of experience and history. Selective, highly impressionistic, and at times verging, in both creative power and distortion, on hallucination, memory is the winner over historical fact, both at the start and throughout. But the plain facts of the matter must not be ignored, down to the names of streets and the occupations of neighbors. When in due time O'Connor focuses on his childhood and especially on his peculiar "education," he identifies in himself something like a war

15. It may seem eccentric to ignore so entirely O'Connor's second autobiographical volume, *My Father's Son*. But it is simply not as interesting and well-made a book; nor is it clear how fully it represents O'Connor's intentions, since, as the prefatory note acknowledges, "when Frank O'Connor died, much of this second volume of his autobiography . . . existed only in early drafts" which were made into a book by Maurice Sheehy. The book enlarges O'Connor's bitter portrait of his father and of the surrogate "fathers" he sought out after leaving Cork, and contains rich portraits of Yeats and George Russell. But those points of interest cannot counterbalance O'Connor's obsessive recapitulation of the literary-political wars in Dublin in the 1930s (especially the internal battles at the Abbey Theatre, of which James Matthews, *Voices*, pp. 124–148, gives a much clearer account) and an increasingly self-pitying narrative voice: "Every humiliation that can be inflicted on a man who tries to live by his imagination and doesn't know the rules of the group to which he aspires I had gone through" (ch. 16).

between imagination and environment: "I shuddered at the difference between the two worlds, the world in my head and the world that really existed." In the real world, the Cork slum of Blarney Lane and Barrack Stream and the bitter marriage of Mick O'Donovan and Minnie O'Connor are the nearest and most threatening.

The book explores how to survive within such a barren and hostile environment; and the predominant resistance to it is the ability to impose, if only briefly, an imagined reality upon the actual. That ability is, early on, identified with storytelling, in the person of O'Connor's uncle-by-marriage Pat Hanlon (ch. 1). Hanlon "made his affliction serve his purposes" by telling stories which, however comic their manner and matter, are in the end a "final commentary on the futility of human existence." But his yarn-spinning accomplishes something distinct and remarkable. For himself, it establishes a kind of human communion ("a couple of hours of intelligent conversation"). For O'Connor, it produces a lasting sense of the possibility, in even the most unlikely of circumstances, of "a real triumph of art over nature." And for his mother, it creates a necessary and briefly effective role as go-between. She, like the usual O'Connor narrator, overhears Pat Hanlon's stories (which are told so rapidly and are so funny that no one else can follow them) and transmits them to her husband and son.

Minnie O'Connor O'Donovan's central role in Pat's storytelling is a small but accurate reflection of her centrality to the book as a whole, which opens with her photograph and concludes with O'Connor's apotheosis of her as the most cherished figure among those "souls that were immortal, that even God, if he wished to, could not diminish or destroy, . . . who for me represented all I should ever know of God." The "celebration" of his mother is to O'Connor the fundamental effort of his own storytelling (ch. 19). Her life as he describes it (ch. 3) is the record—much of it "too terrible" to remember—of a force of character "too strong to have been due to the effect of any environment, and, indeed, [it] resisted a number of environments to which no reasonable person would subject a child." The shape of her life is an obstinate search for home, which derives not only from the bitter circumstances of her own orphan childhood but from a deeper and more universal inward force: "Lust and hunger have no greater grip on human beings than the need for a home" (ch. 7).

The moment (actually, although O'Connor passes over it in a few pages, a period of some eight years) "where she had been happier than at any other time in her life" is her time as a maid in the household of "a butter-and-egg merchant named Barry and his unmarried sister, Alice" (ch. 7). It ends sadly, and rather enigmatically, in a muddle of misunderstanding and exaggerated propriety. That setback, and her subsequent unhappy marriage (in the face of her brother's warning) to the superficially charming Mick O'Donovan, represent precisely the kind of mixed result that human effort and human intention usually produce in O'Connor's fiction. Although Minnie now has an official "home" of her own, it does not bring relief from the pressure of uncongenial environments. In fact the "home" (which enjoys happiness only when Mick is off at war, in a situation exactly parallel to the opening pages of "My Oedipus Complex") is a new field of operation for Minnie. There she resists the impoverishing drunkenness of her husband on behalf of her son, who seems (even to himself) a clumsy disappointment.[16] Minnie's "Mozartean temperament" (ch. 1) cannot transform the circumstances of her marriage and the Cork slum in which it exists, but neither will it be defeated by it.

The measure of effective resistance to an intolerable environment, then, is O'Connor's mother, whose mixture of obstinacy and "a certain simplicity of mind that is characteristic of all noble natures" (ch. 3) is at least part of his inheritance. And resistance is, to O'Connor, the prerequisite not just of the artist, but of any satisfactory life. The necessary battles need not always be external, however; especially for O'Connor, who frequently acknowledges the presence in himself of his father's nature. The war within also takes place in the unprepossessing world of Barrack Stream. The model for it is Minnie Connolly (ch. 8), who blends Pat Hanlon's talent as a mimic, a healthy dollop of wariness with regard to priests, a passionate (if overly literal) belief in fiction, and an ability to translate the actual turmoil of Barrack Stream into verbal "novelettes." Her nature shows "no taste . . . but a fierce, dark, combative masculine intellect" which can overcome even the melancholy which had, at one point, compelled her to spend "some time in the Big House, as she euphemistically called the Lunatic Asylum."

Even the less admirable figures in *An Only Child* demonstrate the power of the human imagination to re-form the circumstances of the world. Mick O'Donovan's conviction that he was "a naturally home-loving body" (ch. 2) persists in the face of recurrent evidence of his drunken and violent

16. There is a quiet geographic circularity to Minnie's quest for a home, and a parallel to her son's life as well; for, although she was raised and educated in the Good Shepherd Convent, she was born "at the top of Blarney Lane" (*An Only Child*, ch. 3)—where O'Connor's memories begin. But she spends most of her married life (and O'Connor most of his childhood) not there but in that alien world of Mick Donovan's family, in the separate and foreign neighborhood of Barrack Stream (*An Only Child*, ch. 1) from which O'Connor seeks to escape, and within which Minnie's indomitable cleanliness and respectability are constantly put to the test.

nature. He is the dark antithesis to Minnie O'Donovan's simplicity, and as well a set-piece of the damnably self-deluding effects of "venial sin":

> I don't think Mother had much pride. Gay people have no need of pride because gaiety is merely the outward sign of inward integrity, but Father had no integrity; as with all mentally sick people, the two sides of his nature hardly communicated and were held together by pins and Hail Marys, and pride was one of the ways in which he protected the false conception of his own character that was one side.
>
> (ch. 2)

Despite the rift in himself, Mick can both confront and demonstrate the truth which is at the heart of *Dutch Interior* and, ultimately, of *An Only Child* as well: "Home was no longer a refuge for him. It had become a prison and a cage" (*An Only Child*, ch. 2), although he would be the last to admit who has made it so.

Mick's willful and ultimately terrifying refusal to acknowledge the facts of his own nature has its corrective mirror-image in Erskine Childers (*An Only Child*, chs. 16 & 17), who approaches the torturous violence of the Irish Civil War through the impenetrable veil of English manners and a romantic outlook, a "grown man who has cut himself apart from life, seems to move entirely by his own inner light, and to face his doom almost with equanimity." And the particular shape which this combat of the imagined self with the real world takes, in the case of the artist, is suggested by the schoolmaster and writer Daniel Corkery, who has remade himself by the force of "self-control" (ch. 12). His fate is ultimately a result of the failure sufficiently to prize the imagination over the "real"; his diminished later life is an instance of the tragedy of a wrong act with a right intent, "the suicidal destruction of the creative faculty as an act of revolt against the worldliness of everyday life" (ch. 15). That tragedy is made all the greater by O'Connor's insistence (in words similar to the way he describes his mother's resistance to circumstances) that Corkery was "a man who, by force of character, had dominated physical difficulties, family circumstances, and a provincial environment that would have broken down anyone but a great man" (ch. 15).

Within the young O'Connor the effort to transform, by way of literature and imagination, the actualities of Cork and of Ireland, shows itself at first largely as a credulous passion for the written word that produces a kind of comic dislocation: "I was always a little bit of what I had picked up from book or song or picture or glimpse of some different life, always half in and half out of the world of reality" (ch. 10). But it soon grows into something more central: "All I wanted was to translate, to feel the unfamiliar become familiar, the familiar take on all the mystery of some dark foreign face I had just glimpsed on the quays" (ch. 14). And remarkably, the progress of the self is supported, even enhanced, by the force of circumstance. The "revolution" that eventually turns the rather silly young "mother's boy" and inept railway clerk Michael Francis O'Donovan into the artist Frank O'Connor is both reflected by and caused by the effort of Ireland to make itself an independent state: "It was a period of political unrest, and, in a way, this was a relief, because it acted as a safety valve for my own angry emotions. Indeed, it would be truer to say that the Irish nation and myself were both engaged in an elaborate process of improvisation," a process which seems doomed, since "the material world was too strong for both of us" (ch. 15).

O'Connor insists upon the word, and the image, of improvisation. It carries a dismissive edge, which the details of his own, largely comic-opera involvement in the guerrilla wars seem to validate, and which is deepened by the ultimate degeneration of the revolution into the "disaster" which is "the death-in-life of the Nationalist Catholic establishment" (*An Only Child*, ch. 19). But the larger failure of the public and political improvisation has the effect of promoting the inner improvisation, emphasizing O'Connor's predisposition to see "life through a veil of literature—the only sort of detachment available to me" (ch. 16), and underscoring the necessity of finding a point of contact between the imagined and the real: a place where the familiar and the unfamiliar may translate one another, and where the limits of the imagination may be seen and understood. O'Connor, seeing how the Irish "improvisation" decays into violent civil war, draws the complex lesson of the lives he has observed in Barrack Lane and elsewhere: that there is an "unimpeachable logic of the imagination, that only what exists in the mind is real" (ch. 16). And sooner or later that reality encounters the other, the external. Here is O'Connor reflecting on his experience as a young rebel: "I was beginning to think that this was all our romanticism came to—a miserable attempt to burn a widow's house, the rifle butts and bayonets of hysterical soldiers, a poor woman of the lanes kneeling in some city church and appealing to a God who could not listen" (ch. 18)—an image which indirectly overpowers even the saintly Minnie O'Connor herself.

The logic of the imagination is centrally necessary to survival, as the lives of Minnie O'Donovan and Gertie Twomey show; but it is also dangerous, as the example of Mick O'Donovan demonstrates with terrible clarity. In a nature like O'Connor's own (which has not inherited, in anything like a pure form, the simplemindedness and "gaiety" that preserves his mother's resistance to circumstance), imagination needs to be leavened, most especially by a comic vision. As the young Michael O'Donovan sees more and more clearly the course of the Irish revolution, he understands better its fatally mixed—and brutally unreflective—nature:

> In spite of all the sentimental high-mindedness, I felt it went side by side with an extraordinary inhumanity. Or maybe angularity is the better word. It was really the lack of humor that seems to accompany every imaginative improvisation.
>
> (*An Only Child*, ch. 18)

Humor provides a kind of balance, undercutting both sentimentality and inhumanity.

And in the end, balance is the vital consideration. However much O'Connor admires imagination and the force of character which will follow its "logic," he is all too aware of the risks it involves. Near the end of *An Only Child* he discusses his "discovery" of grammar. He makes of it "an image of human life" which revives yet again, but with intriguing variation, the importance of the domestic frame as a way of understanding all human behavior, and which proposes quite directly the necessity of a difficult balance of forces:

> Grammar is the bread-winner of language as usage is the housekeeper, and the poor man's efforts at keeping order are for ever being thwarted by his wife's intrigues and her perpetual warnings to the children not to tell Father. But language, like life, is impossible without a father and he is forever returning to his thankless job of restoring authority.
>
> (ch. 18)

What "intrigues"—in several senses of the word—is imagination; what "keeps order" is attention to the actuality of things. The imagination, however rich, has, in isolation, the terrible side effect of "paralys[ing] not only the critical faculty but the ability to act upon the most ordinary instinct of self-preservation" (ch. 18).

The arrangement of the book reflects the shape and necessity of this balance. The first half (parts 1 and 2) focuses not so much on O'Connor himself, who is at most an observer, but on the human context into which he is born, the "environment" upon which his own imaginative and artistic resistance will act. It is here that the "logic of the imagination" unfolds most fully, in Minnie O'Donovan and in two lesser figures who, eccentrically and comically, echo her, Gertie Twomey and Minnie Connolly. Yet even here there are warning signs of the possible failure and terrorizing force of imaginative resistance that is wholly rooted in self-delusion, rather than integrity and gaiety (which O'Connor cannot be certain he has inherited from his mother) or careful attention to things as they are (which he can, albeit slowly, learn). The figure of Mick O'Donovan is in this sense the dark angel at war with the bright angel, his wife. As she has her subsidiary spirits, so does he, in the shape of the neighbor Ellen Farrell, whose hatred of Cork may at first seem admirable, but quickly deepens into an obsessive effort to control neighbors and tenants.

The second half of the book turns to Michael O'Donovan, the son in the grip of conflicting inheritances, by affection drawn to his mother but by temperament sadly like his father. He can—as indeed the detail of the whole first half of the book had demonstrated—observe carefully, but he is mostly driven by imagination, which he must learn to distrust or at least to restrain, but never to abandon. The route to his own Dedalian moment of exile (at least from Cork) takes him, necessarily, through the improvisation of the new and independent Ireland, exemplifying the power of the imagination when it runs its course unanalyzed and not measured against the nightmare of reality. The first half of the book comes down on the side of resistance, of the imaginative re-forming of the world; the second half argues the necessity of disillusionment, with the result that O'Connor can attain a middle ground (ch. 19):

> It took me some time to realize what Mother had seen in that first glimpse of me, that I had crossed another shadow line, and [to] make me wonder if I should ever again been completely at ease with the people I loved, their introverted religion and introverted patriotism.

That the disillusionment is not linear and complete is underscored by the reappearance, at this crucial moment, of the presiding saint of the book's first half, Minnie O'Connor O'Donovan.

The shape of the life which O'Connor defines in *An Only Child* is thus not a progress from childish romanticism to adult skepticism, or from adolescent sentimental patriotism to adult exile; it is something more like a circle, which leaves him poised between affectionate curiosity and hard-eyed criticism, or between nostalgia and disillusionment. At the beginning of part 3, when the portrait of the artist-in-formation, rather than of the world which forms and is to be re-formed by him, truly starts, O'Connor remembers a moment from his childhood:

> I was always very fond of heights, and afterwards it struck me that reading was only another form of height, and a more perilous one. It was a way of looking beyond your own back yard into the neighbors'. Our back yard had a high wall, and by early afternoon it made

the whole kitchen dark, and when the evening was fine, I climbed
the door of the outhouse and up the roof to the top of the wall. It
was on a level with the respectable terrace behind ours, which had
front gardens and a fine view, and I often sat there for hours on terms
of relative equality with the policeman in the first house who dug
close beside me and gave me ugly looks but could not think up a law
to keep me from sitting on my own back wall.

(ch. 10)

If the experience of heights carries into reading, it also applies to writing
as O'Connor does it: isolated and isolating; difficult, even dangerous;
marked often by the disapproval of the respectable world, and at some
distance in time and character from the world it observes, but still within
sight of old and familiar landmarks, at once voyeuristic and neighborly.

That moment—and indeed, the whole of *An Only Child*—is a reasonable
place to end (or, for that matter, to begin) reading O'Connor. It is where
he explicitly confronted the formal challenge of constructing a large con-
tinuous whole without losing the energy and comic edge of an imagination
that was much more at home with character and revelatory anecdotal
incident than with extended plot. And it is his most direct and personal
exploration of issues and themes which had obsessed him from the beginning of his career: the search for, and the escape from, home; the
burdens of human relationship, and especially those between husband and
wife and mother and child; the presence and complex operation of the
forces of imagination and character which can resist, and perhaps even
transform, the grim circumstances of human life. Full of stories, short and
long, many of which echo fictional tales, it is a rich account of O'Connor's
"education" as a storyteller, a process in which environment, history, and
his own effort of will and obsession play vital parts. If he never fully
resolved whether he could—or should—be at ease among those he loved,
the maddening and self-imprisoned, yet enduring and obstinate provincial
Irish, he at least proved again and again the value of viewing life from
that difficult vantage-point.

It might fairly be said of him, as it is said of the dying old man in "The
Story Teller," "There was nothing he cared about only the stories." But
far from being the avenue of escape from life, those stories, rooted in
memory and precise observation, arising from "moral passion" and arousing passionate human sympathy, are the way in which the loneliness of
life can be defeated. Mere speech can too easily become gab (as is worked
out at some length in O'Connor's version of "Ivy Day in the Committee
Room," called "What's Wrong with the Country" and included in *Bones*

of Contention). This is especially true in Ireland, where too many "are conditioned to believe that language was invented to conceal thought" (*Irish Miles,* ch. 18) and where there are too many Father Cassidys who can use words with intentionally brutalizing and diminishing effect. But to O'Connor the lonely human voice speaking truthfully about the particulars of human experience, and using those devices of narrative which are inevitably more complete and more truthful than any act of moral or philosophical generalization, is the most fundamental and passionate agency of human communion and moral judgment.

Afterword

THE CONNECTIONS between these five writers are perhaps most visible in the shared language of disillusionment, loneliness, and a distinctive sort of radical "detachment" from both culture and self. But even at the level of sentences and paragraphs, the manipulation of that language and of elements of the Irish culture of this century produces five powerful and varied responses to a shared sense of impermanence and mortality.

The shared outlook and distinct voices may to some degree derive from particular similarities and differences in their early lives. All were born around the turn of the century (O'Flaherty, the oldest, was born in 1896; O'Connor, the youngest, in 1903), and lived a substantial period of their childhood within the "paralysed" world of Ireland after Parnell. For Elizabeth Bowen and for Kate O'Brien, there remained something idyllic about that period. "Never such innocence again," they might well have said, preempting Philip Larkin; or, more to the point, "never such security again," for certainly both women felt a kind of dislocation after the particular events which interrupted the stability of their childhoods—a dislocation that would not be eased by their ability, as adults, to see the limitations and cruelties of the world within which those childhoods were set. For O'Flaherty, O'Connor, and O'Faolain, the place and time of their childhood was anything by idyllic; but it was nonetheless, and in spite of the visible and proximate presence of avowed "revolutionaries," a time when things were predictable.

That "calm"—whether actual or ironic—came, in each case, to a sudden end. Broadly speaking, all five of these writers lived through (at greater or lesser distance) the turmoil of the revolution and civil war which gave birth to an Irish Republic, and which marked an end to the Ireland which they had known as children. That public upheaval was, to some degree, no more than a rough parallel to the more personal "change" which each underwent. For Bowen and O'Brien it was the death of a parent and the related collapse of what had been a comfortable family life; they were, roughly speaking, acted upon, and their fiction shows the echoes of that event in the prevalence of figures who are similarly the victims (or at least the subjects) rather than the initiators of determining actions. For O'Flaherty, O'Connor, and O'Faolain, the crucial personal event was more closely tied to historical circumstances—World War I for O'Flaherty, the Troubles for O'Connor and O'Faolain—and more clearly identified with the acting out of personal intention through a gesture of rebellion against the desires of their families. These gestures are repeatedly re-enacted in their fiction, which has much to do with the attempt to assert independence and individuality.

For all five writers the world of their childhood was gone, though it returned throughout their fiction. For all five, questions of the direction, value, and nature of change were inescapable; they derived both from the facts of their psychic histories and from events in the culture within which they continued to claim some "living room," as Bowen might have put it. The peculiar nation which resulted from the revolutionary "change" in Ireland in the period 1916–1923 cannot but have emphasized the centrality—and the ambiguity—of those questions. The work of these writers is, in an important way, an effort to map that nation, both sociologically and metaphorically. And at the same time, much of their work is an effort to *address* that nation, to shape and especially to reform it, to continue the work of change which had seemed to stop, so unexpectedly, once the battles of civil war had ended.

For the three sometime revolutionaries O'Connor, O'Flaherty, and O'Faolain, the effort to change the culture within which they found themselves were especially central—and especially problematic. As young men all three had, at some considerable risk, joined passionately and willingly in the effort to make a new Ireland which would redress the oppressive imbalance of the old. They felt all the more sharply the disillusioning result. Their effort seemed to have brought to power a conservative and moralistic culture based on an alliance of church and petty-bourgeoisie that all three had thought was exactly what they were fighting to put an end to.

From stasis to change to a new stasis that in many ways seemed indistinguishable from the old: that is the peculiar shape of the Irish history which all five of these writers lived through, and which left its mark on their work. It is full of problematic explorations of human intention and aspiration, full too of a complex sense of engagement with and detachment from things as they are, a detachment which their lives act out in part by frequent—but never quite Joycean and permanent—physical absences from Ireland. To write freely and in English within and about a theocratic, often censorious, officially Gaelic-speaking society was one of the challenges they accepted—and this challenge remains for all but a few of the significant writers who have followed them. One frequent response has produced a characteristic form of comedy rooted in self-delusion and in excess of language played out against a background of stasis and parochialism, of which Frank O'Connor is a particular master. The distinctive ways in which mythic and historical memory operates upon present circumstance within Ireland makes it nearly inevitable for an Irish writer of any seriousness to focus especially upon the operations of memory and imagination, to make the effort to test dreams and ideals against the observable "facts" of past and present; and it is the case that all five of the writers considered here are, often unwillingly, at once historians and romantics, idealists and skeptics. Both the cultural enclosures of the Ireland of the 1920s and 1930s and the long narrative tradition in Irish culture may have contributed as well to a formal predisposition toward short fiction in which character achieves primacy over plot but in which entrapment regularly conquers revelation. Finally, the challenge of writing within and to Irish culture has more often than not been accepted within an essentially domestic frame. That is to say that the larger cultural conflicts which these writers observe, record, and (implicitly) rebel against are most often played out within the political tensions of the family, often a triangle with a braggart father, a "failed" intellectual son, and a saintly mother. It is the conflict, in other words, of that paradigmatic family of which the Dedaluses are the inescapable model and measure.

To use Joyce as a reference point seems inevitable; but at the same time problematic. There is no question that much Irish fiction written since the 1920s shows the manifest signs of the effort of a number of original and powerful writers to come to grips with the shadow of a looming ancestor. Only a few—Beckett, Flann O'Brien, Francis Stuart, and Aidan Higgins in particular—have battled *Ulysses* on its own complex stuctural terms or clearly accepted the polymathic artistic self-image which Joyce puts forward. To the extent that the bulk of Irish fiction writers have taken up the challenges of Modernism, they have done so by way of what we may have to call the Low or Plain Style. It is therefore no surprise to find Frank O'Connor and Sean O'Faolain, in their efforts to define what is most important in modern short fiction, devoting considerable attention to Hemingway, and to the body of late nineteenth-century Continental Realism whose landmarks include Flaubert, Maupassant, and Turgenev. Of course, insofar as this is an escape from the later Joyce, it is an escape into the earlier Joyce; and if the shadow of *Ulysses* and *Finnegans Wake* is less apparent than we might expect, that of *Dubliners* and *Exiles* and *Portrait* is unmistakable—a particularly immediate burden of the past. Indeed the frequency with which one can encounter echoes of the closing paragraphs of "The Dead" begins, at times, to seem eerie.

But in another sense that burden is less determining than it might seem to the retrospective eye. None of the five writers with which we have been concerned were, for instance, willing to see Dublin as the most Irish and most universal of metaphoric cities. In some sense then they had readily at hand, in their own experience, a way to sidestep Joyce by way of exploring an Ireland, or rather a variety of Irelands, of which the Master knew little. For several of our writers, there were, biographically, much more proximate and visible literary "parents" to be accommodated: Yeats, for O'Flaherty, O'Connor, and O'Faolain; for Bowen, Virginia Woolf and Henry James.

In any case I have intentionally avoided any full attention to the reaction of these writers to Joyce, in part because I feel neither competent nor willing to add to the massive literature centering on Joyce, in part because I believe there is much to be seen in the work of these writers without invoking Joyce, in part in rebellion against the nearly inevitable impulse, in considering any Irish literature written since about 1920, to define and assess it in terms of the work of the Irish Renaissance. That work, and especially the twin monuments, Joyce and Yeats, are at once the great glory and the great curse of recent Irish literature: a glory because of the epic work of imagination and self-invention, both personal and cultural, which it accomplishes; a curse because no writer can now hope for long to escape the faint praise of "the best poet since Yeats" or "the finest writer of fiction since Joyce." And an ironic curse as well, since for so long the effort to follow the creative integrity and honesty of Joyce and Yeats was a sure way to be condemned and censored, within Ireland; an experience which none of our writers escaped.

In the end, it is implicit in the very structure of the preceding chapters that the primary interest to be found in these writers lies within the work itself, not in its connection to the work of others, not even in its relation to the culture which is its point of origin and often its explicit subject. All of these writers attempt to consider life as it is actually lived; all are therefore compelled to draw upon some body of observable actuality, and to all five life in Ireland is such a body, one which they knew well from their own perspective. They share with each other, and with other Irish writers, and indeed with other Modernist writers, certain recurrent concerns about the apocalyptic uncertainties of life and the demonstrable limits of human action; they propose distinctive ways to formulate and to explore those concerns, and offer quite distinctive enactments both of how life is usually lived and how it must or might be lived. They are recognizably conservative, not only in the technical resources they employ but in the fundamental language of memory, love, and responsibility which both they and their characters use. They are all writers whose limitations are perhaps as marked as their accomplishments; but these accomplishments deserve and will amply repay a more full, serious, and consistent attention than they have as yet been granted.

Selected Bibliographies

General Sources

Brown, Terence. *Ireland: A Social and Cultural History 1922–1985* (London: Fontana, 1985).

Deane, Seamus. *A Short History of Irish Literature* (South Bend, Ind.: University of Notre Dame Press, 1986). Not so much a history as a "reading" of Irish literature written in English since about 1650, this is a provocative and valuable example of the reassessment of Irish writing now being undertaken by the so-called Field Day critics. Deane emphasizes especially the ways in which particular writers derive from and respond to the complex and often contradictory political, cultural, and ideological loyalties which have long operated so powerfully within Ireland.

Finneran, Richard J. *Recent Research on Anglo-Irish Writers* (New York: Modern Language Association, 1983). The section on "Modern Fiction," assembled by Diane Tolomeo, is valuable.

Harmon, Maurice, and Roger McHugh. *Short History of Anglo-Irish Literature* (Totowa, N.J.: Barnes and Noble, 1982). Chapter 20, on fiction "after the revival," is both directly relevant and lucid; the bibliography is extensive but not altogether accurate.

Jeffares, A. Norman. *Anglo-Irish Literature* (New York: Shocken, 1982). Much more of a catalog than Harmon and McHugh's book; but a useful one.

Kiely, Benedict. *Modern Irish Fiction—A Critique* (Dublin: Golden Eagle Books, 1950). Short, opinionated, and now nearly thirty years old, this is still a fine introduction to the Irish fiction of the first half of the present century.

LIAM O'FLAHERTY

Starting Points

There is no complete collection of O'Flaherty's stories, nor is there any satisfactory biography. *The Stories of Liam O'Flaherty* (New York: Devin-Adair, 1956) is a substantial collection, containing 42 stories as well as an appreciative brief introduction by Vivien Mercier and a short bibliography of works by O'Flaherty up to 1956. The same introduction, and 29 of the same stories, comprise the collection *The Wounded Cormorant and Other Stories* (New York: Norton, 1973), which is still in print in paperback. Of O'Flaherty's novels, *The Informer* is by far the best known and most widely available, having gone through a number of paperback editions, mostly prompted by the high critical estimation of the film version of the book. *The Black Soul* and *Skerrett* are central to O'Flaherty's work; both have recently been reissued by Wolfhound Press in Dublin, as has the best of his "thrillers," *The Assassin*. Paul O'Doyle's *Liam O'Flaherty: An Annotated Bibliography* (Troy, N.Y.: Whitson Publishing Co., 1972) is a useful resource.

Novels

Thy Neighbour's Wife (London: Jonathan Cape, 1923; New York: Boni and Liveright, 1924)

The Black Soul (London: Cape, 1924: New York: Boni and Liveright, 1925; reissued by Wolfhound Press, Dublin, in 1981)

The Informer (London: Cape, 1925; New York: Knopf, 1925)

The Wilderness. Published serially in 1927, this short novel was not issued in book form until edited by A. A. Kelly for Wolfhound Press, Dublin, in 1978.

Mr. Gilhooley (London: Cape, 1927; New York: Harcourt, Brace, 1927)

The Assassin (London: Cape, 1928; New York: Harcourt, Brace, 1928; reissued by Wolfhound Press, Dublin, in 1983)

The House of Gold (London: Cape, 1929; New York: Harcourt, Brace, 1930)

The Return of the Brute (London: Mandrake Press, 1929; New York: Harcourt, Brace, 1930)

The Ecstasy of Angus (London: Joiner and Steele, 1931 [a limited edition of 365 copies]; Dublin: Wolfhound Press, 1978)

The Puritan (London: Cape, 1931; New York: Harcourt, Brace, 1932)

Skerrett (London: Victor Gollancz, 1932; New York: Long and Smith, 1932; reissued by Wolfhound Press, Dublin, in 1977)

The Martyr (London: Gollancz, 1933; New York: Macmillan, 1933)

Hollywood Cemetery (London: Gollancz, 1935)

Famine (London: Gollancz, 1937; New York: Random House, 1937; reissued, with an introduction by Thomas Flanagan, by David R. Godine, Boston, in 1982)

Land (London: Gollancz, 1946; New York: Random House, 1946)

Insurrection (London: Gollancz, 1951; Boston: Little, Brown, 1951; reissued by Wolfhound Press, Dublin, in 1988)

Stories

Spring Sowing (London: Cape, 1924; New York: Knopf, 1926)

The Tent (London: Cape, 1926)

The Mountain Tavern (London: Cape, 1929; New York: Harcourt, Brace, 1929)

The Short Stories of Liam O'Flaherty (London: Cape, 1937; reprinted in 1948, and reissued in a two-volume paper edition by New English Library, London, in 1970). This includes most (but not quite all) of the stories in the preceding three volumes.

Two Lovely Beasts and Other Stories (London: Gollancz, 1948; New York: Devin-Adair, 1950)

The Stories of Liam O'Flaherty (New York: Devin-Adair, 1956). A substantial (42 stories) but not complete collection up to the mid-1950s, with a short introduction by Vivien Mercier.

The Wounded Cormorant and Other Stories (New York: Norton, 1973). This is a selection of 29 of the 42 stories contained in the previous volume, along with Mercier's introduction.

The Peddlar's Revenge and Other Stories (Dublin: Wolfhound Press, 1976). This is a collection of stories previously not issued in book form. A paperback edition (1981) bears the title *Short Stories by Liam O'Flaherty*.

Biography and Autobiography

The Life of Tim Healy (London: Cape, 1927; New York: Harcourt, Brace, 1927). One of O'Flaherty's most peculiar books, this seems to be, like the first version of Sean O'Faolain's biography of Eamon De Valera, a bit of hired hack-work written for the money. Healy's political maneuvering and his reliance on both Church and capitalism ought to have made him a thoroughly uncongenial figure to his biographer; yet O'Flaherty manages to make of Healy, in politics, what O'Flaherty thought he himself was, in literature: the universally despised (and yet perversely durable and even triumphant) odd man out.

A Tourist's Guide to Ireland (London: Mandrake Press, 1929). An odd and characteristically angry little book.

Two Years (London: Cape, 1930; New York: Harcourt, Brace, 1930). An account of O'Flaherty's life in 1918–1920, and especially of his recovery from his war wounds.

I Went to Russia (London: Cape, 1931; New York: Harcourt, Brace, 1931). An account of O'Flaherty's visit to the home ground of the "new religion" of Communism. In *Shame the Devil* (ch. 8) he condemns it as "a criminal mockery" of a book.

Shame the Devil (London: Grayson and Grayson, 1934; reissued by Wolfhound Press, Dublin, in 1981). An account of O'Flaherty's despair and wanderings in the year 1933. As with *Two Years,* the mood which O'Flaherty defines is of interest and importance, even if the events he describes are largely unverifiable. The book also contains extended recollections of his childhood, of some of his returns to Aran as an adult, and of his experience in World War I. These more-or-less factual sources can usefully be supplemented by several of O'Flaherty's stories—espeically "Mother and Son," "Birth," "The Child of God," "The New Suit," and "The Parting," all in *Stories* (1956), and by O'Flaherty's older brother Tom's book *Aranmen All* (London: Hamish Hamilton, 1934).

Critical and Bibliographic Studies of O'Flaherty's Work

Doyle, Paul. *Liam O'Flaherty: An Annotated Bibliography* (Troy, N.Y.: Whitson Publishing Co., 1972). This necessarily omits the more recent reissuings of O'Flaherty's work by Wolfhound Press and Godine, as well as the story collection *The Peddlar's Revenge;* it seems otherwise complete.

Kelly, A. A. *Liam O'Flaherty: Storyteller* (London: MacMillan, 1976). In conjunction with Wolfhound Press in Dublin, Kelly has waged a long campaign to restore O'Flaherty's books to print and to attract serious attention to his work.

O'Brien, James H. *Liam O'Flaherty* (Lewisburg, Pa.: Bucknell University Press, 1973). An undistinguished volume in the estimable Irish Writers series, it does however provide a reasonably accurate short guide to the verifiable details of O'Flaherty's life.

O'Flaherty, Tom. *Aranmen All* (London: Hamish Hamilton, 1934). This account, by O'Flaherty's older brother, of a return to Aran mentions Liam hardly at all; but the view both of Aran and of the O'Flahertys is variously a direct contrast to, or verification of, O'Flaherty's reminiscences and fictional re-workings. Both "Going into Exile" and "The New Suit" are directly echoed in *Aranmen All,* and Tom confirms Liam's view of his mother and father and of the contentious local schoolmaster David O'Callaghan.

Sheeran, Patrick F. *The Novels of Liam O'Flaherty: A Study in Romantic Realism* (Atlantic Highlands, N.J.: Humanities Press, 1976). A diligent survey of its announced subject, as well as of O'Flaherty's life and the critical reception of his work. Sheeran however excludes *Hollywood Cemetery* and *The Return of the Brute* "as they do not merit serious critical attention." The opening chapters, on the culture of the Aran Islands, are especially informative.

Zneimer, John. *The Literary Vision of Liam O'Flaherty* (Syracuse, N.Y.: University of Syracuse Press, 1970). By far the most complete and least pedestrian study of the whole of O'Flaherty's work, with the exception of a handful of late stories. Zneimer intends to assert O'Flaherty's importance as a "modern" writer, and is therefore somewhat obsessive in his rejection of "Irishness" as an element in O'Flaherty's life or work.

KATE O'BRIEN

Starting Points

For some years after her death, O'Brien's fiction fell into obscurity; it is now reappearing, both in Ireland (under the imprint of Arlen House, Dublin) and in England and America (by way of Virago reprints). Her short memoir of her family, *Presentation Parlour,* is easily the most affectionate and charming of her books. Among her novels, *Mary Lavelle* (reissued in 1985 by Virago in conjunction with Viking Penguin) and *That Lady* (also reissued by Virago/Viking Penguin in 1985) represent an interesting pairing. *The Land of Spices* is also of interest—both for itself, and as something of a counterweight to the more prevalent strand of novels by Irish women writers, most notably Edna O'Brien, which portray both convent education and the lives of nuns as ranging from grim to perverse.

Novels

Without My Cloak (London: Heinemann; Garden City, N.Y.: Doubleday, Doran, 1931; reprinted by Virago in 1986)

The Ante-Room (London: Heinemann; Garden City, N.Y.: Doubleday, Doran, 1934; reprinted in paper by Arlen House, Dublin, in 1980)

Mary Lavelle (London: Heinemann; Garden City, N.Y.: Doubleday, Doran, 1936; reprinted by Virago in 1985)

Pray for the Wanderer (London: Heinemann; Garden City, N.Y.: Doubleday, Doran, 1938)

The Land of Spices (London: Heinemann, 1941)

The Last of Summer (London: Heinemann, 1943; reprinted in paper by Arlen House, Dublin, 1982)

That Lady (London: Heinemann; Garden City, N.Y.: Doubleday, Doran, 1946; reprinted by Virago in 1985). The American edition bore the title *For One Sweet Grape*. This novel was refashioned into a play and later a film, which O'Brien is said to have disliked. It stars Olivia de Havilland and turns up very occasionally on television, usually at odd hours of the day or night.

The Flower of May (London: Heinemann; New York: Harper and Brothers, 1953)

As Music and Splendour (London: Heinemann, 1958)

Travel and Autobiography

Farewell Spain (London: Heinemann, 1937; reprinted by Virago, 1985). This is mostly travelogue, but the chapter entitled "Mainly Personal" includes a recollection of O'Brien's time as a "Miss" in Bilbao in 1922–23.

My Ireland (London: B. T. Batsford, 1962). Chapter 2 offers a brief account of the O'Briens of Limerick; Chapters 2, 3, and 8 include glimpses of O'Brien's childhood. Chapter 8 offers an affectionate characterization of her father; Chapter 6 recalls, in part, Dublin as it was during O'Brien's student years.

Presentation Parlour (London: Heinemann, 1963). This is O'Brien's only extended work of reminiscence, but it is characteristically reticent about O'Brien's own life, focusing instead upon her five aunts. The chapter entitled "Aunt Annie" provides considerable insight into the life and marriage of O'Brien's father and mother.

Biography and Criticism

English Diaries and Journals (London: William Collins, 1943)

Teresa of Avila (New York: Sheed and Ward, 1951)

Criticism of O'Brien

Reynolds, Lorna. *Kate O'Brien: A Literary Portrait* (Gerrards Cross, Eng.: Colin Smythe, 1986). This is the first manifestation of anything like serious critical attention to O'Brien's work.

ELIZABETH BOWEN

Starting Points

All of Bowen's stories have been gathered in one volume, *The Collected Stories of Elizabeth Bowen* (New York: Knopf, 1981), with an appreciative introduction by Angus Wilson. Of her novels, the one she acknowledged, on its republication in 1964, as being "nearest her heart"—and the only one which is set entirely in the world of the County Cork "Big Houses"—is *The Last September,* first published in 1929. It is currently available in a Viking Penguin edition, as are the two novels most widely accounted her best: *The Death of the Heart* and *The Heat of the Day.* One could profitably begin, however, with several less known novels, and especially with *The House in Paris, A World of Love,* and *The Little Girls,* none of which seem to strain so visibly under the desire to be "major" as do *The Death of the Heart* and *The Heat of the Day. Bowen's Court,* her extended study of her family and its seat, first appeared in 1942; in 1964 it was reissued, with the addition of moving remarks on the final sale and destruction of the house. The later version has been reissued by Ecco Press (1979) and more recently (1984) in an English Virago paperback in one volume which also contains *Seven Winters,* Bowen's much shorter memoir of her seasonal residence in Dublin up to the time of her father's illness. Hermione Lee—whose book-length study of Bowen's work is by far the best extended treatment of the subject—has edited a collection of critical and autobiographical essays, prefaces, reviews, and letters in *The Mulberry Tree: Writings of Elizabeth Bowen* (New York: Harcourt, Brace, Jovanovich, 1987). Victoria Glendinning's *Elizabeth Bowen* (London: Weidenfeld and Nicolson, 1977) is a brief, affectionate, and eminently readable biography.

Jonathan Cape undertook the preparation of a Uniform Edition of Bowen's work, beginning in the 1950s. Bowen's reputation has dimmed somewhat since the 1950s, but never gone out entirely—as attested by the persistence of paperback editions, most recently by Avon Books (which issued most of the novels and Glendinning's biography as well; almost all are now out of print) and then by Viking Penguin (their editions of the novels seem rather bewilderingly to disappear and then reappear, at least in America).

Novels

The Hotel (London: Constable, 1927; New York: The Dial Press, 1928)
The Last September (London: Constable; New York: The Dial Press, 1929). Bowen
    added a short preface to the 1952 Cape edition.
Friends and Relations (London: Constable; New York: The Dial Press, 1931)
To the North (London: Gollancz, 1932; New York: Knopf, 1933)
The House in Paris (London: Gollancz, 1935; New York: Knopf, 1936)
The Death of the Heart (London: Gollancz, 1935; New York: Knopf, 1936)
The Heat of the Day (London: Cape; New York: Knopf, 1949)
A World of Love (London: Cape; New York: Knopf, 1955)
The Little Girls (London: Cape; New York: Knopf, 1964)
Eva Trout (New York: Knopf, 1968; London: Cape, 1969)

Stories

Encounters (London: Sidgwick and Jackson, 1923; New York: Boni and Liveright,
    1925; reissued as part of *Early Stories,* below)
Ann Lee's and Other Stories (London: Sidgwick and Jackson; New York: Boni and
    Liveright, 1926; reissued as part of *Early Stories,* below)
Joining Charles and Other Stories (London: Constable; New York: The Dial Press,
    1929)
The Cat Jumps and Other Stories (London: Gollancz, 1934)
Look at All Those Roses (London: Gollancz; New York: Knopf, 1941)
The Demon Lover and Other Stories (London: Cape, 1945; New York: Knopf, 1946).
    The American edition was entitled *Ivy Gripped the Steps.*
Early Stories (New York: Knopf, 1951). This includes all the stories in *Encounters*
    and *Ann Lee's* as well as a preface by Bowen.
A Day in the Dark and Other Stories (London: Cape, 1965). This includes stories

previously collected in *The Cat Jumps* and later collections, plus four new stories and a preface by Bowen.

The Collected Stories of Elizabeth Bowen (London: Cape; New York: Knopf, 1981). This includes all of Bowen's published stories, arranged in order of first book appearance, as well as an introduction by Angus Wilson.

Autobiography, Reminiscence, History, and Criticism (by Bowen)

Bowen's Court (London: Longmans, Green; New York: Knopf, 1942). In 1964 Bowen revised the book and added an important "Afterword" about the demolition of the house.

Seven Winters: Memories of a Dublin Childhood (Dublin: Cuala Press, 1942). Reprinted as part of *Seven Winters: Memories of a Dublin Childhood and Afterthoughts: Pieces on Writing* (New York: Knopf, 1962).

Collected Impressions (London: Longmans, Green; New York: Knopf, 1950)

The Shelbourne Hotel (London: George G. Harrap; New York: Knopf, 1951)

A Time in Rome (London: Longmans, Green; New York: Knopf, 1960)

Afterthoughts (London: Longmans, Green, 1962; for the American edition, see *Seven Winters,* just above)

Pictures and Conversations (London: Cape; New York: Knopf, 1975). This is a posthumous and miscellaneous volume, assembled and with an extended introduction by Bowen's literary executor, Spencer Curtis Brown. It includes a fragment of Bowen's unfinished autobiography ("Pictures and Conversations"), the first chapter of an unfinished novel ("The Move-In"), a lengthy essay ("The Art of Bergotte") and a Nativity play, and finally a reprinting of "Notes on Writing a Novel," first published in 1945.

The Mulberry Tree: Writings of Elizabeth Bowen (New York: Harcourt Brace Jovanovich, 1987). This collection, edited by Hermione Lee, pulls together the most important items in *Collected Impressions, Afterthoughts,* and *Pictures and Conversations* and adds a number of pieces which had not been collected before. The first section, which reprints both the important autobiographical essays "The Mulberry Tree" (about Downe House School), "London, 1940," and "Coming to London," as well as Bowen's most important essays on fiction ("Notes on Writing a Novel," "The Bend Back," and "The Roving Eye"), is especially informative.

Biographical and Critical Studies of Bowen

Craig, Patricia. *Elizabeth Bowen* (New York: Viking Penguin, 1986). This slender biography adds nothing to the account assembled by Victoria Glendinning.

Glendinning, Victoria. *Elizabeth Bowen: Portrait of a Writer* (London: Weidenfeld and Nicolson, 1977). A fine short biography, which does not, however, try to substantiate its high claims for Bowen's place in twentieth-century literature.

Heath, William. *Elizabeth Bowen: An Introduction to Her Novels* (Madison: University of Wisconsin Press, 1961). As the subtitle indicates, this study makes only occasional reference to Bowen's short stories; and, given its date of publication, necessarily deals only with the novels down through *A World of Love.* Heath develops—sometimes at self-defeating length—the links between

Bowen's work and that of Jane Austen, Henry James, Virginia Woolf, and E. M. Forster. He has useful things to say about Bowen's complex use of "propositions," or epigrammatic moral statements.

Kenney, Edwin J. *Elizabeth Bowen* (Lewisburg, Pa.: Bucknell University Press, 1975). This is a careful brief chronological survey of both life and works, perhaps too universally admiring in its approach (especially to *Eva Trout*) and somewhat limited in its insistence on the centrality of the Fall of Man as a focus of Bowen's work.

Lee, Hermione. *Elizabeth Bowen: An Estimation* (New York: Barnes and Noble, 1981). By far the most substantial study of the whole of Bowen's work, including an extensive bibliography of works by and about Bowen. Like Heath and Kenney, Lee makes a case for a high estimation of Bowen's work as a whole, but is not afraid to confront the limitations and even the failures of particular works. The analysis is on the whole more clearheaded and far more complete than Heath, and it does not try, as Kenney does, to defend the improbabilities of *Eva Trout*.

SEAN O'FAOLAIN

Starting Points

The Collected Stories of Sean O'Faolain (Boston: Little, Brown, 1983) includes in one volume all the stories that had been published in book form. The English edition, published by Constable under the same title, is in three volumes. In America these three separate volumes have been published in paperback by Viking Penguin under the titles *Midsummer Night Madness, The Heat of the Sun,* and *Foreign Affairs*. Two of O'Faolain's novels are reasonably available and well worth reading: *And Again?* (reprinted by Viking Penguin in 1982) and *Bird Alone* (republished by Oxford University Press in 1985, with an appreciative introduction by Benedict Kiely). O'Faolain's eminently readable (and gracefully polemical) *The Irish: A Character Study* is still in print. There is as yet no full biography of O'Faolain; his autobiography, *Vive Moi!* deals only—but richly—with his life up to his return to Ireland from England in the early 1930s. Maurice Harmon's revised study of O'Faolain's work, listed below, contains the best available bibliography, although it has three problems: it does not clearly sort out differences between English and American editions and does not adequately distinguish stories from critical essays, reviews, and travel pieces, nor does it clearly identify the periodical title of works which appear under a different name in *Collected Stories*.

Stories

Midsummer Night Madness and Other Stories (London: Cape, 1932). Not to be confused with the Viking Penguin paperback reprinting of the first volume of O'Faolain's *Collected Stories,* which includes these stories and those in the next two collections O'Faolain published.

A Purse of Coppers: Short Stories (London: Cape, 1937)

Teresa and Other Stories (London: Cape, 1947). An American edition, adding two stories ("Up the Bare Stairs" and "The Fur Coat") was published under the title *The Man Who Invented Sin and Other Stories* (New York: Devin-Adair, 1948).

The Finest Stories of Sean O'Faolain (Boston: Little, Brown, 1957). O'Faolain provides a foreword to this volume which is a brief review of his career to that point. Among other things he explains why he—like Frank O'Connor—preferred to omit most of the stories from his first collection. The English edition bears a slightly less assertive title: *The Stories of Sean O'Faolain* (London: Rupert Hart-Davis, 1958).

I Remember! I Remember! (Boston: Little, Brown, 1961)

The Heat of the Sun (Boston: Little, Brown, 1966). Not to be confused with the Viking Penguin reprinting of the second volume of *Collected Stories,* which includes the stories in *The Finest Stories, I Remember! I Remember!,* and *The Heat of the Sun,* as well as O'Faolain's preface to the last-named collection.

The Talking Trees and Other Stories (Boston: Little, Brown, 1970; London: Cape, 1971)

Foreign Affairs and Other Stories (London: Constable; Boston: Little, Brown, 1976). Not to be confused with the Viking Penguin reprinting of the third volume of *Collected Stories,* which includes the stories first published in *The Talking Trees* and *Foreign Affairs,* as well as several previously unpublished stories.

Selected Stories (London: Constable; Boston: Little, Brown, 1978)

The Collected Stories of Sean O'Faolain (London: Constable [3 vols.], 1980–82; Boston: Little, Brown [1 vol.], 1983)

Midsummer Night Madness (London and New York: Penguin, 1982). This is a paperback edition of volume I of *The Collected Stories.*

The Heat of the Sun (London and New York: Penguin, 1983). This is a paperback edition of volume II of *The Collected Stories.*

Foreign Affairs (London and New York: Penguin, 1986). This is a paperback edition of volume III of *The Collected Stories.*

Novels and Autobiography

A Nest of Simple Folk (New York: Viking, 1934)

Bird Alone (London: Cape, 1936; republished by Oxford University Press in 1985, with an introduction by Benedict Kiely)

Come Back to Erin (New York: Viking, 1940)

Vive Moi! (Boston: Little, Brown, 1964)

And Again? (London: Constable, 1979; republished in paper by Penguin in 1982)

Biography and History

Constance Markievicz (London: Cape, 1934; a significantly revised edition was issued by Sphere Books [London] in 1967)

King of the Beggars: A Life of Daniel O'Connell (New York: Viking, 1938). This has been reprinted several times, most recently by Poolbeg Press, Dublin, in 1980.

De Valera (Harmondsworth, Middlesex: Penguin Books, 1939). This is a substantially revised and enlarged version of O'Faolain's adulatory shorter biography of De Valera (1934)—a work which resembles, to American eyes, nothing so much as an unabashed campaign biography. In his search for approving models, O'Faolain in the earlier biography finds De Valera, at various points, to be like Parnell, like the rebel-martyr Mayor of Cork Terence Mac Swiney, like Samson, and—most strikingly of all, perhaps, to an American reader—like both Robert E. Lee and Abraham Lincoln.

The Great O'Neill: a Life of Hugh O'Neill, Earl of Tyrone 1550–1616 (New York: Duell, Sloan and Pearce, 1942; republished by Mercier Press, Cork, in 1970)

The Irish: A Character Study (West Drayton, Middlesex: Penguin, 1947; New York: Devin-Adair, 1948)

Newman's Way: The Odyssey of John Henry Newman (London: Longmans, Green, 1952)

Criticism by O'Faolain

The Short Story (London: William Collins Sons, 1948; New York: Devin-Adair, 1951)

The Vanishing Hero: Studies in the Novelists of the Twenties (London: Eyre and Spottiswode, 1956; Boston: Little, Brown, 1957)

Travel Writing

An Irish Journey (London: Longmans, Green, 1940)

A Summer in Italy (London: Eyre and Spottiswode, 1949)

An Autumn in Italy (New York: Devin-Adair, 1953; the English edition is entitled *South to Sicily* and was published by William Collins Sons in 1953)

Critical Studies of O'Faolain

Maurice Harmon. *Sean O'Faolain: A Critical Introduction* (Dublin: Wolfhound Press, 1984). This is a significantly revised and expanded version of the book issued, under the same title, by Notre Dame University Press in 1966. It is an extended and appreciative study of the whole of O'Faolain's work—by far the best, and essentially the only such study currently extant.

Joseph Storey Rippier. *The Short Stories of Sean O'Faolain: A Study in Descriptive Technique* (New York: Barnes and Noble, 1976). This book is much less extensive than its title suggests; it deals with only eight stories, and entirely with matters of technique and structure.

FRANK O'CONNOR

Starting Points

Collected Stories (New York: Knopf, 1981; reprinted by Random House as a Vintage paperback in 1982) is a substantial but not complete collection of O'Connor's short fiction. Among the omissions are almost all of the stories in O'Connor's first collection, *Guests of the Nation;* as well as his longest story, "The Holy Door," and (inexplicably) one of his best-known, "In the Train." O'Connor's superb reminiscence, *An Only Child,* has been reprinted in paper by G. K. Hall (Boston, 1985). *The Lonely Voice: A Study of the Short Story* has also been brought back into print, with an introduction by Russell Banks, as a Harper and Row paperback (1985). James Matthews, *Voices: A Life of Frank O'Connor* (New York: Atheneum, 1983) is valuable both as biography and as criticism; it must be said as well that it is a rather depressing book—which may only be a sign of its integrity in reporting the hard facts of O'Connor's life and nature.

Stories

Guests of the Nation (London and New York: Macmillan, 1931)

Bones of Contention (New York: Macmillan, 1936; London: 1938)

Crab Apple Jelly (London: Macmillan, 1944; New York: Knopf, 1944)

The Common Chord (London: Macmillan, 1947; New York: Knopf, 1948)

Traveller's Samples (London: Macmillan, 1951; New York: Knopf, 1951)

The Stories of Frank O'Connor (New York: Knopf, 1952; London: Hamish Hamilton, 1953)

More Stories by Frank O'Connor (New York: Knopf, 1954); a very similar volume was published in England in 1964 by Macmillan under the title *Collection Two*.

Domestic Relations (London: Hamish Hamilton, 1957; New York: Knopf, 1957)

A Set of Variations (New York: Knopf, 1969). O'Connor's widow assembled this collection as well as *The Cornet Player Who Betrayed Ireland;* apparently, as no other editor is listed, she also gathered the 1981 *Collected Stories*. The English volume *Collection Three* (London: Macmillan, 1969) includes the same introduction by Harriet Sheehy O'Connor, and a very similar, but not quite identical, selection of stories.

Collected Stories (New York: Knopf, 1981; reprinted by Random House as a Vintage paperback in 1982). The largest collection of O'Connor's stories, but still by no means complete.

The Cornet Player Who Betrayed Ireland (Dublin: Poolbeg Press, 1981)

Novels and Autobiography

The Saint and Mary Kate (London and New York: Macmillan, 1932)

Dutch Interior (London: Macmillan, 1940; New York: Knopf, 1940)

An Only Child (New York: Knopf, 1961; London: Macmillan, 1962; reprinted in paper by G. K. Hall, Boston, in 1985)

My Father's Son (London: Macmillan, 1968; New York: Knopf, 1969; reprinted in paper by G. K. Hall, Boston, in 1985). This is a continuation of, or sequel to, *An Only Child,* which O'Connor planned but did not live to finish. Portions were published in *The New Yorker* during O'Connor's lifetime, and were assembled into a book after his death by Maurice Sheehy.

Books about Literature and Ireland

Irish Miles (London: Macmillan, 1947)

Leinster, Munster, and Connaught (London: Robert Hale, 1950)

The Mirror in the Roadway: A Study of the Modern Novel (New York: Knopf, 1956; London: Hamish Hamilton, 1957)

The Lonely Voice: A Study of the Short Story (Cleveland: World Publishing Co., 1962; London: Macmillan, 1963; enlarged edition New York: Bantam, 1968; reprinted, with an introduction by Russell Banks, as a Harper and Row paperback in 1985)

A Short History of Irish Literature: A Backward Look (New York: G. P. Putnam's

Sons, 1967). The English edition (London: Macmillan, 1967) bears the title *The Backward Look: A Survey of Irish Literature.*

Biographical and Critical Studies of O'Connor

James Matthews. *Frank O'Connor* (Lewisburg, Pa.: Bucknell University Press, 1976). This has been supplanted by the much larger critical biography by Matthews, but it remains a fine short survey of O'Connor's work.

James Matthews. *Voices: A Life of Frank O'Connor* (New York: Atheneum, 1983). A full and honest biography, with excellent observations about O'Connor's work as well.

Maurice Sheehy, editor. *Michael Frank: Studies on Frank O'Connor* (New York: Knopf, 1969). This is a memorial volume, full of reminiscences (of which James Matthews makes ample and intelligent use). It also has a useful bibliography.

Maurice Wohlgelernter. *Frank O'Connor: An Introduction* (New York: Columbia University Press, 1977). A sound, argumentative, and extensive critical study.

THE REST OF THE STORIES

In what follows I do not seek to encompass all that is of value in the work of Irish fiction writers since the generation which is the concern of this study, but rather to suggest some predominant aspects of the fictional terrain—themes that recurrently attract the attention of short-story writers and novelists, and writers whose work has attracted and merited attention. I have restricted myself to writers who are primarily writers of fiction; excluding therefore such very interesting works as the novel and the autobiography written by the poet Patrick Kavanagh and the short stories of the playwright Brian Friel. My comments after each listing are intended as much to make my own biases plain as to summarize the character of the listing. To the trained eye, the unreasonable omissions may be all too clear.

The Short Story

The form continues to attract the vast majority of significant Irish writers of fiction; it is in fact easier to list those writers who did *not* write any considerable number of short stories (Flann O'Brien and Brian Moore stand almost alone). But even in that crowded field several writers stand out, in terms both of sheer bulk and in terms of their distinct uses of the form; in addition, a representative sample of each writer's work is relatively easy to come by.

Benedict Kiely. *The State of Ireland* (Boston: David R. Godine, 1980; New York and London: Penguin, 1982). A fine selection of Kiely's short fiction, it also contains the superb novella *Proxopera,* mentioned below.

Mary Lavin. *Selected Stories* (London: Constable [2 vols.], 1964 and 1974; New York and London: Penguin, 1981). This offers the title story of each of the eleven collections Lavin had published up to 1977; and it includes what may be her finest stories, "The Becker Wives" and "Happiness." A more complete collection, *The Stories of Mary Lavin,* has been issued in three volumes by

Constable (1964–1985); and since then she has published one new collection, *A Family Likeness* (London: Constable, 1985).

John McGahern. *Getting Through* (London: Faber and Faber; New York: Harper and Row, 1980). This was McGahern's second collection of stories. The title alone makes it a useful representation of McGahern's rather grim fictional world; and the volume includes the fine story "The Slip-Up."

Edna O'Brien. *A Fanatic Heart* (New York: Farrar Straus Giroux, 1984). This includes all of the stories in her 1981 collection *Returning*, a selection from her three prior collections, and four previously unpublished stories; the volume as a whole is an ample representation both of O'Brien's power and of her tendency to repeat herself.

William Trevor. *The Stories of William Trevor* (New York and London: Penguin, 1983). A bulky Penguin paperback that includes all of Trevor's five prior collections. Trevor's nationality may fairly be questioned; born and educated in Ireland, he has long lived in England, and for many years Ireland figured only occasionally in his work (it is the setting, for instance, of his novel *Mrs. Eckdorf in O'Neill's Hotel*). But his recent novel, *Fools of Fortune,* and his collection of stories, *News from Ireland* (New York: Viking, 1986), both represent an explicit return, in terms of subject and setting, to his birthplace.

Portraits of the Artist

It is arguable that Joyce's influence on Irish fiction has been most visible in terms of the shadow cast by *Portrait of the Artist as a Young Man*. In any case, the ongoing effort to understand the place (if any) of the creative intellect within modern Irish culture has produced a large number of important novels; and many of those novels seem consciously aware of the life and character of Stephen Dedalus.

Desmond Hogan. *The Ikon-Maker* (New York: George Braziller, 1976). Hogan rather too quickly acquired the title of "promising young writer" (he was only twenty-five when this, his first novel, appeared, and he had already attracted attention as a playwright). It is not clear that the promise has been fulfilled; but his view of Galway and the Irish midlands is worth some attention.

John McGahern. *The Dark* (London: Faber and Faber, 1965; New York: Knopf, 1966). A powerful, if heavily psychological, portrayal of a young man and his farmer father; it is McGahern's first novel and especially worth comparing to Edna O'Brien's *A Pagan Place* (see below). His later novel *The Leavetaking* (London: Faber, 1974) is in some senses, although not explicitly, a sequel; in it a young teacher encounters Ireland's prejudices against divorce and mixed marriage, but the novel's attempts at lyricism seem forced.

Brian Moore. *The Emperor of Ice Cream* (London: Andre Deutsch, 1966). Like Joyce's *Portrait,* Moore's book is in part a defense of the necessity of exile; its hero grows up in circumstances much like Moore's own (a childhood in a doctor's family in Belfast during World War II) and finds little enough to sustain him there, intellectually or spiritually. Moore's own escape took him to Canada; *The Luck of Ginger Coffey* (Boston: Little, Brown, 1960) is in part an ironic reconsideration of that venture, just as *The Feast of Lupercal* (Boston:

Little, Brown, 1957; London: Andre Deutsch, 1958) makes it clear that to have stayed in Ireland would have been no better. Many of Moore's novels—among them *An Answer from Limbo* (Boston: Little, Brown, 1962; London: Andre Deutsch, 1963) and *Fergus* (New York: Holt, Rinehart and Winston, 1970; London: Cape, 1971)—seem especially troubled by the ghosts who continue to haunt those who live in exile from Ireland.

Edna O'Brien. *A Pagan Place* (New York: Knopf, 1970; London: Weidenfeld and Nicolson, 1970; reissued in paper by Graywolf Press in 1984). This novel has been refashioned by O'Brien into a play. Like Julia O'Faolain's *Three Lovers* it seems directly responsive to *Portrait*. It concerns (as does much of O'Brien's fiction) the difficulties in the life of a young girl being raised in the horse country near Ballinasloe; it undertakes as well an experiment parallel to that of the first chapter of *Portrait*, in that the style and syntax of the narrative change as the protagonist grows into awareness.

Flann O'Brien. *At Swim-Two-Birds* (London: Longmans, Green, 1938; reissued in paper by New American Library in 1976). This book desperately—and often hilariously—resists labeling; it is either a tribute to or a send-up of certain High Modernist notions of art and life, and has at its heart a young man who is perpetually a student and purportedly a writer.

Julia O'Faolain. *Three Lovers* (New York: Coward, McCann and Geoghegan, 1971). This appeared in England under the less bland title *Godded and Codded,* and seems unquestionably to be a response to Joyce—in fact doubly so, first by taking as its protagonist a young Irish intellectual encountering Paris (but the intellectual is a young *woman* on a Fulbright), second by including a young man who, in his sense of vocation and his tendency to self-dramatize, is a translation into more modern dress of Stephen Dedalus himself.

The State of the Nation

For many, if not all, of the writers born and raised in an "independent" Ireland which long refused to join the world community (choosing, for instance, to turn away from involvement in the Second World War), the character of Irish life seems often to be a reincarnation of the paralysis of *Dubliners*. But the effort to define (and implicitly to criticize and perhaps even to change) the condition of life in Ireland remains a productive line of attention, both for writers and readers.

Aidan Higgins. *Balcony of Europe* (London: Calder and Boyars, 1972). Almost uniquely with recent Irish fiction, this novel accepts many of the devices of High Modernism, from epigraphs to complex shifts of time and voice; one can with relative ease identify the notes borrowed from Joyce (and from F. Scott Fitzgerald, for that matter). But the novel retains a very real richness and force. Higgins's shorter next novel, *Scenes from a Receding Past* (London: John Calder, 1977) might fairly be listed among the portraits of the artist; it deals with several of the same characters as *Balcony of Europe*, but is set entirely in Ireland—in fact in Celbridge, north of Dublin, although Higgins chooses, for his own reasons, to transpose that world to somewhere near Sligo.

Desmond Hogan. *A Curious Street* (New York: George Braziller, 1984). A short novel which nonetheless endeavors to interweave the rather bleak present with the historical and the mythic past—with predictably mixed results.

Jennifer Johnston. *The Gates* (London: Hamish Hamilton, 1973). A short, deft, and genuinely funny novel about shabby-genteel "old" Ireland coming in contact with a more energetic younger generation.

Molly Keane. *Good Behavior* (New York: Knopf, 1981). This novel marked Keane's re-emergence into print; it stands, along with many of Mary Lavin's stories, much of Edna O'Brien's work, and John McGahern's *The Barracks* as a diagnosis of the particular deforming pressure of Irish society upon the lives of women.

Benedict Kiely. *The Captain with the Whiskers* (London: Methuen, 1960). The best-known of Kiely's novels, it has been reissued (1980) by Poolbeg Press. It centers on a character who seems at times to be willfully melancholy, but it does not altogether forego the energy of voice and description which marks Kiely's short fiction.

John McGahern. *The Barracks* (London: Faber and Faber, 1963) and *The Pornographer* (London: Faber, 1979; New York: Harper and Row, 1979). The first of these two is, in my opinion, the most powerful, and also the darkest, of McGahern's portrayals of the world of the Irish agricultural midlands; the second is only marginally less bleak but does incorporate a greater variety of voice and tone than is usual in McGahern's fiction.

Patrick McGinley. *Bogmail* (London: Martin Brian and O'Keeffe, 1978; New York: Ticknor and Fields, 1981) and *Foggage* (New York: St. Martin's Press, 1983). McGinley's novels may be an acquired taste; and it must be admitted that it is never easy to distinguish what is merely facile and bitterly manipulative within them from what is of more weight. But their very oddity, of style as well as of subject and plot, make them worth reading, if only as distinct elaborations of the common Irish presumption that, in the end, nothing works out as it should.

Brian Moore. *The Mangan Inheritance* (New York: Farrar, Straus and Giroux, 1979). One of the few novels in which one of Moore's emigrés returns to Ireland—with extremely disorienting results.

Edna O'Brien. *The Country Girls Trilogy* (New York: Farrar, Straus and Giroux, 1986). This brings together in one volume the three short novels which O'Brien published between 1960 and 1964 under the titles *The Country Girls, The Lonely Girl* (reissued as *The Girl with the Green Eyes* after a film of that name had been made of it), and *Girls in Their Married Bliss*. O'Brien has now added a brief "epilogue" which continues the interrelated stories of Baba and Kate, convent-educated, whose lives take them from the horse country of the west of Ireland to Dublin, with largely disastrous results. The novels are worth reading in part because of the great stir they created in Ireland when they appeared—they were for the most part viewed as scandalous and irredeemable, a charge which Benedit Kiely considered in a now-famous (and brilliantly titled) essay review, "The Whores on the Half Doors." O'Brien's complex reaction to Ireland—a loving bitterness, one might say—is laid out without the trappings of fiction in her book *Mother Ireland* (London: Weidenfeld and Nicolson, 1976; New York and London: Penguin, 1978): part autobiography, part travelogue, part indictment.

Flann O'Brien. *The Third Policeman* (London: MacGibbon and Key, 1967; reissued in paper by New American Library in 1976). The novel was written in 1940, but not published until much later—a victim not of the Irish censorship but of the obtuseness of O'Brien's British publishers, who found it neither intelligible nor funny. It is both, and portrays life in the Irish countryside by way of a mix of farce and nightmare. It should also be read, as a corrective, by anyone who has ever composed a serious "scholarly" footnote.

The Old Troubles and the New

Ireland has once again become known, and not for stasis. Political violence is an almost inescapable subject for contemporary Irish writers—poets and playwrights as well as writers of fiction. And it is often viewed through the lens of the older Troubles of the 'teens and twenties, which in fact provide at least some of its historical roots.

M. J. Farrell [Molly Keane]. *Mad Puppetstown* (London: William Collins Sons, 1931; New York: Farrar and Rinehart, 1932) and *Two Days in Aragon* (London: Collins, 1941). Molly Keane has had at least three careers—first as a writer of very horsy popular novels, then as a somehwat more serious writer whose work seems at times an Irish version of Evelyn Waugh, then (after a long silence and finally under her own name) as the author of two recent and well-received novels. The two books listed here are both views of the Troubles from within the Big House; they, along with a number of the other novels which Keane wrote under the psuedonym M. J. Farrell, have been brought back into print by the invaluable Virago series.

Jennifer Johnston. *The Railway Station Man* (New York: Viking, 1985). Set in contemporary Ireland, very near the Ulster border, it powerfully considers the possibilities—and the limits—of "insulation" from political violence.

Benedict Kiely. *Proxopera* (1972; most readily available in the collection *The State of Ireland,* listed above) and *Nothing Happens in Carmincross* (Boston: David R. Godine, 1985). The first is a masterful novella describing the accidental encounter between "normal" Irish life and terrorism; the second is a novel which approaches the same situations somewhat less economically. The novel in particular raises the question of the degree to which the traditionally "Irish" (or one might say Joycean) defenses of wit and eclectic learning can withstand the shocks of violence, which seem particularly to take their toll among innocent bystanders.

Bernard MacLaverty. *Cal* (London: Cape, 1983; New York: George Braziller, 1983). A view of sectarian conflict from within, and from the North, MacLaverty's novel centers on an unemployed Belfast Catholic who becomes involved in terrorism and then tries to withdraw from it. The novel has been made into a film, which is true to its source but which makes perhaps a bit too visible the melodramatic underpinnings of MacLaverty's plot.

Julia O'Faolain. *No Country for Young Men* (London: Allen Lane, 1980; New York Carroll and Graf, 1987). This is an especially convincing portrayal of the ways in which the political mythologies established or confirmed in the 1920s can still have a profound and even fatal power.

William Trevor. *Fools of Fortune* (New York: Viking, 1983). This is a rather quirky book which seems to consider how much imagination and political faith may influence, even distort human lives. It offers as well a replaying, in terms of individuals, of the long-standing "embrace" of England and Ireland.

Matters of Faith and Doubt

The continuing force, within Irish culture, of religious belief and religious observance (not to mention clerical power) is a particular aspect of the state of the nation which deserves separate notice. Among the very many works that deal directly with problems of religious belief and religious vocation (how many Irish writers are lapsed seminarians!), the following manage to transcend merely sectarian interest.

Benedict Kiely. *There Was an Ancient House* (London: Methuen, 1955). A convincing, partly autobiographical, account of what draws young men into—and then often out of—the clerical life.

Benedict MacLaverty. *Lamb* (New York: George Braziller, 1980). MacLaverty's short first novel raises in an especially powerful way the conflicts between love and faith.

Brian Moore. *The Lonely Passion of Judith Hearne* (London: Andre Deutsch, 1955). Moore's first novel, the story of a devout Belfast spinster whose faith is as much a prison as it is a solace. Moore's very short novel *Catholics* (New York: Holt, Rinehart, and Winston, 1972) poses a variety of important questions about the possibility of "reforming" religious faith; but it stops well short of doing more than framing the problem. Both *The Great Victorian Collection* (London: Cape, 1975) and *Cold Heaven* (New York: Holt, Rinehart, and Winston, 1983) confront the conflict of faith and doubt by way of recognizably modern and skeptical protagonists into whose lives apparent miracles (not necessarily of an explicitly religious character) intrude.

Julia O'Faolain. *Women in the Wall* (New York: Viking, 1975). An effective historical novel which treats religious mysticism and secular (and feminine) power in sixth-century Gaul.

Francis Stuart. *Black List/Section H* (London: Martin, Brian and O'Keeffe, 1975; Carbondale, Il.: Southern Illinois University Press, 1975). Unquestionably the best of Stuart's many novels, it is a unique mixture of fictionalized autobiography, cultural history, and parable. The "faith" here is as much political as religious; but in an Irish context one can never disentangle the religious and the political.

Index